SURVIVING CHANGE
A Survey of Educational Change Models

James B. Ellsworth

ERIC ® Clearinghouse on Information & Technology
Syracuse University • Syracuse, New York
IR-109

Surviving Change:
A Survey of Educational Change Models

James B. Ellsworth

This publication is available from Information Resources Publications, ERIC Clearinghouse on Information & Technology, Syracuse University, 621 Skytop Road, Suite 160, Syracuse, NY 13244-5290; 1-800-464-9107 (IR-109)

ISBN: 0-937597-50-3

U.S. Department of Education
Office of Educational Research and Improvement
National Library of Education

This product was funded in part with Federal funds from the U.S. Department of Education under contract no. ED-99-C0-0005. The content of this publication does not necessarily reflect the views or policies of the U.S. Department of Education nor does mention of trade names, commercial products, or organizations imply endorsement by the U.S. government. The U.S. Department of Education's web address is: http://www.ed.gov/

Editorial Staff: R.D. Lankes, Eric Plotnick,
    Susann L. Wurster, Nicole Catgenova
Designer: Lloyd Lathrop

Acknowledgement

The publishers have generously given permission to use numerous quotations and adaptations from the following copyrighted works. From *Diffusion of Innovations*, 4th ed., by E.M. Rogers. Copyright 1995 by Everett M. Rogers. Copyright 1962, 1971, 1983 by The Free Press. Reprinted by permission of The Free Press, a division of Simon & Schuster. From "Conditions that Facilitate the Implementation of Educational Technology Innovations," by D. Ely, in the *Journal of Research on Computing in Education*, 23 (2), pp. 298-305. Copyright 1990 by ISTE (the International Society for Technology in Education). Reprinted by permission of the publisher. From *The New Meaning of Educational Change*, by M.G. Fullan and S.M. Steigelbauer. Copyright 1991 by Teachers College, Columbia University. Reprinted by permission of Teachers College Press. From *The Change Agent's Guide*, 2nd ed., by R.G. Havelock and S. Zlotolow. Copyright 1995 by Educational Technology Publications, Inc. Reprinted by permission of Educational Technology Publications. From *Change in Schools: Facilitating the Process*, edited by Gene E. Hall and Shirley M. Hord. Reprinted by permission of the State University of New York Press © 1987, State University of New York. All rights reserved. From *Strategies for Planned Change*, by G. Zaltman and R. Duncan. Copyright 1977 by John Wiley & Sons, Inc. Reprinted by permission of John Wiley & Sons, Inc. From *Systemic Change in Education*, by C. Reigeluth and R. Garfinkle (Eds.). Copyright 1994 by Educational Technology Publications, Inc. Reprinted by permission of Educational Technology Publications.

Dedication

Donald P. Ely was president of the Association for Educational Communications and Technology (AECT) the year I was born. His decades of leadership and scholarship in the educational technology field have helped clarify our definitions, synthesize our research findings, and identify the conditions contributing to successful educational change. His guidance has also shaped the professional lives of countless graduates of Syracuse University's Instructional Design, Development, and Evaluation program. I was one of them.

Thanks, Don.

James B. Ellsworth

About the Author

James B. Ellsworth is Chief of Evaluation Research and Development for the U.S. Army's Intelligence Center at Fort Huachuca, Arizona. In his off-duty time, he teaches with the Educational Psychology/ Educational Technology program at the University of Arizona's Sierra Vista Campus and serves as Communications Officer for the Association for Educational Communications and Technology's (AECT) Council on Systemic Change. He holds degrees from Clarkson University and Syracuse University. His current areas of interest

James B. Ellsworth

include educational reengineering, program evaluation, and the teacher's role in systemic reform. Dr. Ellsworth has written numerous publications; is a frequent invited speaker on education systems for information-based society; and serves as Managing Editor for IST*Online*, a project to create a peer-reviewed annotated bibliography of scholarly educational resources on the Internet. He is an active member of several professional associations including AECT, the International Society for Performance Improvement (ISPI), and the American Educational Research Association (AERA).

Table of Contents

Figures

Foreword

Change. It happens. Why should we care or try to understand its nature? Change surrounds us; we are immersed regularly in its process. Each day we encounter new information and experiences that affect our perceptions of the world. The advent of an information-based society has precipitated change at a rate never before seen. We are now recognizing change as a regular part of our lives–and often questioning how to deal with it.

To make sense of change, organizations like the Association for Educational Communications and Technology (AECT), have created sections, publications, and program tracks devoted to the discussion of change theory and practice. Within AECT's Council on Systemic Change (formerly the CHANGE Division), we have explored the differences and commonalties of change theory. No one theory has arisen as "correct." Instead, we have found that educators must understand and draw from the range of approaches in order to guide the process of change.

Educators are constantly dealing with change as they strive to be responsive to the needs of their students and society. At times the task is overwhelming. The constancy of change–or a lack of understanding of its course–can lead them to take a "wait and see" stance: to respond only to serious crises as they emerge. Banathy[1] suggests that the ship of education may be on troubled waters, with its crew attempting isolated, piecemeal efforts to repair individual components rather than changing course to avoid the icebergs ahead.

This book explores change theory from multiple perspectives seen in decades of its research and practice. Jim Ellsworth does indeed offer educators theoretical blueprints or maps that will enable them to understand and guide change. After surveying the topography of its theory, Ellsworth suggests that rather than seeking a single "best" approach to guiding change, the practitioner should use the approaches together in service of an overall strategy, using the tools each provides to address the needs for which they are best suited.

To aid this integration, he provides the reader with a map relating each approach to the practitioner's likely questions. Combined with his comprehensive overview of the change process, this offers ready access to an outstanding set of tools for applying change theory to real world innovation and reform.

Mary C. Herring
AECT Council on Systemic Change, President, 1999-2000

---

[1] Banathy, B.H. (1993). Systems Design: A Creative Response to the Current Educational Predicament. In C. M. Reigeluth, B. H. Banathy, & J. R. Olson (Eds.), Comprehensive Systems Design: A New Educational Technology (pp. 9-49). Berlin: Springer-Verlag.

Introduction

Purpose

This Educational Resources Information Center (ERIC) book is offered as a resource to educators who must deal with change. It is a practitioner's tool, intended as a road map for the teacher, professor, or administrator seeking guidance from the literature on change. Change isn't new, and neither is its study. Consequently, a rich set of frameworks is available to guide us, often solidly grounded in empirical studies and practical applications. This book seeks to bring them together as a practitioner's toolbox: it offers a brief history; presents educational change frameworks, with examples; and describes trends in the theory and practice of change. It concludes with an annotated bibliography of key change literature.

While the volume of published literature concerning educational change is staggering (an ERIC search as of this writing yielded 31,018 hits) most of these contributions can be classified under a much more manageable set of major perspectives, which I am loosely calling "models" of change. These perspectives were selected based on their prevalence in the research, and their ability to be combined to yield a 360° view of the change process. In each case, one author's, or group of authors', work has been selected to represent that perspective. Other authors, who have provided crucial elaborations and updates to these main examples, are also included in the corresponding chapter. A small group of studies from disciplines outside educational change (in some cases outside education) were also selected based on their contribution of key concepts not found elsewhere in the literature.

Assumptions

This book makes several implicit assumptions about the nature of change, and thus about the characteristics of an effective approach to its management. Most obviously, it assumes that change can be understood and managed. When change is approached in this fashion, it is sometimes referred to as *planned* change.

At a subtler level, though, is the second fundamental assumption that the key to understanding and managing change successfully is to bring the diverse models together in a "toolbox," rather than to select only one model. Doing so will equip the practitioner with a full set of specialized tools for managing change. Supporting this belief are the following explicit assumptions:

- Planned change is a specialized instance of the general communication model (Rogers, 1995, pp. 5-6).
- The understanding and application of frameworks describing planned change can be facilitated by examining the portion of the change communication model on which each framework is focused.
- The closer the match between the framework on which interventions are based and the portion of the change communication model on which a practitioner desires to operate using those interventions, the more likely they are to produce the desired effects.
- The application of multiple, coordinated interventions to a given portion of the change communication model is more likely to produce the desired effects than the application of a single intervention, or of multiple, uncoordinated interventions (Hall & Hord, 1987, p. 144).
- Coordinated operation on multiple portions of the change communication model is more likely to result in successful and enduring change than an effort which operates on only one portion, or operates on multiple portions in an uncoordinated fashion.

These assumptions all relate to efforts to implement a *single innovation*, however that is conceived. This book's third fundamental assumption is that effective, lasting change is best facilitated by multiple, coordinated innovations addressing the priorities and concerns of multiple stakeholder groups (Hirumi, 1995, in the section "How do you restructure education through systemic change?").

Early Traditions of Change Research

Current research in educational change can trace its roots to two philosophical "ancestors." The first of these, emerging as its own discipline in the 1940s, is most commonly referred to as the *Diffusion of Innovations* tradition. The second, articulated in the 1950s, is the *general systems theory* tradition. The organizing philosophy underlying my book resulted from a fusion of these two traditions in the late 1980s and early 1990s, and is called *systemic change in education.*

The Diffusion of Innovations tradition is generally considered to have begun with the Ryan and Gross study (1943) of the diffusion of hybrid seed corn in Iowa between 1928 and 1941, although less formal studies go back as far as Gabriel de Tarde (1903) and his book, *The Laws of Imitation* (Rogers, 1995, pp. 31, 39-40). Early diffusion research was itself reflected in several more focused traditions, particularly anthropology, sociology, and communication. It is from the study of communication that the phrase "Diffusion of Innovations" emerged as representative of the field of study (Rogers, 1962). Everett Rogers currently identifies ten such traditions under the umbrella of diffusion, accounting for over 3,000 research studies (1995, pp. 42-43). In education, diffusion research reached prominence in the early 1970s; in fact, each of the main examples (except Rogers) selected to represent the various perspectives in my book originated with a publication during this time.

The general systems theory tradition effectively began with the launch of Ludwig von Bertalanffy's journal, *General Systems* (1956). Early studies and publications tended to focus on management science, for example C. West Churchman's book, *The Systems Approach* (1968) or general science, for example George Klir's book, *An Approach to General Systems Theory* (1969). General systems theory was introduced into educational research in 1973 by Bela Banathy's book, *Developing a Systems View of Education* (1973). Interest in the systems approach surged briefly, and some works in that timeframe usually classified under the Diffusion tradition even incorporated related frameworks in their design (for example, the use of Adaptive Systems Theory in Hall, Wallace & Dossett, 1973). However, it emerged as a major focus of educational research fifteen years later, with the publication of Banathy's paper "Systems Inquiry in Education" (1988), in the journal *Systems Practice*.

Other Reviews of Change Research

This book is not the first major publication to review the change literature, nor even the first to do so using systems theory as an organizing framework. See Salisbury's *Five Technologies for Educational Change* (1996). Salisbury's chapters dealing with systems thinking, systems design, and change management (three of his "five technologies") are particularly effective at bringing together the contributions of research in these areas in a concise overview, and cover both the diffusion and systems research traditions. Jerrold Kemp's *A School Changes* (1995) is strong in references to recent publications dealing explicitly with systemic change in education, as well as to publications outside of change research, in the context of a particular school's successful change effort. Reigeluth and Garfinkle, in their 1994 book, *Systemic Change in Education* focus exclusively on this area, providing chapters on theory, models, and support components, as well as examples of a systemic approach to education reform that were successful.

Another recent publication of interest is Means, et al. (1993), Using Technology to Support Education Reform. This publication, which synthesizes educational technology research in support of education reform, does not explicitly treat either the mainstream diffusion or systems literature. However it is implicitly systemic in its approach and clearly deals with educational change. It may be chiefly of use to those involved in technology-based reform who are seeking an outline of what a systemic effort of this type might consider.

Practical Application of Educational Change Theory

In any field of human inquiry, we tend to proceed somewhat like the fabled blind men examining the elephant. Early in our research, someone excitedly tells us there's an elephant "over there," and points us in the right direction. We feel our way into the right vicinity until we stumble into some part of the creature, and proceed to explore it from that perspective. Over time as we grope beyond this part, we begin to encounter other questing hands. We all pause together to compare notes. At first, because no one has the same description, we are certain everyone else is wrong. We know what we felt; any disparate results can only come from flawed methodology or a focus too different to be relevant to *us!*

Eventually, though, someone arrives on the scene to find us quarreling, and this newcomer and those who follow begin to wonder how it all fits together, and start to try to reconcile the conflicting descriptions. I believe this is the stage at which research on change in education has arrived. I "see" no more clearly than my predecessors, certainly. But thanks to their diligent examinations and thorough descriptions I am making this attempt to fit the descriptions together.

My effort is qualitatively different from that of the early systems theorists. They are a bit like a sighted man just coming upon the scene and delivering a flowing description of a whole elephant. Their perspective and understanding allows us to see the creature as a system–to comprehend an elephant as more than the sum of its parts–which is vitally important (Salisbury, 1996, p. 18). Yet I maintain that it is of no less importance for us to hold onto those original descriptions, and to fit them into the context of the whole that is now revealed.

The practitioner wants to do something with this elephant. From the systems theorists, he knows that he wants one: as a whole, it fits his needs. But to build the platform to set upon its back, he still needs to talk to the person who actually felt its back and flanks. To calculate the load it can pull without exhaustion, he needs to talk to the person who examined its powerful legs. To determine the manipulative operations he can train it to perform, he needs to talk to the person who studied its strong and flexible trunk.

Thus it is with educational change. When we are dealing with the operations of a particular part of the change communications model, the empirical knowledge we have from scholars of that part is, in that moment, more important to our success than philosophical knowledge of the whole. Yet we must always return to the insights the systemic perspective gives us into the operation of the gestalt, lest we become so captivated by the strength of the flanks that we believe it a wall, and so entranced by the flexibility of the trunk that we believe it a snake.

I wrote this book to help the practitioner understand the whole and apply the parts. Perhaps together, aided by the authors whose works are presented here, we will at last be able to remove the blindfolds from our eyes, exclaiming, "Voilá! The elephant!"

A Strategy
for
Educational
Change

chapter **1**

Suppose you had a classroom. In this classroom, you had everything necessary for learning to occur. You had kids who were eager to learn. You had textbooks and lab supplies. You had computers, filtered Internet connectivity, and appropriate software. You had lesson plans that were well crafted, and that contained balanced, effective learning activities. You had reliable, valid assessments with which to judge student progress. You had paper, pencils, and all the little things. You had a comfortable, safe environment in which learning could occur. You had a trained, qualified, innovative, and dedicated teacher who could bring it all together.

Now, suppose you had no curriculum. You had no framework to organize those lesson plans, to help the teacher to know when to teach what subjects…or in what order. Suppose, in short, that you had no strategy. What effects do you suppose that would have on the success of the learning experience in that classroom at the end of the year?

Why Change Needs a Strategy

Over the years, the knowledge base of change research has become a bit like this metaphorical classroom. The pioneers erected the structure and their successors have populated it with empirically grounded theory describing every aspect of how change works. Yet as practitioners of educational change, we have no successful strategy to help us apply these theories in support of the change process *as a whole*.

To some extent, this results from a curious and counterproductive tendency in our culture to arrive at a position, stake out our philosophical turf, and defend it stoically against all comers. In the change research community, this was reflected in the formation of what Rogers (1995) has termed "invisible colleges" of change researchers, which for several decades proved remarkably resistant to the exchange of information (p. 38). Many researchers aligned with each of the perspectives discussed in this book have stayed within the frameworks defining their models.

Ironically, when new evidence or a persuasive new model appears, this drive often reverses itself among converts from the old models. Previous loyalties may give way to a sort of "intellectual cannibalism" where what was previously regarded as "high truth" is suddenly dismissed as the deluded belief of a more ignorant time.

In summary, throughout much of the 1990s, change research has seen little exchange among the classical camps (each remaining convinced that its approach is most productive). Thus, no strategy has emerged from inside these camps to unite their parts in service of the change communication model as a whole. Meanwhile, the fresh perspective most capable of doing so from the outside–systemic change–ironically merely wrote them off as not being systemic (perhaps based on the fragmentary presentation of the classical camps).

Fortunately, the past few years have seen an increasing recognition on all sides that there is value in uniting the empirical knowledge base of the classical models within a systemic context. This book attempts to do so, using the concept of change as a specialized instance of the general communications model (Rogers, 1995, pp. 5-6) to illustrate how the tactics represented by the classical models may be fused into a comprehensive, systemic strategy for the change process as a whole.

The Change Communication Model

Let us begin by considering the general communication model (Figure 1). A sender wishes to communicate a *message* to a *receiver.* This is accomplished using a *medium,* which is essentially a means for establishing

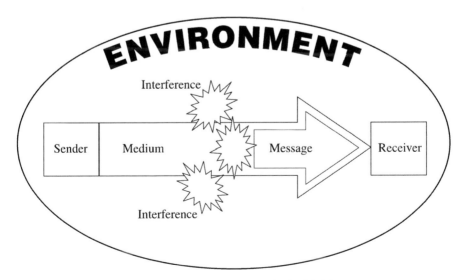

Figure 1. The General Communication Model

a channel through the *environment* between the two communicants. However, this environment also contains *interference* which can disrupt the medium or distort the message.

First, it should be observed that this is a model of a communication *system*. With a message as the unit of analysis, it represents all the major components that interact to form an instance of communication. It should also be noted that many media are capable of simultaneously addressing the same message from the same sender to many receivers. For example, the principal addressing her school over a public address system is engaged in a single communication instance that sends a single message to multiple receivers.

It is also worth pointing out, for this example, that some of these receivers are teachers, while others are students, and still others are administrative or support personnel. Receivers from each of these types have different characteristics, which may cause them to reach differently to the same message. Likewise, receivers perceiving differences between themselves and the sender may also react differently. Many media also reach receivers in or across different environments, each of which may present varying types or levels of interference. Effective communication systems must consider all these factors and may individualize the message or the medium selected for certain types of audiences. This essentially creates a larger communication system in which multiple instances of the model in Figure 1 serve the same communication objective.

With these things in mind, we may now consider the particular instance of this model that is change (Figure 2). In this context, we have a *change agent* who wishes to communicate an *innovation* to an *intended adopter*. This is accomplished using a *change process* that establishes a channel through the *change environment* between the two communicants. However, this environment also contains *resistance* that can disrupt the change process or distort how the innovation appears to the intended adopter.

Once again, as with the general model, this is a depiction of a complete system–in this case of *change* communication. With a single innovation as the unit of analysis, it represents all the major components that interact to form an instance of this form of communication. The classical models discussed in this book address each of these components in turn, thereby providing empirically grounded tactics suited to operation on each. By uniting these tactics in service to a guiding strategy for a particular change effort, we improve our chances of effective, lasting change.

Before we consider what this strategy might entail, one crucial point should be emphasized, which is not so readily apparent in the change communication model as in its more general counterpart. It is easily recognized that communication is (or should be) a two-way process in most instances (Rogers, 1995, p. 6). In the general communication model, this is simply reflected by the two parties changing places: the receiver becomes the sender and vice versa. In the change communication model, however, it might appear to be a one-way process, as the intended adopter is unlikely to switch places with the change agent. This would be a

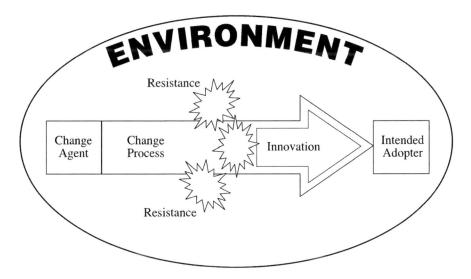

Figure 2. The Change Communication Model

misinterpretation–and often a fatal one–for the change effort. Communication throughout the process must flow in both directions. The flow from intended adopter to change agent is merely an instance of the general communication model rather than the specialized change form! Change practice that does not encourage this feedback is certainly unethical (amounting to a manipulative process anchored in the paternalistic belief that "the change agent knows best") and most likely unsuccessful as well.

This need to tie change practice to the requirements and priorities of its stakeholders is one of the central tenets of systemic change that is not immediately evident from Figure 2. Consequently, it is not enough to simply describe the parts or to show how they fit together. Understanding the relationships among the components illustrated in the change communication model is an important part of the strategy for change presented here, but it is insufficient as a strategy unto itself. What's missing–the portion dealing with the interrelationships between the system or subsystem being changed and its surrounding systems and supra systems–is the topic of the final section in this chapter.

Guiding Change Systemically

It has already been noted that both the general communication model and the change communication model represent a system. Webster's (1979, p. 1853) defines a system as "a set or arrangement of things so related or connected as to form a unity or organic whole." There are three components of this definition of particular importance here:

1. "A set or arrangement of things": Each component of a system can be identified and examined separately. Understanding the system does not demand that the system be seen only as the whole.

2. "So related or connected as to form": These components, however, do not function in isolation. One can identify and examine the inherent interdependencies and interactions between them.

3. "A unity or organic whole": The nature and existence of the relationships between the components presents synergies that cause the operation of the whole to be more effective than the operation of the parts in isolation (Salisbury, 1996, pp. 9-10).

This in no way diminishes the accuracy or importance of empirically-derived knowledge concerning the individual operation of the parts. To consider an obvious example, modern medicine clearly views the human body systemically. Liver disease produces a yellowing of the skin and stomach distress, yet we do not simply treat the skin or the stomach. It is equally important to note that we do not treat the system either (with the exception of holistic medicine): our understanding of the system tells us that these symptoms may best be addressed by treating the liver. So while a focus on the system as a whole is essential for diagnosis, application of that diagnosis by the practitioner requires empirical knowledge of the operation of the individual part (or subsystem) as well, in this case the liver.

In addition to multiple parts, systems often have multiple dimensions that must be understood. Applied as a strategy for guiding educational change, systems thinking is required in order to:
- Integrate the parts of the change communication model
- Select and coordinate the types of changes one makes
- Involve stakeholders and consider their needs and concerns
- Ensure that the end result of these processes constitutes a viable system in the context of its surrounding systems.

The first two dimensions are discussed in this section. The last two are primarily addressed in Chapter 9 on the system.

Integrating the parts of the change communication model requires some additional explanation. Take another look at Figure 2. While at first glance it may appear to be a straightforward linear model, further examination reveals additional complexity. The change agent is not always the developer of the innovation. Frequently, this is simply an individual within the system of intended adopters who wishes to (or is assigned to) facilitate the diffusion of a pre-existing innovation. A linear model might therefore be expected to place the innovation first. But the wise innovation developer, taking the broader systems view discussed in Chapter 9, will have studied the characteristics of the intended adopters, their relationship within the systems of which they are a part, and the environment in which those systems exist. Should those components, then, be placed first?

In fact, the change communication model is not linear. It is organized according to functional (i.e., systemic) relationships, rather than by linear time. A practitioner will need to vary the portion of the model she focuses on, as her objectives bring its different parts into focus. Thus, the order of the chapters in this book is somewhat arbitrary.

What is critical to understand about the components of the change communication model–as a system–is the effects that each is likely to have on the others. For example, much early change research assumed that the primary, if not the exclusive, determinant of diffusion was the "objective" quality of the innovation (Burkman, 1987, p. 437). Yet history is replete with examples where innovations whose effectiveness could be soundly demonstrated failed to diffuse (Rogers, 1995, pp. 7-10). Later research has uncovered many possible reasons for this, which the change communication model will illustrate easily.

First an innovation is "carried" from change agent to intended adopter by the change process. One of the major classical camps of diffusion research arose in recognition that a flawed process can doom the diffusion of an otherwise effective innovation. Likewise the ultimate goal of a single instance of the change communication model is to get a particular intended adopter to "buy into" the innovation and use it in a way that improves some aspect of their lives or the lives of those they serve. (Chapter 3 addresses characteristics of the innovation itself that contribute to this goal, and Chapter 7 discusses the concerns of these adopters and the levels of innovation use they must be guided through before the desired "buy-in" can occur.) It must also be remembered that each instance of the model occurs within an environment, whose conditions will interact with the design of the change process to affect its success. The environment also contains resistance factors that may disrupt the process or distort the message. Finally, the characteristics of the change agent and the level of the system at which he works will interact with the design of the change process and, perhaps, the nature of the innovation. All of these, in turn, affect the intended adopter's perception. Understanding the systemic interaction of these components will facilitate more effective intervention, and will frequently suggest applying a package of interventions whose components are assembled using these interrelationships to reinforce one another.

Selecting and coordinating the types of changes that one makes are also critical aspects of a systemic strategy for change. The problems facing education today rarely reflect a single, "diseased" component that must be restored to its previous state to bring the system back to a healthy equilibrium. Most often they reflect a desire to bring new tools to bear to enable the system to meet new requirements. In such cases, while the success of each individual innovation depends on coordinated attention to the parts discussed above, producing the desired effects may require many coordinated, mutually reinforcing innovations that are bundled and introduced concurrently to produce an essentially new system (Figure 3).

For example, the debate about the effect of reduced class size on student learning has raged for decades with no clear resolution. While the working hypothesis that smaller class size contributes to an enhanced learning experience is intuitively appealing, many empirical studies of this issue show no significant difference (Halloran, 1984; Harvey, 1994) or are inconclusive (Millard, 1977). One reason for this has been that teachers in "experimental" classrooms with smaller class sizes have received little or no training in instructional strategies appropriate for those class sizes (McIntyre & Marion, 1989). With teachers in "control" classrooms lecturing to large groups and teachers in "experimental" classrooms using the same methods to teach the same curricula to small groups, is it any wonder that significant differences were seldom observed?

This situation becomes even more pronounced when the core innovation under discussion is an emerging technology. Successful infusion of such an innovation will generally require accompanying innovations pairing it with appropriate pedagogy, "smart" classroom layouts, power and communication infrastructure improvements, and thorough teacher training with ongoing support (Ellsworth, 1997). Furthermore, it is frequently not sufficient that these innovations merely be complementary and undertaken concurrently. Active coordination between interdependent efforts is required (Hirumi, 1995). This coordination is represented by the bi-directional arrows that connect the parts of the change communication model in Figure 3.

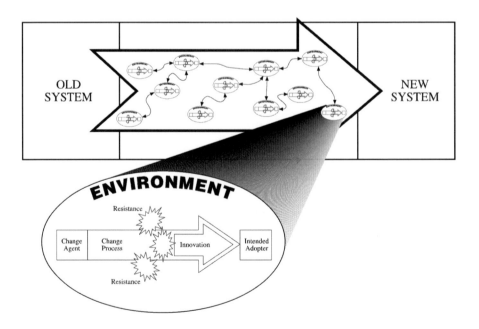

Figure 3. Systemic Application of the Change Communication Model

Summary

Educational change is in need of a strategy. Past research has supplied us with effective methods for "greasing the wheels" of particular portions of a change effort, but little guidance in their integration. Rogers (1995, pp. 5-6) tells us that change is a specialized instance of the general communication model (Figure 1). It therefore seems reasonable that this specialized instance (Figure 2) might prove useful as an organizing framework. In fact research from the Diffusion tradition has clustered around the components of such a model. This book will therefore explore the research using the change communication model as a framework to suggest the common change questions that can best be answered from the perspective of each classical camp of diffusion research.

While it is critical to understand which of the tools in our "change toolbox" can best serve the practitioner under different circumstances, it is equally important not to lose sight of the systemic nature of the change effort as a whole. Simply applying the tactics suggested by a classical model to facilitate the operation of a single component of the change communication model, or applying several in isolation to their corresponding components, will not maximize the overall effort's chance of success. To do this, interventions in support of each component must be integrated. Furthermore, in most cases, multiple, coordinated innovations must be undertaken to ensure that changes in one component of the system are supported and reinforced by changes in interdependent components. These ideas were discussed in this chapter. Two more concepts from the systemic model–stakeholder involvement and ensuring the integrity of the changed system in the context of its surroundings–will be discussed in Chapter 9 on the system.

Educational Change Models

chapter 2

Where does a superintendent who wants to incorporate portfolio assessment in her district go in the change literature for guidance? What framework would help her to anticipate teacher reactions to such a plan and to design appropriate interventions based on their specific needs? What model would help her identify ways to structure the introduction of portfolios that would facilitate teacher adoption? What framework could she turn to for help with identifying psychological, technical, or cultural obstacles that might interfere with effective adoption of portfolios? What model would help her understand the role and constraints most applicable to her in guiding this change?

Where could she turn for tips about issues and constituencies outside her schools that might affect implementation of this innovation, or for information on what other innovations might need to be introduced to support use of portfolios?

These are examples, from one particular perspective, of the issues that each of us confronts regularly as educators who must deal with–if not initiate–change in our environments. They should reinforce the idea–introduced in the preceding chapter–that each innovation will probably require some interventions targeting most components of the change communication model. They should also call to mind that a given innovation may well require other, supporting innovations, such as teacher training or new ways of communicating assessment results to parents. Yet the questions raised in the preceding paragraph continue to stand on their own merit. Where can we go for specific guidance, grounded in research and practice, when faced with an issue in a particular component (or a succession of particular components)? Where can we find the tactics suited specifically to each, which we may then integrate under our comprehensive strategy for intervention?

The Big Picture

The preceding chapter was devoted to an introduction of the change communication model as an overarching strategy for educational change. Its visual depiction of the relationships between the components discussed in the change literature highlighted the interdependence that makes such a systemic strategy so important to effective change. Opening with this "big picture" view allows the remainder of this book to be considered in light of the process it is intended to serve. From this point forward, however, the focus shifts to the type of questions with which this chapter opened. Given a particular question or issue related to a change effort, we will explore starting points in the literature that offer relevant, appropriate guidance for the practitioner.

Question(s)	Component of Change Communication Model	Title of Flagship Publication (or Framework Name, if Different)	Principal Author(s)	Location in Monograph
What *attributes* can I build into the innovation or its implementation strategy to facilitate its acceptance by the intended adopter? How can the presence or absence of these attributes affect the rate of acceptance by the intended adopter (or prevent acceptance altogether)?	Innovation	*Diffusion of Innovations*	Rogers, E.M.	Chapter 3
What are the conditions that should exist or be created in the environment where the innovation is being introduced to facilitate its adoption?	Environment	*Conditions of Change*	Ely, D.P.	Chapter 4
What are the implications of educational change for people or organizations promoting or opposing it at particular levels? What can I, as a(n)... (e.g., teacher, district administrator, parent) do to promote change that addresses my needs and priorities?	Change Agent	*Meaning of Educational Change*	Fullan, M.G. Stiegelbauer, S.M.	Chapter 5
What are the essential stages of the change facilitation process? What activities should the change agent be engaged in during each stage?	Change Process	*Change Agent's Guide*	Havelock, R.G.	Chapter 6
What stages do teachers go through as an innovation is implemented? What will be the major focus of their concerns at each stage? What levels of innovation use are likely to be exhibited at each stage? How do I identify which stage teachers are at right now? How do I assess the extent to which teachers are actually using the innovation as its developers intended?	Intended Adopter	*Concerns-Based Adoption Model (CBAM)*	Hall, G.E. Hord, S.M. Newlove, B.W.	Chapter 7
What are the cultural, social, organizational, and psychological *barriers* to change that can promote resistance to the innovation? What can I do to lower these barriers and encourage adoption?	Resistance	*Strategies for Planned Change*	Zaltman, G. Duncan, R.B.	Chapter 8
What are the factors *outside* the immediate environment in which the innovation is being introduced that can affect its adoption? How can change efforts combine multiple, mutually reinforcing innovations to increase the likelihood of effective, lasting change? What stakeholders and constituencies are likely to see their interests impacted by this change, and how can I work with them to ensure they see their concerns being addressed?	System	*Systemic Change in Education*	Banathy, B.H. Reigeluth, C.M. Garfinkle, R.J. Carr-Chellman, A.A. Jenlink, P.M.	Chapter 9

Figure 4. A Taxonomy of Change Models Based on Common Questions in Practice

In this context, the "big picture" looks a bit different. Rather than an illustration of how the various components of change fit together to form the process as a whole, this new perspective might better be viewed as a tabulation of the models according to the questions they most readily answer. Figure 4 is such a tool. The left-hand column shows common questions related to change practice. (Common questions related to the change communication model are presented in the preceding chapter.) The change framework most suited to answer the question is identified, and the principal authors associated with that framework are listed, along with the chapter in this book in which their work is discussed.

Still, at the end of the day, it is important to remember that all the individual interventions you may select or design based on the guidance of any particular framework must work together as components of your overall change strategy. You may never learn of a cultural incompatibility involving a perceived attribute of your innovation unless you apply an effective approach during the Relate stage of the change process. Furthermore, once you identify and address an incompatibility, you should reinforce your adjustments to the innovation's perceived attributes by addressing the participants' personal concerns.

In short, study the parts of this elephant. Learn what each part can do for you, because you will need the strength of each as you pursue any given change. But never forget that you need the whole elephant to make change work. While it is critical to understand each framework, change is an inherently systemic process and must be treated as such. You may find it useful to return to Figures 2 and 3 as visual reminders of the interrelationships among their components, or to consult Chapter 9 for guidance from systems theory as it applies to change.

The Classical Change Models

It should be re-emphasized that all of the frameworks included here were constructed independently by their authors, and that their hypothesized relationships to the change communication model are my own derivation based on my review of the literature. Regardless of the validity ascribed to my organization of these frameworks in a comprehensive model of educational change, each stands on its own merit and is supported by several decades of research and practice. It is also worth noting that while I believe the aspects of each framework emphasized herein to be the strongest and most commonly emulated in other studies, several of these models also address other aspects not discussed in this book.

While I have tried to expand the change communication model in a roughly sequential order, remember that it is not truly linear. Although an innovation must at least exist in concept before the practitioner will be concerned with dissemination, its developers would likely assess the conditions predisposing the environment toward change during initial planning. This assessment should also address system and adopter needs to determine the type of innovation to develop. Furthermore, some "innovation" characteristics really pertain to the way the innovation is introduced, and can therefore be altered later to enhance support. In short, any component of the change communication model may be revisited many times during a change effort.

With these caveats considered, we will begin with the focus on the innovation itself: the Diffusion of Innovations model. This model identifies the most salient characteristics of innovations, as well as each characteristic's effect on rate of adoption. In the current (fourth) edition of the book from which this model derives its name, Rogers (1995) notes that "much effort has been spent in studying 'people' differences in innovativeness...but that relatively little effort has been devoted to analyzing 'innovation' differences...." (p. 204). The importance of this perspective is reflected in research indicating that innovation attributes account for between 49 and 87 percent of variance in rate of adoption (Rogers, 1995, p. 206).

Practitioners are likely to find this perspective of the greatest use if they are engaged in the actual development of the innovation or if they are deciding whether (or how) to adapt the innovation to meet local requirements. Even when the "actual" form of the innovation is already set, however, Rogers' framework can be useful in determining how it is to be presented to its intended adopters (as mentioned above). For example, perceptions of the innovation can sometimes be improved by highlighting its similarities to other ideas or tools with which the adopter is already comfortable. Failure to consider issues of perception can be equally disastrous. For example, Chevrolet attempted to market the Nova model in Spanish-speaking countries without considering that "No va" means, "It doesn't go" in Spanish.

The focus on the change environment is represented by Ely's Conditions of Change model. This model explores the circumstances that predispose an environment toward change. Prior to Ely's first (1976) introduction of the conditions, research on the change environment had tended to focus on readily quantifiable, demographic, and logistical characteristics. These earlier studies rarely offered insight into the impact of environmental factors on the extent to which members of a social system were psychologically ready to consider change. This latter focus is typical of scholars writing from this perspective, who have produced a rich and consistent knowledge base supporting conditions that appear to apply equally to change in any cultural setting.

Here the practitioner is aided especially in the initial determination of whether change is likely to succeed, and thus whether it is worth pursuing, under the existing circumstances. After assessing the presence or absence of the conditions, the prospective change agent may learn whether or not the project has a good chance of yielding the anticipated benefits. Since failure can bring some very personal consequences for an innovation's advocates and waste the organization's time and resources, it may be best to avoid a project when the conditions are not present. Yet beyond this, Ely's perspective can also be useful for the practitioner who chooses to direct interventions toward improving one or more of the conditions, either before the implementation effort is launched or in response to changes in them as it progresses. This latter application, as a tool for continuous diagnosis and feedback, is a particularly promising use of the conditions that is often overlooked.

Shifting to a focus on the change agent, the *Meaning of Educational Change* model attempts to relate educational change to the perspectives of its major players at both the local/regional or national levels. This framework is the only one to treat individual actors in educational settings according to their diverse characteristics. In its namesake book (now titled *The New Meaning of Educational Change*), Fullan and Stiegelbauer (1991) present guidelines for resisting, coping with, or leading change efforts from perspectives ranging from the student to the national government. These guidelines are frequently preceded by an assessment of where each of these stakeholders stands as a group, with regard to demographics, attitudes, and other characteristics related to disposition toward school change. They are also accompanied, in each case, by a discussion of cautions and limitations related to each role and its activities in support of or resistance to educational change. This model is also considered to include studies focusing on the change agent at one particular level or perspective, for example the teacher (Nies & LaBrecque, 1980), the principal (Haynes & Blomstedt, 1986), or the consultant (Goddu, 1976).

This perspective is likely to serve the practitioner best in suggesting types of change activities that are typically associated with or especially effective for change agents in their particular role. These activities may then be situated within the change process (discussed in the next chapter) as they are pursued. Conversely, the discussion of limitations and constraints associated with their roles may enable them to avoid activities that are unlikely to produce a positive effect. It may even provoke resistance due to a perceived agenda stereotypically associated with their positions. Because Fullan and Stiegelbauer address the characteristics and change "postures" of many different roles, their framework may help the practitioner to understand the perspectives of others with whom the implementation effort requires collaboration. It may also help the practitioner to understand those who resist the desired change.

A focus on the change process is seen in the *Change Agent's Guide* model, which is based on a classic book by Havelock first published in 1973. While at first glance it would seem to represent the change agent focus, it is in fact a book about "the process of innovation," as authors Havelock and Zlotolow state in the introduction to its current (1995) edition. The book's central theme and structure are supplied by a model of this process built around the *stages of planned change*. Perhaps introduced in response to literature reviews lamenting the lack of reliable, dependable guidance on the educational change process (e.g., Olivier, 1971), this model has gained a wide following and produced many follow-up studies confirming and elaborating on its principles. *The Change Agent's Guide* (Havelock & Zlotolow, 1995) itself incorporates four running case studies, which are used to illustrate the principles discussed.

With this model, the practitioner who is beginning to plan an implementation effort can find guidance for structuring it around the stages required to lay a solid foundation for lasting and effective change. As the effort progresses, this framework will also offer ideas, examples, and sometimes step-by-step guidance for activities and interventions at each stage. As the stages are presented, the author's discuss the importance of their associated activities, how they fit within the process as a whole, and relationships between them. In some cases, relationships with other change frameworks are also discussed.

One of the most useful features of this model is that it was designed expressly for the practitioner. It begins with a simplified, sequential perspective on the change process that makes it easy to grasp its basic flow. It then helps the change agent develop a more sophisticated understanding by identifying and explaining where and why these linear assumptions do not hold. Havelock and Zlotolow also address two critical topics rarely treated in the literature: the process by which change agents determine when their work with a given innovation is done and how they can guide its successful transition from implementation to institutionalization as a routine and accepted part of the client system.

The focus on the intended adopter is presented in the *Concerns-Based Adoption Model*, or *CBAM*, originally proposed by Hall, Wallace, and Dossett (1973). Scholars writing from this perspective proceed from the assumption that teachers are the key adopters of concern. This model has several unique strengths, including having dimensions which are each paired with a valid and reliable instrument for diagnosing current status (Hall, 1978, p. 2). It has also benefited from a large number of contributors, who have generally continued their CBAM research even after leaving the core group (e.g., Loucks, 1983; Rutherford, 1986). Coupled with new researchers and practitioners adopting the CBAM perspective, these characteristics have yielded an exceptionally rich knowledge base with strong empirical support.

Because CBAM can be used to track adopters' concerns and behaviors related to innovation use, it is a powerful tool for diagnosing the implementation effort's progress. This perspective can also be useful as the effort is launched, to assess whether prior exposure from other sources (like the media, or colleagues at other schools) has caused portions of the population to advance into subsequent Stages of Concern or Levels of Use. One of the key lessons of CBAM research is that the most effective interventions will vary accordingly, because adopter concerns evolve over time to focus on different issues. For example, if most adopters are experiencing intense personal concerns, a campaign aimed at highlighting the innovation's impact on student learning is unlikely to have much effect. Another useful feature of this framework is the Innovation Configuration (IC) Component Checklist, which allows the practitioner to communicate what effective innovation use actually looks like in its intended setting (e.g., the classroom) and even to specify what (if any) adaptations can be made to reduce strangeness or complexity without rendering the innovation ineffective.

The final framework explicitly represented in the change communication model's most basic form (see Figure 2), built around a focus on resistance to change, is the *Strategies for Planned Change* model that is represented the best by Zaltman and Duncan's book (1977) of the same name. From the title, one may correctly conclude that the term "strategies" covers a broader range than just resistance, but its thorough classification of barriers to change marks it as the classic representation of this genre. Their chapter on this subject identifies eighteen factors, comprising four major categories, which disrupt change efforts and distort adopter perceptions of innovations. While many of these factors–and their counterparts in other research following this perspective–merely reflect the absence of positive factors discussed in the preceding models, many others represent true negative factors working against change. From the standpoint of the change communication model, overcoming these obstacles is as necessary as any other component for the success of the change effort as a whole.

This framework can be useful to the practitioner because it explores change from the opposite perspective of most other models. By focusing attention on factors that erect barriers to change, Zaltman and Duncan help the practitioner to recognize such obstacles as they arise, or even to identify and address their underlying issues before they arise. It is important to note that a given individual can harbor intense pro-change and pro-resistance sentiments simultaneously. Therefore, while Ely's conditions, for example, may largely be present, they may be negated to some extent by the presence of social values that argue against adoption. The ability to diagnose the presence of resistance factors and act to reduce them is therefore just as essential as the ability to assess and develop factors promoting change.

While not a part of the change communication model reflecting a single innovation, the focus on the system added in Figure 3 and represented by the Systemic Change in Education model is an essential component of the overall change strategy described in this book. Recall that several coordinated and mutually reinforcing innovations, such as infrastructure, curriculum, pedagogy, and technology, are usually necessary to support effective, lasting change (Hinnant & Oliva, 1997; Hirumi, 1995). This principle, together with interactions among components of the change communication model itself (i.e., the non-linear interrelationships discussed earlier) and the involvement of stakeholders and surrounding systems external to the immediate environment into which innovations are being introduced, calls for the holistic perspective supplied by this model. Systemic change in educational contexts generally traces its roots to Banathy (1973, 1988, 1991), but has been greatly expanded and clarified by other scholars. Most notably this includes Reigeluth and Garfinkle (1994b), who assembled a translation of Banathy's basic research into a form more accessible to the practitioner.

Reigeluth and Garfinkle's perspective may be of particular use to the practitioner at this point because this framework is illustrated in a series of exemplars, or case-based examples that show its key points in practice. Having read the more theoretical discussion of the other frameworks in the preceding chapters, the reader may recognize some of their principles in the cases illustrating the systemic model. The practitioner should study the systemic paradigm as an integrating framework, within which all the tools and tactics introduced elsewhere in this book may be brought to bear.

Much human learning occurs when the real-world complexity of a subject is first artificially reduced to a manageable level, then gradually restored until a complete understanding is achieved. Similarly, the community of change practice has learned about its operation through independent study of the components of the change communication model, and is now beginning to examine the complex interrelationships that exist in its authentic settings. My book is organized to build on examination of each individual component with a "guided tour" of some contexts in which they are applied and in which those relationships can be illustrated. If I have succeeded, as you read in Chapter 9 about the perspectives of practitioners that Reigeluth and Garfinkle have assembled in their edited volume, one or more of these contexts will tie the lessons of the other models to your own experience. And you, too, will say, "Voilá! The elephant!"

Summary

The visual representation of the change communication model in the preceding chapter provided an organizer for what follows by illustrating the relationships among its components. This chapter, in contrast, presented the literature we will use as resources for answering questions frequently associated with the components. Figure 4 offered a one-page guide to this book, based on those questions. Each of the major perspectives represented in the literature was introduced with an overview of its history and orientation. In each case, the tools and tactics offered by the individual models were tied to the most salient benefits the practitioner can expect from studying and learning about them.

The major perspectives introduced are:

- Rogers' (1995) Diffusion of Innovations, focusing on innovation attributes
- Ely's (1990a) Conditions of Change, focusing on the social system's receptiveness to change
- Fullan and Stiegelbauer's (1991) perspective in *The New Meaning of Educational Change*, focusing on change agents
- Havelock and Zlotolow's (1995) perspective in *The Change Agent's Guide*, focusing on the change process
- Hall, Wallace, and Dossett's (1973) Concerns-Based Adoption Model, focusing on adopters

- Zaltman and Duncan's (1977) perspective in *Strategies for Planned Change*, focusing on resistance
- Reigeluth and Garfinkle's (1994b) perspective in *Systemic Change in Education*, focusing on the system.

The Innovation

An instructional software company is preparing a simulation to help teach human anatomy. Some of the programmers are excited about the advanced features they could add by integrating their program with some state-of-the-art virtual reality gear made by another company. The marketing team says the program is complicated already, and is afraid the add-on gear would make it too difficult to set up. What guidance does the change literature have to offer?

The project leader just got a call from a major textbook publisher who would like to collaborate on integrating the simulation with their text on human anatomy at that grade level. This would require some changes to the programming, but many schools that might want to adopt a simulation like this are currently using that textbook. Does change research suggest that this could make a significant difference in adoption?

A principal has seen marketing literature on the soon-to-be-released simulation, and is impressed. His science department thinks it will go well with the text and curricular materials they're already using, but it's divided over whether to throw out the old, manual exercises right away, or run them in tandem for a year. What would change research recommend?

These are some of the common situations arising in change practice, which call for a knowledge of how an innovation's attributes affect adoption. Whether you're the innovation's developer, a change agent responsible for its dissemination, or a teacher or educational leader who wants to implement it, you will make decisions affecting either the physical innovation or the way that innovation is perceived by those who you'd like to see adopt it. Such decisions require a focus on the innovation framed within the context of the overall change effort.

Rogers' Diffusion of Innovations

Among the most comprehensive discussions of this type is Rogers' book, *Diffusion of Innovations* (1995). In addition to being an excellent general practitioner's guide, this work contains an entire chapter on innovation attributes and their effect on adoption rate. Rogers developed and refined his framework in several studies over the last thirty years, feeling that "We need a standard classification scheme for describing the perceived attributes of innovations in universal terms" (p. 208). This conclusion had a very practical basis: as the preceding chapter noted, these attributes account for between 49 and 87 percent of variance in adoption rate (p. 206).

Rogers' framework consists of five characteristics which these inquiries suggest achieve "maximum generality and succinctness…(1) *relative advantage*, (2) *compatibility*, (3) *complexity*, (4) *trialability*, and (5) *observability*" (p. 208). In the 1995 edition of his book, *Diffusion of Innovations*, he prefaces his discussion of these attributes with a section titled "Explaining Rate of Adoption" (pp. 206-208), which combines the main effect of innovation attributes with four other factors. As part of this discussion, he presents an illustration (Figure 5), which relates these factors and the five attributes to rate of adoption (p. 207).

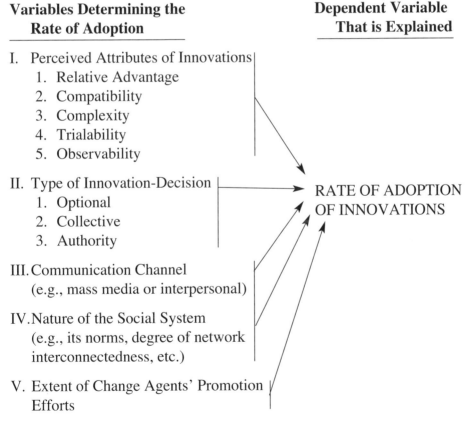

Figure 5. Rogers (1995). Variables Determining the Rate of Adoption of Innovations. *Note.* From *Diffusion of Innovations*, 4th ed. (p. 207), by E. M. Rogers, 1995, New York: The Free Press, a Division of Simon & Schuster. Copyright © 1995 by Everett M. Rogers. Copyright © 1962, 1971, 1983 by The Free Press. Reprinted by permission.

Although the variables Rogers identifies in this figure are described somewhat differently, a relationship to a component of the change communication model in Figure 2 is frequently clear. These other factors will therefore be discussed in more detail in subsequent chapters. Where such a relationship suggests itself, *Diffusion of Innovations* may also be useful as a supplement to the literature discussed in those chapters. For the moment, however, let us concentrate on the five attributes of innovations.

Relative advantage is perhaps the most obvious of these attributes. Simply put, this attribute represents the extent to which the innovation in question is perceived as being better than the tool or practice it replaces (Rogers, 1995, p. 212). This can represent itself in many ways. Perhaps the innovation can make its adopters jobs easier, or help them perform better without additional effort. Maybe it can free adopters of menial or administrative chores associated with a job, freeing them for the activities they find challenging or rewarding. Possibly it allows its adopters to do what they're already doing, but in half the time or at half the cost. Other benefits are more difficult to argue as desirable for the system as a whole, such as raising the prestige or perceived social status of the adopter. However, in some cases they may make useful incentives to supplement the benefit of adoption to the system in ways that may be more persuasive to the individuals who will make the adoption/rejection decision.

In general terms, Rogers identifies six "sub-dimensions" of relative advantage (p. 216):
  1. Economic profitability
  2. Low initial cost
  3. Decreased discomfort
  4. Social prestige
  5. Savings in time and effort
  6. Immediacy of reward.

Rogers notes that which types of relative advantage are most important will vary based on the nature of the innovation and the characteristics and values of the intended adopters (1995, p. 212).

Rogers makes three specific points concerning relative advantage that may be of particular importance to practitioners of educational change. These relate to *overadoption, preventive innovations,* and *use of incentives* (1995, pp. 215-221).

Rogers has long pointed out the "pro-innovation bias" of diffusion research (p. 100) and urged those involved in change efforts to guard against assuming that adoption is always good or appropriate. Overadoption refers to the decision to adopt an innovation when those knowledgeable of both innovation and context would recommend rejection (p. 215). In other words, there is no objective, tangible advantage to adoption in that context, but rather some subjective, intangible benefit, such as being seen as progressive or cutting edge. Rogers therefore notes "that one role of the change agent is to prevent too much adoption of an innovation, as well as to try to speed up the diffusion process" (p. 215). Applied to the practitioner of educational change, this cautions us to apply an informed skepticism when the chief argument for an innovation is to avoid being thought of as "stuck in the past" and no more substantive rationale is forthcoming!

Preventive innovations include those where the reward occurs long after adoption and those where the only reward is avoidance of an unpleasant event. Both of these circumstances are frequently found in educational innovations, particularly large-scale reforms. Rogers observes that these innovations diffuse slowly because individuals have difficulty perceiving their relative advantage (1995, p. 217). Nonetheless, he lists several instances of such innovations that diffused relatively quickly, and describes several aspects of their strategies that may have contributed to their success (pp. 218-219).

Use of incentives is a diffusion strategy that has been both controversial and common. Rogers notes that incentives can be monetary or non-monetary, and that they may be paid directly to the intended adopter, to someone in the system who can influence the intended adopters, or to the system as a whole (1995, pp. 219-220). While there are serious ethical, legal, and financial issues that must be considered before offering incentives for adopting educational changes, one conclusion from empirical research concerning their use (Rogers, 1973) merits their mention. In his book, *Diffusion of Innovations*, Rogers relates that innovators and early adopters tend to be of higher socioeconomic status than those who adopt later in the process. Therefore, use of incentives can be a powerful force for equity, as this technique causes more individuals of lower socioeconomic status to adopt (1995, p. 221).

Applied to education, this might be best considered at the system level: for example, by supplying one innovation, such as computers or Internet access, as an incentive for schools in poorer districts to adopt another, related innovation, such as a curriculum emphasizing higher-order thinking skills that uses multimedia or Internet-based resources. Of course, it should also be remembered that if incentives contribute strongly to a decision to adopt, there may be little relative advantage to continued use after the incentive has been obtained (1995, p. 221). Strategies employing linked innovations like the preceding example may offset this problem somewhat.

The second attribute, compatibility, describes the congruence of the innovation with the values, experience, and perceived needs of the intended adopters (Rogers, 1995, p. 224). The implications of some forms of compatibility are relatively clear. For example, few would want to be the change agent assigned to persuade Amish schools to adopt the computer-based simulation described at the beginning of this chapter! Yet other forms of compatibility can work just as strongly for–or against–an innovation. The project leader in this chapter's introduction had a major advantage in the publisher's desire to collaborate: since many schools' science curricula were already built around that publisher's textbook, these potential customers would perceive her innovation to be highly compatible. Imagine how much more difficult Marketing's job would be if the program's pedagogic assumptions conflicted with those of the curricula currently in place. Adopting the simulation might actually require adopting an entire new science curriculum for those grades, which would be a prohibitive cost for many schools.

In his discussion of compatibility, Rogers describes four related concepts that may be especially useful to practitioners of educational change: *technology clusters, naming of innovations, positioning of innovations,* and *indigenous knowledge systems* (1995, pp. 235-242).

The concept of technology clusters reflects the systemic notion of introducing multiple, mutually reinforcing innovations as a package, as represented in Figure 3. Rogers notes that "innovations often are not viewed singularly by individuals. They may be perceived as an interrelated bundle of new ideas" (1995, p. 235). This complex concept has many implications for educational change. Returning again to the example in this chapter's introduction, schools may view textbooks, curricula, and exercises (computer-based or not) as a technology cluster. An innovation seen as compatible with the cluster might be adopted singularly because of that compatibility, whereas an innovation incompatible with the rest of the cluster might be rejected. If new theoretical or technological developments require introducing an innovation that inherently conflicts with a cluster with which it is associated, it may be best to package it with other innovations to replace the entire cluster.

Naming of innovations is often careless, but issues of compatibility can ruin a poorly named innovation (Rogers, 1995, p. 236). Some names and descriptive phrases have value-loaded meanings—or no meaning at all—in a particular setting. Scientific or technical terms may simply not be understood. Imagine a school board member, who is concerned about an appropriate range of learning objectives in the curriculum, being asked to adopt "Bloom's Taxonomy," for example. In some communities, terms like "constructivism" or "systemic reform" carry highly charged connotations. This issue is also discussed in Havelock and Zlotolow's book *The Change Agent's Guide* (see Chapter 6), which uses the examples of sensitivity training, sex education, and black studies (1995, p. 123).

The other concepts, positioning of innovations and indigenous knowledge systems, are closely related. An indigenous knowledge system is comprised of the perceptions–or shared understanding–held by the members of the environment in which an innovation is to be introduced. Positioning of innovations is an application of perceived similarities between innovations and existing products or ideas. Positioning strategies may be used to bring the innovation into direct competition with a familiar idea or product (e.g., by describing it as "just like" something currently used, yet better in some key way). Alternatively, they may carefully establish it as "sufficiently similar" to be compatible (e.g., with other elements of a technology cluster but not competitive. Since positioning alters potential adopters' perceptions of the innovation itself, it represents a way for a non-developer (e.g., principal or change agent) to essentially alter the compatibility attribute of an existing innovation (Rogers, 1995, p. 238).

One point Rogers makes concerning indigenous knowledge systems is especially relevant to educational change. Past change efforts have frequently approached dissemination from the competitive perspective discussed above, assuming that indigenous knowledge systems have nothing of value to offer. This approach has frequently succeeded with ample marketing and badgering ("everybody who keeps up with the current development is doing it"). Yet it has also led to techniques or technologies being discontinued even though they may still be optimal for some subset of their original users. Change agents should use positioning to avoid needlessly displacing current practices that remain valid. Rogers also notes that indigenous knowledge systems generally have "master practitioners" who are regarded as experts by others in their social system. If an innovation is introduced as competing with the knowledge base that confers this status upon them, relative advantage issues may be triggered (see above) in a subpopulation with the influence and interpersonal network to erode compatibility perceptions among intended adopters (Rogers, 1995, pp. 241-242).

Complexity is Rogers' third attribute, and it is relatively self-explanatory. Innovations that are seen as difficult to understand or adopt will diffuse more slowly, as few will voluntarily embrace change that makes their lives more difficult (1995, p. 242). In the example introducing this chapter, addition of the virtual reality gear to the simulation would be likely to significantly increase its apparent complexity to the intended adopter, and this expectation sparked concerns in the Marketing Department. Difficulty in understanding what the innovation is intended to be is one aspect of complexity that is frequently overlooked. This is especially true of theoretical innovations, where the exact nature and description of the innovation is frequently refined for several years in light of subsequent studies before it stabilizes. One technique for making a theoretical or procedural innovation clearer to its intended adopters is Hall and Hord's (1987) *Innovation Configuration (IC) Component Checklist*, discussed in Chapter 7.

Rogers' final two innovation attributes are somewhat subtler. The fourth, trialability, refers to the extent to which a prospective adopter can "try out" an innovation before committing to full adoption. To some extent, this involves the ability to adopt the innovation a little at a time rather than all at once (Rogers, 1995, p. 243). The Harvard Business School's case studies in the 1970s is such an example, since they were introduced as a single activity in a lecture-based classroom, and then infused over time as an integral part of the course. Innovations such as these are likely to diffuse more rapidly than those that must immediately replace past practice in toto. An equally important aspect of this attribute, however, is the extent to which negative consequences of early, difficult, or failed adoption (discontinuance) can be minimized. The example at the beginning of this chapter illustrates both of these principles. A decision to retain the existing exercises for a year would allow the simulation to be adopted a little at a time, and would offer science teachers a fallback option in case technical or pedagogic difficulties encountered during implementation required its discontinuance in mid-year. Similarly, the administration should afford teachers and other stakeholders (e.g., students) maximum flexibility during implementation, so that they don't perceive themselves being "punished" for adopting. (This relates especially to the Management Stage of Concern discussed in Chapter 7, when teachers must juggle the mechanical aspects of innovation use with the continuing, often competing demands of the classroom.)

Observability is the last innovation attribute Rogers discusses, and it frequently interacts with the other four. It pertains to the intended adopter's ability to actually see the innovation being used by others. This "vicarious trialability" (Rogers, 1995, p. 244) makes that attribute less critical for later adopters of an innovation, but significantly more important to innovators and early adopters. One aspect of this reduces complexity: later adopters may find it easier to learn innovation use by watching it, rather than merely reading about it or having it described to them. Another aspect pertains to the consequences of adoption: innovations exhibiting relative advantage that are highly (and immediately) observable may diffuse more quickly than those whose positive consequences are invisible or delayed, such as preventive innovations.

Other Studies

In the years since Rogers first articulated these five attributes, other research more specifically focused on educational change has built upon his findings. Among the earliest and most interesting is a study by Holloway (1978) of the reactions of 100 high school principals to an innovative, cooperative high school-college program. This study is especially noteworthy because it employed a quantitative methodology (factor analysis), while Rogers' original study used the qualitative, rural sociology approach (Rogers, 1995, p. 209). Holloway's findings generally support Rogers, although he identified "status/prestige" as a separate factor from relative advantage and found little distinction between the effects of relative advantage and compatibility (Holloway, 1978, pp. 19, 27-28). Several other studies have also used statistical analysis techniques to arrive at innovation characteristics influencing adoption (Clinton, 1973; Hahn, 1974).

Other authors have arrived at similar findings independently. For example, in *Science Teachers' Perspectives on Alternate Assessment*, Newell (1992) cites no work by Rogers, yet concludes with the following observations (parallels from Rogers' findings are shown in brackets):

> "To improve the chances for long-term adoption of the new practice, one should focus on issues of practicality [complexity] and on helping teachers see the benefits of alternative assessment to student learning [relative advantage]. Teachers need opportunities to understand conceptually what is meant by alternative assessment [compatibility]. They need to see other teachers use it [observability] and to have an opportunity to try it themselves.... Consequences for not getting it right the first time should be minimal [trialability]." (p. 18)

Kearns (1992), examining the diffusion of eight computer-based systems in suburban Pittsburgh, took another interesting approach. Wary of accepting Rogers' attributes as the de facto critical characteristics, he elicited key attributes from study participants prior to measuring their effect on rate of adoption. He discovered twenty-five attributes, which included the five identified by Rogers. Interestingly, his subsequent analysis indicated that all twenty-five attributes accounted for only one additional percent of variance in rate of adoption over Rogers' five. Nonetheless, the general method of deriving a set of attributes grounded in the setting under study is noteworthy.

Another interesting twist on Rogers' perspective comes from Burkman, writing in Gagné's *Instructional Technology: Foundations* (1987). He provides a treatment of *factors affecting utilization*, which relies heavily on Rogers' model, but examines factors from the user's point of view, rather than the change agent's. Burkman refers to this approach as *User-Oriented Instructional Development* or *UOID*. The result is typified by his discussion of Rogers' relative advantage factor, which he looks at explicitly from both the instructor's and the organization's point of view (pp. 443-444).

Still other contributions are methodological: Moore and Benbasat (1990) have derived a standardized questionnaire to measure innovation characteristics based on the attributes Rogers identified. Continued use of such an instrument in research and practice will benefit the rigor of Rogers' model much as it has that of CBAM (Chapter 7).

Other work applies Rogers' framework to specific educational contexts or problems. In a unique, cross-disciplinary and cross-cultural study of distance education at Taiwan's National Open University, Shih and Zvacek (1991) combined Rogers' concept of diffusion with a curriculum development framework and Banathy's original (1973) concept of the systems view of education. This study may be especially useful as an illustration of the successful, combined application of two of the models discussed here. For a look at how adopter perceptions of innovation attributes can change over time, Hamilton and Thompson's (1992) study of Iowa State University's Electronic Educational Exchange program offers an interesting perspective which also considers adopter characteristics. Van Fleet and Durrance (1993) explore a different setting in their use of Rogers' five innovation attributes to develop strategies for closing a perceived communication gap between leaders of public libraries and the research community. Finally, Harris (1997) uses Rogers' model in conjunction with social systems theory to develop approaches useful for school technology leaders in facilitating the adoption of technological innovation.

Summary

Rogers, in his original edition of *Diffusion of Innovations* (1962), spearheaded research that emphasized the role of innovation characteristics (attributes) in the change process. This text–currently in its fourth edition (1995)–remains the epitome of the focus on the innovation. Rogers also identifies other factors affecting rate of adoption (Figure 5) in an interesting foreshadowing of the change communication model proposed here, although he gives less attention to their relationships with one another and uses slightly different terms. Rogers identified five attributes, which have been validated both by further qualitative inquiry (e.g., Newell, 1992) and by sophisticated quantitative techniques (e.g., Holloway, 1978). Rogers' innovation attributes (Rogers, 1995, p. 208) are:

- Relative advantage ("Is it better than what I've got now?")
- Compatibility ("Does it conflict with my values, practices, or needs?")
- Complexity ("Is it too difficult to understand or use in authentic settings?")
- Trialability ("Can I try it out first, and can I go back to what I was doing if I don't like it?")
- Observability ("Can I watch someone else using it before I decide whether to adopt?")

Over the years, research in educational change has applied Rogers' model to a wide variety of settings. Practitioners engaged in change efforts in these contexts are encouraged to explore these and related studies in greater detail. (Terms in italics are ERIC descriptors, with * indicating *major* descriptors–the primary subjects of the document or article.)

- Hamilton, J., & Thompson, A. (1992). The adoption and diffusion of an electronic network for education. In M. Simonson and K. Jurasek (Eds.), *Proceedings of selected research paper presentations at the convention of the Association for Educational Communications and Technology, Washington, DC.* (ED 347 991)

*Adoption (Ideas); *Attitudes; *Change Agents; College Faculty; *Computer Networks; *Educational Change; Elementary Secondary Education; Higher Education; Information Dissemination; *Information Networks; Student Teachers; Teachers; Telecommunications; Use Studies

- Harris, J. (1997). Who to hook and how: Advice for teacher trainers. *Learning and Leading with Technology, 24*(7), 54-57. (EJ 544 740)

Adoption (Ideas); *Change Agents; *Educational Change; Educational Technology; *Innovation; Models; Personality Traits; Social Characteristics; *Technology Transfer

- Shih, M., & Zvacek, S. (1991). Distance education in Taiwan: A model validated. In M. Simonson & C. Hargrave (Eds.), *Proceedings of selected research paper presentations at the convention of the Association for Educational Communications and Technology, Orlando, FL.* (ED 335 013)

Attitudes; Cultural Influences; Delivery Systems; *Distance Education; Educational Change; Educational Objectives; Educational Technology; *Educational Theories; Foreign Countries; Higher Education; *Models; Open Universities; Program Evaluation

- van Fleet, C., & Durrance, J. (1993). Public library leaders and research: Mechanisms, perceptions, and strategies. *Journal of Education for Library and Information Science, 34*(2), 137-152. (EJ 464 414)

*Change Strategies; *Communication (Thought Transfer); *Librarians; Library Research; Models; Periodicals; *Public Libraries; Research Utilization; *Researchers; Telephone Surveys; *Theory Practice Relationship*

The
Change
Environment

chapter 4

After extensive research and development, an innovative instructional practice is ready for dissemination. The developers were familiar with Rogers' Diffusion of Innovations model discussed in the preceding chapter, so the innovation's attributes (and their marketing strategies) have been carefully crafted to facilitate rapid adoption. Independent studies have shown the new practice to produce statistically significant increases in learning over the most comparable practice currently in use.

The lead developer leans back in her chair and smiles. She knows how much effort goes into a successful change effort; she's had to work hard for her successes. But this one should be easy. With a sound pedagogy backed by such favorable validation results, what else is necessary?

The developers in this example are confident of a straightforward and successful dissemination effort, and with good reason. It has long been conventional wisdom that the most important factor in determining an innovation's success is the quality of the innovation itself. Build a better mousetrap, and the world will beat a path to your door. Early models of educational change often reinforced this assumption (Burkman, 1987, p. 437). Still, attempts to diffuse innovations of "proven" or "obvious" effectiveness have failed, and sometimes repeatedly, throughout history (see Rogers, 1995, pp. 7-10). Understanding what else is necessary sometimes demands a focus on the change environment situated within the change effort as a whole.

Ely's Conditions of Change

Ely was the first to emphasize the environmental conditions that promote change. In his pioneering study (1976) of change in libraries, he uses the term *Conditions for Change* to refer to a set of factors he uses to describe the environment. This study has also been refined over the years, and broadened to cover "the implementation of educational technology in a variety of education-related contexts" (Ely, 1990a, p. 299). Ely's approach recognizes that the characteristics of the innovation are not the only factors influencing its adoption. His research suggests that the environment in which the innovation is to be introduced can play an equally important role in determining a change effort's success.

Ely's studies have identified eight of these conditions, and validated them across various educational and cultural settings: (1) there must be "dissatisfaction with the status quo"; (2) "the people who will ultimately implement any innovation must possess sufficient knowledge and skills to do the job"; (3) "the things that are needed to make the innovation work should be easily accessible"; (4) "implementers must have time to learn, adapt, integrate, and reflect on what they are doing"; (5) "rewards or incentives [must] exist for participants"; (6) "participation [in the change process must be] expected and encouraged"; (7) "an unqualified go-ahead and vocal support for the innovation by key players and other stakeholders is necessary"; and (8) "leadership [must be] evident." Ely advocates these guidelines as "suggestions for successful implementation," but cautions that they are not "formulæ or rules," and that they cannot all be realistically achieved for all innovations in all environments (Ely, 1990a, pp. 300-303).

Ely's Conditions of Change model is arguably the broadest and most far-reaching of the classical change models. Turning again to the change communication model proposed in Figure 2, it is easy to see why. As a framework of environmental conditions, it seeks to represent the context within which the constructs defined by the other classical models operate. This necessarily makes its guidelines relatively general. This also suggests that its primary utility may be diagnostic, although Ely does state that, "The goal is to attain each of the eight conditions during implementation" (1990a, p. 303). It is important to understand that few change agents will have direct control over all the environmental variables this framework implies, so it may not be possible to affect all of them in the suggested manner. However, it seems reasonable to expect that improved knowledge of the current status of each of the conditions will enhance the ability of participants in the change effort to make more effective decisions. This, in turn, may often translate into an improved capacity for influencing the conditions in the desired direction. With that in mind, let us turn to the conditions themselves, and their implications for educational change efforts.

The first, and the most obvious, is *dissatisfaction with the status quo*. Change is uncomfortable: a wise saying holds that "the only person who welcomes change is a wet baby." For change to be voluntarily embraced, participants must perceive the status quo to be even less comfortable. Ely considers this issue on a deeper level, noting a wide range of possible causes for this dissatisfaction (1990a, p. 300). This has some important implications for those associated with educational change efforts.

From a diagnostic perspective, measuring dissatisfaction with the status quo can provide much more than just a number. Is the source of dissatisfaction internal, such as frustration with textbooks full of outdated information, or is it external, such as pressure from the state level because of test scores that are consistently low? Just who is dissatisfied, anyhow? Is it teachers, or parents, or the school board? The answers to these questions can help those involved with change efforts to understand who is supporting them and why, and what changes might cause that support to shift.

From a marketing perspective, understanding sources and levels of dissatisfaction can help the change agent's efforts to position the innovation to be more compatible with what Rogers calls "felt needs" (1995, p. 228; see also discussion of "compatibility" in Chapter 3, herein). For example, if a change agent was attempting to persuade teachers to accept properly validated Internet sources in student research, and she knew that particular teachers were dissatisfied with dated information in their textbook, she might emphasize the potential of high-quality Internet sources to include the latest research.

The second condition in Ely's framework recognizes that "the people who will ultimately implement any innovation must possess *sufficient knowledge and skills* to do the job" (1995, p. 300). Ely notes, "People may believe that changes are in order, but without the specific knowledge and skills to bring about the change the individual is helpless" (p. 300). Yet the importance of this condition is often overlooked in education change efforts. Unfortunately, this is probably the least likely of the conditions to exist in the environment as the change agent finds it. One of the most common causes of non-adoption or discontinuance is insufficient training of teachers and staff. Ironically, this training is often presented as an ill-conceived, last minute add-on to the implementation plan. Those associated with change efforts have many tools at their disposal for accomplishing this training, including in-service programs, technical support, or peer support. It is our responsibility when we undertake educational change to ensure that effective training is provided to all intended adopters.

Ely's own nomination for the most obvious of the conditions is the third, which requires that resources are available. While this certainly covers "big ticket" items, such as computers, classroom remodeling, personnel salaries, and teacher/staff training, it also covers things so small that they may be overlooked or seen as inconsequential. For example, some schools are unable to supply every student with a textbook, and are relying increasingly on students to supply materials. These practices have disturbing implications for students of lower socioeconomic status. As Ely states, "Resources are broadly defined as those tools and other relevant materials that are accessible to assist learners to acquire learning objectives" (1990a, p. 300). If those resources are unavailable, acquisition of those learning objectives will be significantly impeded. Those involved in educational change must work to ensure that necessary resources are both generally available (i.e., to the change effort) and equitably available to each student and teacher.

The fourth condition requires that *time* is available, that "implementers must have time to learn, adapt, integrate, and reflect on what they are doing" (Ely, 1990a, p. 300). Change by definition requires development of new competencies to support the new product, procedure, or principle being introduced. Those expected to adopt the innovation will need time for this, and also for developing or redeveloping supporting materials (e.g., Web-based training). Ely notes that "time is a vital element in the total process of educational change," further concluding that this should be "Good time. Company time. Paid time" (pp. 300-301). While it may be necessary, from a practical perspective, for employers and employees to share the time investment in lifelong learning required by an information-based society, there are equally practical disadvantages to shifting this investment further onto employees. This is especially true during times of change. Employees may be more likely to resist or reject the innovation if they believe that adoption will require an investment of time for which they will not be compensated. Alternatively, they may simply refuse to invest that time, resulting in a superficial implementation equally destructive of the innovation's intent. For example, the mid-1990s saw many presentations and paper-based lesson plans indiscriminately "converted" to the Web with no adjustments to pedagogy, because there simply wasn't any time provided to understand and adapt to the characteristics and requirements of the new medium.

Ely's fifth condition requires that *rewards or incentives* exist for participants (1990a, p. 301). This requirement is clearly related to Rogers' "relative advantage," but more explicitly acknowledges the possibility that such rewards may be entirely contrived. In general, as Rogers noted, relative advantage generated by innovation use is more cost-effective in creating lasting change than an incentive paid to promote adoption, because the latter may need to be repeated indefinitely to prevent discontinuance (Rogers, 1995, p. 221). However, for some innovations, there simply may be no relative advantage to adoption that is relevant to a particular participant. A tenured teacher, who has produced good test scores for thirty years through lectures and drills, for example, may not see the benefit in adopting a more participatory or constructivist pedagogy. In a situation like this, a linked reward may be appropriate, such as a reduced teaching load, increased secretarial help to revise materials, a budget increase, or a salary bonus. Regardless of whether the reward is intrinsic or extrinsic, or whether it is seen as the result or the cause of innovation use, it should be there in some form (Ely, 1990a, p. 301).

In an interesting parallel to the systemic model's emphasis on stakeholder involvement (see Chapter 9), the sixth condition is that *participation* is expected and encouraged (Ely, 1990a, p. 301). Ely begins by establishing that "This means shared decision making, communication among all parties involved, and representation where individual participation is difficult" (p. 301). At the very least, such a policy helps ensure "that each person feels that he or she has had an opportunity to comment on innovations that will directly affect his or her work" (p. 301). "Buying in" to the process with one's own time, effort, and ideas in this way contributes to a sense of ownership in the innovation. This makes it difficult for participants to advocate rejection, since doing so would essentially render their own investment wasted. Another important implication of this condition is that recognized leaders, both formal and informal, in the environment must communicate explicitly that general participation in (i.e., adoption of) the innovation is expected. While this may be implied, especially if those leaders introduce the innovation, failure to make such an expectation clear has contributed to large-scale neglect even of innovations that were mandated. Consider the official "adoption" of the metric system by the United States in the 1970s, for example, and its limited impact in daily life almost three decades later.

Ely's seventh condition highlights the importance of *commitment* by those who are involved. This acknowledges that "an unqualified go-ahead and vocal support for the innovation by key players and other stakeholders is necessary" for successful change (Ely, 1990a, p. 301). This takes the "expectation and encouragement" of the preceding condition to another important level. Educators are well acquainted with the "flavor of the month" or "panacea du jour" phenomena, where a given innovation is "the institution's most important initiative" for a few months to a couple of years, yet never heard of again when it is suddenly replaced by the next "most important initiative." Change requires effort. Potential adopters, who are being asked to commit time and effort to the innovation's success, will be looking to their leaders for evidence of long term backing. For example, teachers may be reluctant to develop competencies in computer-based learning if the school's budget does not contain money for maintenance, upgrades, new software, or technical support. As Ely observes, they are not looking for "blind commitment, but firm and visible evidence that there is endorsement and continuing support for implementation" (p. 302). Such support must also be reinforced at all levels of leadership (p. 301), since an innovation supported by just one individual can fall into disuse as soon as he leaves the organization (Ellsworth, 1998, p. 131). If supervisors close to the intended adopters do not support implementation, old practices will continue unmodified, except for a façade hastily erected whenever the supportive leader enters the area (Ellsworth, 1998, p. 9).

The final condition in Ely's model requires that *leadership* is evident. While at one level this echoes the importance of the leaders' expectations and commitment discussed in the preceding two conditions, Ely focuses more heavily on a subtler implication. Whereas the cognitive or "rational" impact of leadership in the change environment may be summed up according to the rest of the framework (i.e., leaders' promotion or provision of those conditions), leaders also exert significant affective influences. Whether they are official supervisors or informal role models, mentors, or advisors, these individuals provide those around them with inspiration and encouragement throughout all phases of implementation. "They are available for consultation when discouragement or failure occur; and they continually communicate their enthusiasm for the work at hand" (Ely, 1990a, p. 302). This reinforcement is particularly crucial in educational settings, where individual practitioners generally act with great autonomy. However, identifying respected peers to provide it is frequently not seen as a priority until a crisis arrives. As Hall observes, "Change is a process, not an event" (1978, p. 1). Availability of affective support throughout this process is a key factor in avoiding discontinuance and achieving institutionalization. Thus, those who will provide it should be present and clearly visible to all participants from the beginning (Ely, 1990a, p. 302).

Other Studies

Prior to Ely's initial proposal of this framework (1976), studies of environmental characteristics facilitating change were typified by Volume II of the Rand Change Agent Study (Berman & Pauly, 1975), which focused chiefly on quantifiable, demographic characteristics of the school environment, such as enrollment and finances. While these studies provided useful insights on the logistical aspects of the environment that impact the change process, they largely ignored the organizational, structural, and motivational aspects, as well as the aspects which start people thinking about change to begin with. This is the gap that Ely filled.

Ely's findings are held in similar regard to Rogers' innovation attributes. Other researchers have pursued Ely's approach, and their work originally tends to follow the qualitative, rural sociology approach more common to diffusion research (Rogers, p. 51). Essentially, Ely's framework was molded through "modified analytic induction" (Bogdan & Biklen, 1992, pp. 69-72). His initial description of the conditions was "held up to the light" of data from new studies in divergent settings, and the conditions and their definitions were continually refined until they formed a comprehensive model of environmental conditions facilitating change.

Typical of this genre is Haryono's (1990) investigation of higher education improvement programs in Indonesia. This study surveyed participants in a Course Reconstruction Workshop to assess the presence of Ely's conditions and explore their effect on the extent to which they implemented a new instructional method. Haryono found that the conditions were present in varying degrees, and that the extent to which they were present exerted a strong, positive effect on depth of implementation. This research is also significant in what it did not find–significant differences in Ely's conditions based on either inter-cultural differences or on intra-cultural demographics. In fact, Ely himself has explored these same issues, and further verified the stability of the conditions across cultures as diverse as those of Indonesia, Chile, and Peru (Ely, 1990b).

Another important issue is raised by Newton's (1992) study of the implementation of whole language teaching methods. She used observations and interviews to collect case information on two reading specialists, a teacher, and a reading coordinator who were involved in such an implementation. Her analysis confirmed that Ely's conditions were in fact present, although she also identified ten additional conditions pertaining specifically to whole language contexts. Not all studies of this type have revealed significant factors beyond the eight Ely identifies, however (e.g., Read, 1994), so it would be premature to conclude that other factors are necessarily present in all settings. Nevertheless, Newton's findings emphasize the risk in assuming that any existing model provides an exhaustive list of relevant factors in any particular environment other than that from which it is derived. Likewise, it may also be inaccurate to assume that all factors identified in an existing model are present in all settings. In fact, Read's study further suggests that, in some environments, as few as two of Ely's conditions may account for almost half the observed variance at implementation level.

As Ely's conditions have become more firmly defined, more researchers have incorporated them into advanced quantitative inquiries, just as they did with Rogers' work. For example, Read (1994) used multiple regression analysis, as did Bauder (1993). Bauder's study also used factor analysis; the results suggested refinements to the conditions' operational definitions (especially participation and leadership), although the conditions themselves were supported.

Some studies have also sought to derive such conditions without presupposing Ely's findings. While these studies may use different labels, their findings are generally consistent. For example, Kell, Harvey, and Drexler (1990, p. 5) cite five conditions including "a vision for reform" (Ely's first condition), "leadership and support from...administrators" (a combination of his seventh and eighth conditions), "conditions that allow teachers... flexibility, time, and incentives" (his fourth and fifth conditions), and so on.

Other research merely reflects Ely's perspective, neither presupposing his conditions nor in fact seeking to derive conditions at all. One such study is Kaufman and Paulston's (1991) report, *Hungarian Education in Transition*. This inquiry sought to identify the impact of sociopolitical change on Hungary's educational system following the break with socialism. One of the key findings was that while reform had enabled educational change at the local level, it had by and large not been actualized (p. 7). The authors' explanation of this phenomenon mainly reflects the absence of Ely's conditions. History has conditioned the Hungarian people to accept the status quo, since disaffection has always brought punishment, according to the authors (p. 12). The citizens who are expected to elect school boards to make local decisions have no concept of what this means, and the teachers who are expected to suggest reforms have no experience doing so (p. 7). The plan for "retooling" schools and faculty to reflect new social priorities, in most cases, provides insufficient time (p. 11). Rewards and incentives for change, where they exist, are countered by conditioned fear about "making trouble" (p. 16). As a result of these factors, both support and leadership are seen as lacking (p. 12). While Ely's conditions are not cited, such independent validation of their underlying principles (especially in another culture) strengthens their credibility.

A final category of study is particularly salient here: research suggesting that use of Ely's conditions in conjunction with other models may provide fertile ground for future inquiry. One such study, conducted by Riley (1995), examines the implementation of an innovative career development program promoting gender equity in New York State middle/junior high schools. She concludes that while Ely's conditions were useful in examining implementation efforts, their combination with other approaches might yield even greater insight. Marovitz (1994) also reaches similar conclusions in his study of educational television at West Point. In addition to Ely, Marovitz uses the work of Rogers, Burkman, and others to synthesize a more robust model of organizational diffusion, one that describes a four-phase process and addresses the influence of their integrated findings upon it. This strategy was required, he notes, because the individual supporting models varied in their ability to explain observed results at different stages of the change process.

Summary

In his exploration of the situational factors contributing to successful change in libraries (1976), Ely pioneered the investigation of environmental conditions and their influence on the change process. The systemic model (see Chapter 9) provides key insight into the nested levels of systems and stakeholders in the macro-environment. However, Ely's framework, updated and generalized in a 1990 article on educational technology innovation, continues to offer the greatest insight into the micro-environment immediately surrounding a single change effort. The phrase, "conditions of change" has come to represent this method of inquiry. Ely (1990a) identified eight conditions that facilitate an innovation's diffusion and adoption. Supported by subsequent research using both qualitative (e.g., Newton, 1992) and quantitative (e.g., Bauder, 1993) methods, these eight conditions are:

1. Dissatisfaction with the status quo ("There has to be a better way.")
2. Knowledge and skills exist ("I can do this" or "I can learn quickly.")
3. Resources are available ("I have everything I need to make it work.")
4. Time is available ("I have time to figure this out, and to adapt my other practices.")
5. Rewards or incentives exist for participants ("I'm going to get something out of this too.")
6. Participation is expected and encouraged ("This is important, and I have a voice in it.")
7. Commitment by those who are involved ("Administrators and faculty leaders support it.")

8. Leadership is evident ("I know who to turn to for encouragement, and they're available.")

Ely's model has been applied to change research in a wide range of settings, especially international. Practitioners engaged in change efforts in these contexts are encouraged to explore these and related studies in greater detail. (Terms in italics are ERIC descriptors, with * indicating *major* descriptors–the primary subjects of the document or article.)

- Ely, D. (1990b). The diffusion and implementation of educational technology in developing nations: Cross-cultural comparisons of Indonesia, Chile, and Peru. *Instructional Developments, 1*(1), 9-12. (ED 331 469)

  *Adoption (Ideas); Change Agents; *Cross Cultural Studies; *Developing Nations; *Diffusion (Communication); Educational Change; *Educational Innovation; *Educational Technology; Elementary Secondary Education; Foreign Countries; Higher Education; Questionnaires; Surveys*

- Kaufman, C., & Paulston, R. (1991). *Hungarian education in transition.* Paper presented at the annual conference of the American Educational Research Association, Chicago, IL. (ED 335 275)

  *Educational Change; Elementary Secondary Education; Foreign Countries; Foreign Culture; *International Education; *Social Change; World Affairs*

• Kell, D., Harvey, G., & Drexler, N. (1990). *Educational Technology and the restructuring movement: Lessons from research on computers in classrooms.* Paper presented at the annual conference of the American Educational Research Association, Boston, MA. (ED 326 195)

*Adoption (Ideas); Computer Assisted Instruction; *Educational Change; Educational Technology; Elementary Education; *Instructional Innovation; *Microcomputers; *Program Implementation; Teacher Attitudes; Teacher Role*

• Newton, D. (1992). *Whole language: What is it?* (ED 354 494)

*Case Studies; *Educational Change; Elementary Education; Interviews; Models; *Program Implementation; Teacher Attitudes; Teacher Role; *Whole Language Approach*

The Change Agent

chapter 5

Change, or the pressure to change, is in the air in our educational systems. The effects touch everyone at all levels, from national governments to students. What can–and should–the stakeholders at each of these levels do when they choose to become involved and have a voice in their future? What does it mean at each of these levels to become an agent for–or against–a particular change effort? Where does each of these stakeholder groups now stand in relation to educational change, and what strengths, limitations, or potential biases do these starting points imply? How might the answers to these questions for each of the groups involved be different from one another? How might they be similar?

The environment is ready for educational change in many ways. Many of the conditions discussed in the preceding chapter already exist. Dissatisfaction with the status quo is heightened with each report criticizing our graduates' readiness for information-based society. Our levels of knowledge and skill in understanding and enhancing human learning have never been higher, and in many institutions we are reaching a "critical mass" of technology-savvy educators and students. Both public and private agencies are offering resources through grants, sometimes in millions of dollars.

What can you do to bolster these and the other conditions, and use them in support of effective, meaningful educational change? What can you do to prevent hasty adoption of unnecessary or ineffective change? Having weighed an innovation's characteristics and decided which of these two alternatives applies to the innovation you are facing, what should you do about it? Answering these questions, and attending to their implications, requires a focus on the change agent.

Fullan and Stiegelbauer's *New Meaning of Educational Change*

While *The Meaning of Educational Change* was first published in 1982, Fullan has been writing about the subject since the 1970s, providing his model with a research lineage as rich as each of the others discussed here. Unlike Rogers, Fullan has focused his work explicitly on educational change. Stiegelbauer, a noted scholar of change, joined Fullan to write the second edition (1991) titled, *The New Meaning of Educational Change*, which offers a comprehensive discussion of "stakeholder-as-change-agent" perspectives. This model is one of two expressly focused on the human participants taking part in the change process. (The other is the Concerns-Based Adoption Model discussed in Chapter 7.)

Readers are encouraged to read the first part of *The New Meaning of Educational Change*, which discusses the causes and nature of change in an educational context in a manner unequalled by any other framework, apart from the systemic model discussed in Chapter 9. Readers will note many interesting correspondences with Rogers' (1995) description (especially if you read his whole book) and with Ely's (1990a) conditions of change. In fact, Fullan and Stiegelbauer present a model of factors affecting implementation (Figure 6) that resembles these frameworks in its consideration of "characteristics of change" and "local characteristics."

For our purposes here, however, we will primarily consider the second part and some of the third of Fullan and Stiegelbauer (1991). These parts present a thorough treatment of the characteristics and limitations

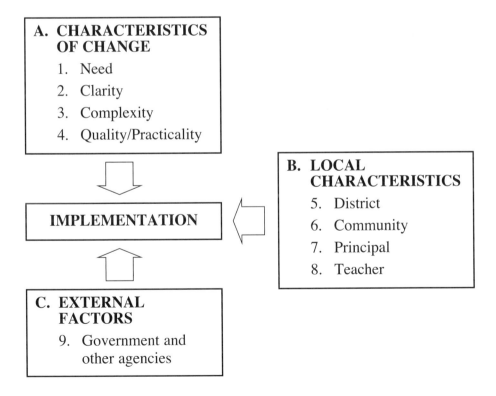

Figure 6. Interactive Factors Affecting Implementation. *Note.* From *The New Meaning of Educational Change*, (p. 68), by M. G. Fullan and S. M. Steigelbauer, 1991, New York: Teachers College Press. Copyright © 1991 by Teachers College Press, Columbia University. Reprinted by permission.

associated with each level of stakeholder represented in the "local characteristics" and "external factors" portions of Figure 6. Each chapter of Part II is devoted to one level or class of stakeholder, and each shows how these traits affect the manner in which those stakeholders can best relate to educational change, as agents either for or against a particular effort. The first chapter of Part III addresses governmental stakeholders, specifically in the United States and Canada. Portions of the other chapters will be drawn upon as well, where they relate to characteristics and limitations corresponding to those discussed for other stakeholders.

The authors identify six types of stakeholders with change agent roles at the local level: (1) *the teacher*, (2) *the principal*, (3) *the student*, (4) *the district administrator*, (5) *the consultant*, and (6) *the community, including the parent*. Governmental stakeholders are addressed at the federal and state levels (United States) and the federal and provincial levels (Canada). The remaining chapters of Part III cover professional preparation of teachers, professional development of educators, and the future of educational change (Fullan & Stiegelbauer, 1991, pp. viii-ix).

In discussing the first stakeholder class, the teacher, Fullan and Stiegelbauer begin with the observation that "educational change depends on what teachers do and think" (1991, p. 117). This is grounded in the fact that–regardless of what governments, school boards, or administrators require–it is the teacher who is in the classroom day after day with the students. If the teacher resists implementation, implements without critical components, or merely maintains a façade of implementation, then educational change will not succeed. (This is discussed in further detail in Chapter 7, which is on the Concerns-Based Adoption Model.) Yet most teachers today are faced with "routine, overload, and limits to reform" (p. 118). This leads to what is perhaps one of Fullan and Stiegelbauer's most important characterizations of change for teachers: "It can either aggravate the teachers' problems or provide a glimmer of hope" (p. 126). For the teacher struggling to both maintain order and teach, change places additional demands on an already crowded schedule. This makes attention to the other components of the change communication model all the more critical, and is why an entire framework (see Chapter 7) is devoted to identifying and addressing teacher concerns.

Fullan and Stiegelbauer identify six major issues that teachers should consider before committing to, or rejecting, a change effort (1991, pp. 137-139):

1. Does the change address an important need? Is there evidence that the innovation has worked elsewhere, and contributed toward more effective learning? If so, is the change therefore elevated in importance above the alternatives competing for resources?

2. Is the administration supporting the innovation–and why (or why not)? What are the administration's competing priorities, and how receptive is it to viewpoints by faculty that differ from theirs? What techniques have you actually tried to get your views heard?

3. Are fellow teachers likely to support (or oppose) the innovation? How do you know?

4. What collaborative efforts might you lead, with other teachers, to support the innovation or a possible alternative course of action? Have you actively collaborated with other teachers in previous efforts?

5. How will you keep the innovation in perspective if you become a leader in its support or opposition? What techniques will you use to help avoid becoming distanced from the teachers, students, and learning?

6. What assistance from teacher unions or professional associations might you obtain to help you support (or oppose) the innovation? What bargaining chips are realistically available to help secure more important concessions governing implementation?

Interestingly, Fullan and Stiegelbauer conclude with an instructive contrast with the statement that begins their chapter on the teacher. "School improvement," they say, "is related not just to what the teachers do and think" (1991, p. 143). Several of the issues in the preceding list clearly imply the role of other stakeholders and components of the educational system in determining a change effort's fate.

One of these other stakeholders, which research (e.g., Fullan, 1988; Hall & Hord, 1987; Leithwood & Montgomery, 1982; Smith & Andrews, 1989) shows holds an especially crucial role, is the principal. Principals act as buffers, balancing the competing needs and contributions of teachers with those of other stakeholders outside of the school. This makes their role especially difficult. Individuals on both sides may feel that a change effort is moving too quickly, or not quickly enough. Both sides may blame the principal (Fullan & Stiegelbauer, 1991, p. 144).

Fullan and Stiegelbauer also note that the routine demands of the principalship have increased to the point where most principals admit their inability to meet everyone's needs all the time (1991, pp. 146-148). Thus, for the principal, as well as for the teacher, change may be seen as just one more thing intruding on the more essential commitments of keeping day-to-day instruction on track. However, the fact remains that principals are frequently effective agents of change. The greatest constraint on the principal's freedom to act is, in many cases, his perception of the systemic constraints inhibiting action. As Sarason (1982) notes, "'the system' is frequently conceived by the individual in a way that obscures, many times unwittingly, the range of possibilities available to him or her" (p. 164). Principals may also suffer from the same sort of "isolated autonomy" described earlier for teachers, and thus may be unaware of the flexibility that their own district regularly accepts. According to Sarason, "The range of practices among principals within the same system is sufficiently great to suggest that the system permits and tolerates passivity and activity, conformity and boldness, dullness and excitement, incompetency and competency" (p. 171).

One of the most authoritative studies of the principal's role, to which Fullan and Stiegelbauer accord several pages, is Hall and Hord's (1987) *Change in Schools: Facilitating the Process*. While I emphasize that book's chief focus in Chapter 7, the teacher concerns underlying the Concerns-Based Adoption Model, those desiring additional information about the principal's role in change may want to consult Change in Schools as well. Fullan and Stiegelbauer state, "Principals are middle managers" (p. 152). While this section is devoted to the principal, per se, these issues may translate equally well to middle managers (e.g., deans or division chiefs) in educational settings other than K-12 schools.

Fullan and Stiegelbauer identify ten major guidelines for the principal who takes the change agent's role (1991, pp. 167-168):

1. Brainstorm possibilities, but avoid wishful thinking. Avoid blaming others or the system for implementation difficulties before you try to act.
2. Think big, but start small. Don't micromanage, but don't plan for more than you can support.
3. Focus on something tangible and essential like curriculum and instruction.
4. Work on enhancing fundamentals, like the professional culture of your school.
5. Build your comfort with responsible risk-taking through long-term practice.
6. Empower your faculty and staff: encourage their innovations, and support them with time and resources.
7. Establish and communicate a clear vision, both in terms of objectives and the change process.
8. Prioritize objectives and decide what projects you are not going to pursue.
9. Build alliances with those in the district office, other principals, key faculty, and outside groups that can help.

10. Be alert to feedback from other stakeholders, and know when
    to be cautious.

Fullan and Stiegelbauer conclude their chapter on the principal with a
bottom-line prescription for effective change leadership at that level. The
most effective principals figure out ways to reduce and contain the time
they spend on routine administrative functions. They ask of each
management task, "Does this really require the principal's attention, or can
it be delegated?" Just as importantly, they invest the time saved in this
manner in "talking with teachers, planning, helping teachers get together,
and being knowledgeable about what was happening" (1991, p. 168). This
shift in and control of emphasis is essential, because

> Serious reform, as we have seen, is not implementing single
> innovations. It is changing the culture and structure of the
> school. Once that is said, it should be self-evident that the
> principal as head of the organization is crucial. As long as
> we have schools and principals, if the principal does not
> lead changes in the culture of the school, or if he or she
> leaves it to others, it normally will not get done. That is,
> improvement will not happen. (p. 169)

The authors next take a step back to consider an important stakeholder
rarely addressed in change models: the student. It may be difficult, as they
note, to paint a coherent picture of the student's role in educational change
because of their numbers and diversity (Fullan & Stiegelbauer, 1991, p.
170), and because of their lack of representation in the power structure of
the traditional educational model (pp. 171, 176, 178-179). Yet students may
have the most at stake in the educational system, and how (or if) it changes
or maintains equilibrium.

This paradox would not be tolerated in any other subsystem of a free
society: it is widely understood that systems operate most effectively when
those who have the most to gain or lose from their success or failure have

a proportionate voice in their governance. This is equally true for change, which may be seen as the adaptive component of governance. In one of the few studies directly examining the effect of student perceptions on change, Hull and Rudduck (1980) found students' expectations to be a significant influence on the success of some innovations.

Interestingly, students–even more than teachers and principals–have been found to experience school as isolated individuals (Fullan & Stiegelbauer, 1991, p. 173). Cusick's study (1973) found that most students are "passive watchers and waiters who pay a minimal amount of attention to formal classroom work while channeling their energy and enthusiasm into their groups of close friends" (p. 222). These studies suggest that students have little support coping with change, even as followers.

Since students in most schools have not had any experience or training as participants in educational change, they will not have the skills and knowledge to independently elect to take the change agent role. Students can, and do, exert considerable negative influence to reject changes they perceive as undesirable, however (Fullan & Stiegelbauer, 1991, p. 180). The authors' discussion of implications for students is targeted at issues teachers or administrators must consider to get students engaged in change (and in their education as a whole), and to help students gain the experience and skills to participate as change agents in the future (pp. 188-190):

- Identify the ways in which the innovation will alter the relationship between you and your students.
- Plan strategies for enhancing student motivation and understanding concerning both the innovation and the change process. Levels of both directly affect whether, and to what extent, they make the necessary changes in their behavior for implementation to occur.
- Consider students not only in terms of learning outcomes, but also as partners in learning who are being asked–as you are–to change their activities in some meaningful way.

- Consider explicitly how you will introduce the innovation to your students and how you will obtain student reactions throughout the change process.
- Plan specific strategies for building students' competencies in the changed roles the innovation will require.

Fullan and Stiegelbauer conclude their chapter on the students by observing that "effective educational change and effective education overlap in significant ways" (1991, p. 190). Students should be encouraged and empowered to participate as active partners in shaping their learning experience and the school that supports it. This does not equate to "letting the students run the school," but rather, as the authors observe, to treating the student "as someone whose opinion mattered in the introduction and implementation of reform in schools" (p. 170). They close by noting

> Teachers who blend education and change, periodically discuss the meaning of activities with students, work on the skills the students need to participate in new educational reforms, and consider the relationship between old and new, will be going a long way in accomplishing some of the more complex cognitive and social educational objectives contained in the policy statements and curricula of most school districts. (p. 190)

Having considered the student, at "the bottom of the heap" (p. 189), Fullan and Stiegelbauer (1991) next turn to the top of the heap within the school structure itself: the district administrator. More than any other, the authors' treatment of this role highlights the relationship between their framework and the change communication model, particularly its systemic application shown in Figure 3. The authors maintain that the greatest change-related problem in today's schools is not, in general, resistance to innovation but rather "uncritical and uncoordinated acceptance of too many different innovations" (p. 197). They hold, therefore, that among the most critical roles of district administration is to help schools sort out the multiplicity of proffered changes and implement the right ones. This leads the authors to the broader recognition that meaningful, lasting change depends on the district administrator's ability to coordinate multiple innovations simultaneously within their districts, which is the problem I have illustrated in Figure 3.

One aspect of this role that Fullan and Stiegelbauer emphasize involves the launch of particular programs within the district. They note that "district administrators are usually the critical source of initiating specific innovations" (1991, p. 197). Even when an innovation is launched from within a particular school, its transfer from one school to another depends strongly on the district administrator's unambiguous support, in terms of both emphasis and resources (p. 198).

The district administration is, quite possibly, the level at which the current American educational structure is worst suited to meaningful change. Attempting serious change can end a district administrator's career, since small groups opposed to the reforms can pressure school boards and voters to turn him or her out. Needless to say, the successor to an administrator fired for supporting a particular reform is likely to state clearly, public opposition for that reform, and embark upon a program in direct opposition to his predecessor's intent. The continuity which is critical for the long term, organizational changes required for serious reforms (pp. 200, 210) becomes almost impossible to maintain in such an environment. One is tempted to wonder if district administrators should be elected or appointed for life, as judges are!

Fullan and Stiegelbauer offer seven guidelines for district administrators embarking on their careers, or becoming more active as change agents in a district where they are already employed (1991, pp. 212-214):

1. Choose a district where the school board and constituents have been relatively united as a force for change.
2. Once in a district, develop the capacity of key subordinates (such as other district administrators and principals) to work with teachers and to lead change.
3. Directly and through principals, provide the vision, resources, and training that communicate clearly that schools (e.g., teachers, principals, students) are valued as the main centers of change.
4. Maintain a focus on improving instruction–teaching and learning–and on building a collaborative, engaged social culture in schools.
5. Understand that in this context, a strategy for improvement is itself an innovation and must be effectively communicated in the same manner as any other change.
6. Establish a clear accountability system and accessible feedback channels. Monitor and assess the improvement process.
7. Most of all, develop your own expertise in the change process, and use this knowledge to build a culture of engagement and improvement that extends through–and beyond–the central office.

Fullan frequently writes from a systemic perspective, so it is not surprising that he and Stiegelbauer note in their book, *The New Meaning of Educational Change*, that all of the above guidelines are in service of building the capacity for continuous improvement into the district's culture (1991, p. 214). In their chapter on the district administrator, Fullan and Stiegelbauer illustrate how the stakeholders within the school system, must work in concert for effective change. The remaining chapters discussed here begin to turn to key stakeholders outside the school proper.

It is perhaps fitting that the transition from internal to external stakeholders should pivot around a stakeholder who may be either: the consultant. Some consultants are, in fact, internal or district consultants in curricular or resource support roles. While these individuals, in theory, have the most direct interaction with the stakeholders in the district on whom successful implementation will depend, research paints a depressingly different picture (Fullan & Stiegelbauer, 1991, p. 216). In many cases, the role of such district consultants is nebulous, even for the consultants themselves. Teachers frequently have even less understanding of the consultant's role. There is generally little congruence between consultants' descriptions of their own roles and teachers' perceptions of those roles. Furthermore, most such consultants neither have specialized training for their innovation duties when they are hired, nor are they provided with it before beginning those duties (pp. 216-219).

Still, when these obstacles are overcome, the internal consultant or facilitator can be a powerful force for meaningful change. District consultants who have accumulated successful experience in those roles are often teachers' only source of continuing support throughout all stages of the implementation process. It is these facilitators who work closely with other district personnel to provide the intensive, repeated, and coordinated interventions necessary for change to become institutionalized (Fullan & Stiegelbauer, 1991, p. 225).

Other consultants are outside experts, either in a specific innovation to be introduced or in the process of educational change itself, and occasionally in both. Such external consultants have the potential to bring advanced knowledge to bear, which would not otherwise be available to the district. However, they have historically achieved this potential no better than their internal counterparts (Aoki, Langford, Williams, & Wilson, 1977, p. 41). Fullan and Stiegelbauer observe that "Some external consultants are not good; others offer packaged 'solutions,' which even when appropriate do not go very far; and still others are inspiring, but nothing comes of the ideas when they leave" (1991, p. 225). The latter two cases, in particular, highlight challenges inherent in the external role: lack of situational awareness resulting from the outsider status and lack of long-term presence and follow-through.

Significantly, the external consultant's weaknesses are the internal consultant's strengths, and vice versa. Fullan and Stiegelbauer summarize this section most effectively in a single sentence: "The primary task of the school district should be to develop its own internal capacity to assist and manage both the content and the process of change, relying selectively on external assistance to train insiders and to provide specific program expertise in combination with internal follow-through" (1991, p. 225). Through such collaboration, the external facilitator's knowledge of both the innovation and the change process is handed over and carried through in a manner that ensures continued, longitudinal support that is focused on the key contextual factors specific to the implementation site.

The authors also provide specific guidelines for the facilitator–internal or external–seeking to take a leadership role in the change process (Fullan & Stiegelbauer, 1991, pp. 217-226), based on field research on the characteristics of effective consultant practice (Corbett, Dawson, & Firestone, 1984; Cox, 1983; Louis & Rosenblum, 1981; Ross & Regan, 1990):

- Familiarize yourself with student needs in each of the schools within the district.
- Participate in location and selection of the innovation, when possible.
- Understand the innovation, its purpose, and the benefits it is intended to produce.
- Conduct wide and thorough searches for information to assist in implementation.
- Help develop a system plan for integrating the innovation with existing practice.
- Assess staff expectations concerning the change process, based on their experience with previous innovations.
- Help arrange and conduct training in use of the innovation, in collaboration with your counterparts internal or external to the

district.

- Plan a series of workshops to facilitate assessment and follow-up; avoid one-shot events.
- Tailor implementation strategies to the range of individuals and contexts involved, and make adjustments based on feedback received.
- Focus on working with teams and organizations, rather than working alone or with individual teachers.
- Identify resources available to support implementation activities, especially staff time, knowledge, and clerical/administrative support.
- Identify any competing visions among staff factions and assess the prevalence/severity of resulting tensions.
- Determine the frequency of staff turnover and bureaucratic disruptions to daily conduct of the school's mission.
- Arrange funding or other support from the district or other sources.
- Obtain endorsements of the innovation from key district leaders (e.g., superintendent, school board, principal) and opinion leaders (e.g., respected teachers or staff).
- Work with teachers using the innovation in the classroom, and help them work out "bugs" and overcome obstacles.
- Assist in evaluating the innovation's effectiveness.
- Plan a strategy for implementation and institutionalization of the innovation, in collaboration with your counterparts internal or external to the district.
- Encourage personnel within the district to reach decision points and continue the implementation process; schedule meetings and obtain outside information as needed.
- Assist district personnel in matching alternatives to local needs.

In closing their chapter on the consultant, Fullan and Stiegelbauer reemphasize the importance of collaboration between internal and external facilitators–and their district–to balance the competing demands of comprehensive and continuing assistance:

> Indeed, the dilemma faced by both internal and external consultants is one of scope vs. intensity. Although effective change requires intensive, ongoing contact, the number of clients is far beyond the available time and energy of consultants. Like most dilemmas, it is not solvable; but by employing principles of social change, including the setting up of peer support systems, consultants (whether internal or external) can reach and respond to more people more effectively that they currently do. (p. 226)

At this point, the authors turn their attention to stakeholders explicitly outside the school itself, but no less critical to the success of its change efforts: the parent and the community. There is considerable irony in the fact that the typical educational change effort has historically ignored its clients more than any other group. Like the internal client–the student–these external clients have a great deal at stake in the performance of the school system. Unlike the student, however, parents and the community represent education's investors: they provide, the school's funding (through taxes or tuition) in the expectation that it will produce certain outcomes. In recognition of this relationship, they are typically accorded representation–in the form of a school board–that in theory provides them with a great deal of control over that funding and the goals toward which it is spent.

It may be surprising, therefore, that almost two thirds of typical curriculum decisions involve no community participation (Boyd, 1978, p. 613). Yet when the community does become engaged, it almost always prevails. Although, depending on the community's demographics and the extent to which it is informed, this can just as likely result in avoidance of necessary change as in rejection of unsound innovation (Fullan & Stiegelbauer, 1991, p. 244).

Taken together, these facts underlie one of the authors' central points concerning the involvement of parents and the community in change efforts: this is a very powerful, yet systematically untapped resource for school improvement (Fullan & Stiegelbauer, 1991, p. 246). By mobilizing these stakeholders and providing them with relevant information–and training in appropriate skills–parents, school boards, and other community groups can play a key role in guiding implementation and reducing turbulence. Conversely, without such attention they will intervene of their own accord (perhaps unexpectedly) when they feel their interests are jeopardized. They will probably also prevail, even though their intervention may be uninformed, counter to the direction adopted by other stakeholders, or both!

Fullan and Stiegelbauer also devote considerable attention to the potential roles of the parent that are explicitly instructional. Research suggests that these kinds of interventions by parents consistently increase the level of favorable learning outcomes for the student in the most cost-effective manner, which is (or should be) the ultimate goal of any educational change effort (Fullan & Stiegelbauer, 1991, pp. 235-237). In contrast, because research evidence is lacking that parental involvement in non-instructional activities (i.e., activities linked only indirectly to teaching and learning) consistently produces superior educational outcomes (pp. 237-238), numerous questions remain concerning the relationship between the indirect outcomes of such efforts and the change process. The authors note that this does not mean such involvement is without merit, only that its value is in its "mutually reinforcing, synergistic positive impact" in conjunction with instructional initiatives (p. 240).

For parents and other community members desiring to take a more active role in shaping the education of their children, Fullan and Stiegelbauer offer these specific suggestions, which may also be useful to those within the school who seek to encourage such involvement (1991, pp. 247-249):

- Where a choice of schools is available (e.g., public, private, or charter), look into the history and attitude of each with regard to parent and community involvement.
- Once established in a community where the schools welcome and value parent and community involvement, be responsive and participate.
- Never assume that teachers don't want parent or community participation. They may simply be assuming that parents don't want to participate, or they may be overwhelmed by the competing demands of change and day-to-day teaching and be reluctant to ask for help.
- Familiarize yourself with some of the curriculum (through books, discussions, and/or electronic resources).
- Ask those at the school if there is anything you can do at home for your own children, or in the classroom, to help with instruction. If they are receptive, suggest a small workshop to help you, and others like you, to learn about effective instruction and tutoring.
- If the curriculum and instructional innovations in the school appear overwhelming at first, do not despair. It takes experience and interaction with the rest of the educational system to develop a good understanding.
- The most positive effect on learning outcomes will occur when the school, parents, and the wider community collaborate to use their respective strengths. Talk regularly with teachers to learn activities that will support their efforts and to share information about your children's learning and behavior that only one of you may see.
- Work with teachers and administrators to make parent involvement at the school and classroom levels a fundamental part of the school's mission.
- Work with teachers and administrators to establish specific programs and practices for involvement at the individual teacher

level. Teachers need clear, understandable materials to use with parents.

- Urge the specification of clear objectives, the provision of good materials and training, and the continuous gathering of feedback that involves parents in selecting innovations and assessing their effectiveness.
- Suggest the establishment of a part-time coordinator for school-wide parent involvement, with regular access to teachers and the principal.
- Work with other parents and community groups to apply pressure for change, if the school is unresponsive to these collaborative strategies.

Fullan & Stiegelbauer (1991) conclude with two key points about parent and community involvement:

> In the meantime, the simple conclusion of this chapter is twofold. First, the vast majority of parents find meaning in activities related to their own children rather than in school- or system-wide endeavors [yet these activities must be coordinated at those levels]. Second, educational reform requires the conjoint efforts of families and schools. Parents and teachers should recognize the critical complementary importance of each other in the life of the student. Otherwise, we are placing limitations on the prospects for improvement that may be impossible to overcome. (p. 250)

After discussing the six types of stakeholders with change agent roles at the local level, Fullan and Stiegelbauer then explore the change agent role played by governments. This role is fraught with paradoxes and dilemmas, as governments have simultaneously great authority in establishing policy and dictating change and very little direct influence on what gets implemented (1991, pp. 253-254, 262). Yet when governmental agencies attempt to close this gap by becoming preoccupied with monitoring compliance with requirements, they often have the effect of reducing outcomes by forcing schools to use their available resources to demonstrate compliance, drawing from resources that would otherwise support implementation (p. 283).

The authors argue that governments do have a necessary and productive role in educational change, however. First, "problems of equity and program quality are unlikely to be resolved at the local level" (Fullan & Stiegelbauer, 1991, p. 288) because they are the result of decisions or byproducts of decisions made at that level, or of inadequate resources available for their resolution. Second, educational change efforts have resulted in significantly stronger positive effects on outcomes when governments provide effective encouragement and coordination (pp. 263, 269), than when their role is weak and disjointed outside of policy formulation and compliance, such as in implementation (pp. 272, 274-276).

In many ways, Fullan and Stiegelbauer treat the relationship between governments and schools in a fashion parallel to their discussion of external and internal consultants. Governments are presented as a crucial source for direction and support, but implementation success largely depends on the extent to which they can hand the effort over to districts and schools who understand what implementation is to look like, and who have the skills and resources to make it happen. They note that the desire to make it happen is often not a problem. In fact, local districts frequently go beyond government requirements if appropriate support and information are made available (Fullan & Stiegelbauer, 1991, pp. 267, 269, 284). Some research has even noted that the most effective government-initiated reforms occur when governments collaborate with local districts to identify how a given reform or set of policies can be coordinated to help achieve local goals (Fuhrman, Clune, & Elmore, 1988, p. 247).

Based on these observations, Fullan and Stiegelbauer offer six guidelines for governments in facilitating meaningful and successful educational change (1991, pp. 282-288):

1. Focus on building the local capacity (e.g., knowledge, resources, infrastructure) to actually implement changes. ["Implementation depends more on capacity than compliance" (Elmore, 1980, p. 37).]

2. Provide a clear description of what the innovation is, and looks like, in practice (see the discussion of the IC Component Checklist in Chapter 7). Invest the time to interact with local agencies about meaning, expectations, and needs of implementation.

3. Design and disseminate an explicit, but flexible, implementation plan to guide the process of change in practice.

4. Ensure that government staff involved with the change effort, especially those who will interact directly with local districts, develop adequate knowledge and competence regarding both the innovation itself and the process of facilitating change.

5. Emphasize innovations leading to meaningful changes in the practice of teaching and learning, rather than simply defining abstract goals and competencies without regard for how they will be accomplished.

6. Recognize that meaningful change is complex and takes time (see the related discussion in Chapter 7).

In summarizing the government role, it is fitting that it should be discussed last, because real change is implemented (or rejected) at the hands of the other stakeholders discussed earlier. Yet those stakeholders, with their day-to-day responsibilities for maintaining the status quo, will often need innovation to be developed, orchestrated, and supported by governments and/or government-funded research and development agencies. Fullan and Stiegelbauer conclude their chapter on the government and reform by observing that "The role of governments is to enlarge the problem-solving arena and to provide the kinds of pressure and support that force and reinforce local districts to pursue continuous improvements" (1991, p. 288).

While governments are the last form of change agency whose role is explicitly discussed as such, Fullan and Stiegelbauer make some important points concerning professional development in the remainder of Part III. It may be somewhat misleading to present this issue under a distinct "teacher-educator" role, because some aspects of this discussion pertain to teachers themselves, while others are responsibilities accruing to district administrators or to governments. However, the authors note that, "Educational change involves learning how to do something new. Given this, if there is any single factor crucial to change it is professional development" (Fullan & Stiegelbauer, 1991, p. 289).

Unfortunately, professional development is also one of the factors most universally neglected. Governments focused on monitoring compliance, administrators struggling to fund certain aspects of change, taxpayers more receptive to lowering standards for new teachers than paying them a professional wage, and teachers shackled to a growing certification bureaucracy are unlikely to make sure that resources are available for educating educators in support of change. Yet the cost of not doing so is almost certain failure, as change is a lifelong reality in an information-based society, for teachers as well as their charges (Fullan & Stiegelbauer, 1991, pp. 344-345).

Fullan and Stiegelbauer consolidate their advice for the various stakeholders involved in teacher education at the end of their penultimate chapter. They offer three fundamental recommendations (1991, pp. 341-344):

1. Professional development must align with the needs of the teaching profession and with the improvement of schools, not merely with new developments in abstract theory.
2. Professional development must become a fundamental part of the district/school culture. It must be expected of, and supported by, all faculty and staff, regardless of position. It must be coordinated, integrated, and applied throughout the curriculum; it

must not consist of isolated events without follow-through.

3. All professional development activities should follow two fundamental principles. First, they should reinforce the attributes of successful performance through as many activities as possible. Second, they should be geared less toward implementing a particular innovation than toward fostering individual and institutional habits and structures that infuse lifelong learning as a core value throughout the school culture.

Other Studies

Fullan provides a good introduction to the wider body of work investigating the roles and strategies of various types of change agents. His 1980 literature review, *The Role of Human Agents Internal to School Districts in Knowledge Utilization*, examines research in this area with regard to most of the change agent types discussed here, and provides an outstanding gateway to the wider literature. Fullan and Newton (1988) also offer three case studies highlighting the pivotal role of the principal in the implementation of an innovative system of classroom instruction in three urban high schools. These case studies also illustrate the roles of teachers and internal district consultants.

The principal's crucial role in leading school reform efforts is also explored by Powell and Hyle (1997) in their study of three secondary schools in the Midwest and their attempts to implement inclusive programs for students with disabilities. This study stands out as a dissection of failed reform based on Fullan's model, and also highlights his emphasis on the importance of a clearly communicated understanding of what an innovation looks like in practice. It is complemented by a contemporaneous study by Tilkin and Hyle (1997) of principals adopting inclusion that showcases successful implementation of the same innovation by building administrators using Fullan's suggestions.

Those interested in similar leadership for change at the district level may wish to review Zakariya's (1996) study of the superintendent's role as a change agent. This study shows how the district administrator can apply Fullan's approach to implement stakeholder involvement and strategic planning in support of suburban school renewal.

Another perspective worth exploring in greater detail is that of the teacher as change agent. Fullan and Hargreaves (1996) provide what may be the classic resource in exploring this role, in the revised edition of *What's Worth Fighting for in Your School.* The authors present a revealing, holistic look at the problems facing teachers and principals in initiating and leading meaningful change, as well as strategies for addressing them aimed at teachers, principals, and educators outside the school. Another interesting look at this perspective is provided by the proceedings of a conference designed to allow teachers to share their views on innovative programs with administrators and university faculty (Southeastern Regional Vision for Education, 1992). The proceedings, titled *What Teachers Have to Say about Creating Innovations in Education,* offer recommendations from teachers to administrators, policymakers, teacher-educators, and government-sponsored educational research agencies.

Fullan (1993) also devotes additional attention to the role of the teacher-educator as change agent in his article, "Why Teachers Must Become Change Agents." Here he urges teacher preparation programs to infuse strategies into their curricula that beginning teachers will need not only to become effective teachers, but effective agents of educational change as well. Those interested in professional development and school reform may also wish to consult the various reports of the Holmes Group, especially *Tomorrow's Schools of Education* (1995). Fullan takes a similarly holistic approach in *Change Forces: Probing the Depths of Educational Reform* (Fullan, 1994). In this volume, which is part of the School Development and the Management of Change Series, Fullan extends his approach to the change agent in a manner suggestive of our discussion of the systemic paradigm in Chapter 9. Extensive references are also provided.

Summary

If there is one consistent theme throughout Fullan and Stiegelbauer's discussion, it is that school is, for each person, a place of "quiet isolation." Yet, in many cases, each is striving toward the same goals. The authors find that the "meaning of educational change" is remarkably consistent for different individuals in different roles. So the promise for the change agent is that there is enormous potential for true, meaningful change simply in building coalitions with other change agents, both within one's own group and across all groups. The challenge is to begin: to reach out, to establish areas of common interest, and to move forward. Fullan and Stiegelbauer identify six key levels of local stakeholders-as-change-agents, plus two outside the local community:

1. The teacher (who has the most direct control over what happens in his classroom)
2. The principal (who is positioned to set the climate for change in her school)
3. The student (who, if his learning is not served, renders implementation moot)
4. The district administrator (who has significant autonomy in establishing district policy)
5. The consultant (who brings specialized change knowledge and/or enables follow-through)
6. The parent and the community (who rarely get involved, but usually prevail when they do)
7. The government (who can mandate action and provide, or withhold, support)
8. The teacher-educator (who can equip the faculty and staff with tools for leading change).

Fullan has aggressively continued development and extension of his model, and his framework has also been applied in a variety of settings by other researchers. Practitioners engaged in change efforts in these contexts are encouraged to explore these and related studies in greater detail. (Terms in italics are ERIC descriptors, with * indicating *major* descriptors–the primary subjects of the document or article.)

- Fullan, M. (1980). *The role of human agents internal to school districts in knowledge utilization.* San Francisco, CA: Far West Laboratory For Educational Research and Development. (ED 203 459)

  *Administrator Role; *Change Agents; Educational Environment; *Educational Innovation; Elementary Secondary Education; Principals; Research Needs; Resource Staff; School Districts; Superintendents; *Teacher Role*

- Fullan, M. (1993). Why teachers must become change agents. *Educational Leadership, 50(6),* 12-17. (EJ 459 419)

  *Beginning Teachers; *Change Agents; Cooperation; Elementary Secondary Education; Inquiry; Lifelong Learning; Mastery Learning; *Moral Values; *Professional Development; *Teacher Education; *Teacher Effectiveness; Teaching Conditions*

- Fullan, M. (1994). *School development and the management of change series: Vol. 10. Change forces: Probing the depths of educational reform.* Bristol, PA: Falmer Press. (ED 373 391)

  *Agency Cooperation; *Change Agents; *Educational Change; *Educational Environment; Elementary Secondary Education; Misconceptions; *Moral Values; *Organizational Change; Resistance to Change; Teacher Education*

• Fullan, M., & Hargreaves, A. (1996). *What's worth fighting for in your school?* (Rev. ed.). New York, NY: Teachers College Press. (ED 401 622)

*Collegiality; Educational Environment; *Educational Improvement; Elementary Secondary Education; *Participative Decision Making; School Restructuring; Teacher Responsibility; *Teacher Role; Teaching Conditions; *Teaching (Occupation)*

• Fullan, M., & Newton, E. (1988). School principals and change processes in the secondary school. *Canadian Journal of Education, 13*(3), 404-422. (EJ 396 071)

*Administrator Role; *Change Agents; Change Strategies; Classroom Techniques; *Educational Change; Foreign Countries; *High Schools; *Instructional Leadership; Longitudinal Studies; *Principals; Secondary Education*

• Holmes Group. (1995). *Tomorrow's schools of education: A report of the Holmes Group.* East Lansing, MI: Author. (ED 399 220)

*College School Cooperation; Educational Change; *Educational Improvement; Elementary Secondary Education; Faculty Development; Higher Education; Knowledge Base for Teaching; Partnerships in Education; Position Papers; *Professional Development Schools; *Schools of Education; *Teacher Education; *Teacher Education Curriculum; Teacher Educators*

• Powell, D., & Hyle, A. (1997). Principals and school reform: Barriers to inclusion in three secondary schools. *Journal of School Leadership, 7*(4), 301-326. (EJ 547 325)

*Administrator Role; Case Studies; *Change Agents; Definitions; Disabilities; Educational Change; *Inclusive Schools; *Principals; *Program Implementation; *Resistance to Change; Secondary Education; Special Education*

- Southeastern Regional Vision for Education. (1992). *What teachers have to say about creating innovations in education: Proceedings from the Sharing Success Forum, Orlando, FL.* (ED 348 755)

*Change Agents; Change Strategies; *Educational Change; *Educational Innovation; Educational Planning; Elementary Secondary Education; *Program Effectiveness; Program Implementation; *School Restructuring*

- Tilkin, S., & Hyle, A. (1997). *The change to inclusion: Five case studies in one district.* Paper presented at the annual meeting of the University Council of Educational Administration, Orlando, FL. (ED 415 635)

*Case Studies; Change Agents; *Change Strategies; *Disabilities; *Educational Change; Educational Methods; Elementary Secondary Education; *Inclusive Schools; Mainstreaming; Models; Program Development; Program Implementation; School Administration; School Districts; School Restructuring*

- Zakariya, S. (1996). Change agent. *Executive Educator, 18*(1), 10-15. (EJ 516 062)

*Change Agents; Change Strategies; *Educational Change; Elementary Secondary Education; *School Culture; *Strategic Planning; *Superintendents; *Teamwork*

The
Change
Process

chapter 6

So, you want to be a change agent, eh? You've found–or maybe even created–an innovation, and you're confident it exhibits the attributes Rogers talks about. You're familiar with the environment in which you want to implement it, and it appears to meet enough of Ely's conditions for you to be confident "the time is right" for change. You've read Fullan's suggestions for a change agent in your role, and you're ready to go. But where do you start, and what should you expect? What can the literature tell you about where you should focus your attention as the effort proceeds?

Some things are fairly clear. You're going to need to study the problems that call for change. You'll need to identify the key stakeholders in the environment, and get to know their hopes and concerns. Even with an innovation already in mind, you should probably explore alternative solutions, if only so you'll be able to defend why your recommendation is best. You'll also want to reach out and identify resources that can help you and your clients implement your innovation successfully. Finally, of course, there will come a time when you must move on, returning to your normal duties or seeking new situations that call for change. You'll want the system you leave behind to be able to sustain itself, and continue to evolve, in your absence.

These steps and others may naturally come to mind as you consider what is necessary to implement change, but how do they relate to one another? Is there any typical sequence in which they should be undertaken? What activities and interventions are involved in each step? Planning your approach to each particular implementation project, and carrying it out successfully requires a focus on the change process and the role it plays in service of the total change effort.

Havelock and Zlotolow's *Change Agent's Guide*

One might imagine from the title that this framework might serve as the best representative of the focus on the change agent discussed in the preceding chapter. But the second edition of *The Change Agent's Guide* (Havelock & Zlotolow, 1995) does not emphasize guidelines for various categories of change agents, in the manner of Fullan and Stiegelbauer. It is, in fact, the change agent's guide to the change process. Returning to the change communication model in Figure 2, it is the channel by which the innovation is conveyed to its intended users. Since publication in 1973 of the original edition, which was written by Havelock only and entitled *The Change Agent's Guide to Innovation in Education*, Havelock's work has offered change agents a concise look at the phases by which educational innovations are communicated and how those phases interrelate.

Havelock and Zlotolow (1995) present "seven ideas in a circle" (see Figure 7), which form the core of the framework presented in their book. These ideas–really phases–are generally referred to as the *C-R-E-A-T-E-R model* (also as Re-CREATE or CREATE and Renew). The seven stages are: *Care, Relate, Examine, Acquire, Try, Extend,* and *Renew* (Havelock & Zlotolow, 1995, p. 2). The authors note that despite the linear appearance of such a list, the process is more accurately seen as a cycle or even a series of cycles. Each phase may be studied separately to highlight the corresponding major

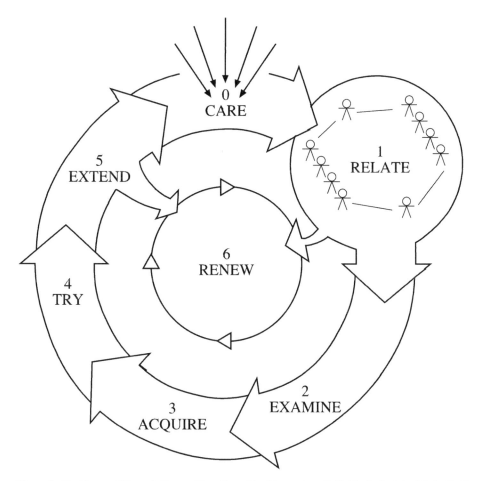

Figure 7. The Stages of Planned Change. *Note.* From The Change Agent's Guide, 2nd ed. (p. 11), by R. G. Havelock and S. Zlotolow, 1995, Englewood Cliffs, NJ: Educational Technology Publications. Copyright © 1995 by Educational Technology Publications, Inc. Reprinted by permission.

set of implementation issues. Yet all the phases must also be viewed holistically to gain an appropriate understanding of the change process in its entirety (pp. 10, 12). The authors also observe that it is sometimes appropriate to jump ahead to subsequent stages, "provided we realize that we will eventually have to circle back to confront these issues" (p.5). For example, we might try a tentative solution and observe the system's reactions as part of our plan to examine and diagnose its needs (p. 5).

In *The Change Agent's Guide*, the authors provide a brief introduction to these core concepts, as well as to different approaches to change agentry, such as "catalyst," "solution giver," "process helper," and "resource linker (Havelock & Zlotolow, 1995, pp. 9-10). They then interweave four case studies through the rest of the *Guide* to illustrate key points as they arise. The sections at the end of the book offer valuable resources and contacts, as well as some advice on constituting an implementation team and choosing a strategy. For our purposes here, however, we will focus on Part Two of the *Guide*, which explores the stages of the change process that form the C-R-E-A-T-E-R model.

The authors designate the first of these stages as "zero" rather than number "one," "because it is ground zero, the rock bottom prerequisite for a change activity, often taken for granted…" (Havelock & Zlotolow, 1995, p. 6). This Care stage is closely related to the first of Ely's conditions, dissatisfaction with the status quo. Innovation is generally undertaken because someone perceives something is wrong, or at least that something could be better. Havelock and Zlotolow describe this stage as "establishing the need for action." They begin with an introduction to social systems (pp. 43-46), explaining that caring must start with an understanding of why, and how, systems change, and of the system to be changed. For example, in what sense are its members a group? To what extent do they share a consensus on the concern(s) that cause the change agent to be involved?

The authors introduce Kurt Lewin's "unfreeze-move-refreeze" concept of social change next. They explain that "unfreezing," or making the system receptive to change, is the focus of stages 0 and 1, which are Care and Relate respectively. "Moving," or introducing the change, occurs during stages 2-5, which are Examine, Acquire, Try, and Extend. "Refreezing," or creating a new, stable state incorporating the change, happens in stage 6, which is Renew (Havelock & Zlotolow, 1995, p. 49).

With this understanding of social system change as a foundation, the change agent is ready to consider both the cares that motivate the system (or some of its members) to want change and those that can serve to alert the change agent to potential obstacles at each stage. Havelock and Zlotolow present two such lists, one each for client and change agent concerns, to offer the change agent some possible starting points in this effort (1995, pp. 51-54).

Interestingly, while their client concerns are all initiating concerns (those which may set change in motion), their change agent concerns are organized along a time dimension: the stages of the C-R-E-A-T-E-R model. This may establish a basis for using C-R-E-A-T-E-R in conjunction with the Concerns-Based Adoption Model (CBAM) discussed in Chapter 7. It should be noted that the unit of analysis in CBAM is the individual adopter, whereas in C-R-E-A-T-E-R it is the adopting system as a whole; nevertheless, the "red flags" Havelock and Zlotolow list often correspond at least loosely to CBAM's stages. This correspondence may assist the change agent in identifying potential system-level obstacles to look for based on the concerns being evidenced at the time by individual adopters within that system.

Havelock and Zlotolow conclude their discussion of the Care stage with two sections that the change agent may find especially intriguing. The first, titled "How People Show and Don't Show They Are in Trouble," explores four situations the change agent may encounter that signal different system postures toward change. The authors discuss the implications under varying circumstances: when everything seems fine; when widely differing concerns are held throughout the system; when the expressed concerns appear to be symptoms of another unstated concern; and when concerns are extremely intense (Havelock & Zlotolow, 1995, pp. 55-57).

The final section under the Care stage considers the ethics of change agentry. Havelock and Zlotolow note that while change agents may be given "license" by those in legitimate authority over the client system, their work often leads them to discover more fundamental dysfunctions that may lie outside the scope of such charters. Furthermore, they observe, while the change agent may attempt to guide his actions by the physician's maxim, "above all, do no harm," he cannot actually guarantee this when his work involves tinkering with complex interrelationships in living systems. Therefore, they conclude, the change agent more realistically is obligated both to strive to minimize the risk of harm and to obtain informed consent from the members of the client system before proceeding (Havelock & Zlotolow, 1995, p. 57).

Havelock and Zlotolow describe stage one, Relate, as "building relationships to [sic] and among clients" (1995, p.59). The importance of this stage cannot be overstated. It is certainly critical for the change agent to build and maintain a productive relationship with all key stakeholders or their representatives, but it is equally vital (and more often overlooked) to facilitate greater collaboration among members of the client system. As we shall see in Chapter 9, one of the most common causes of failure in school reform has been that different groups within the system are not united in their efforts, but rather each working separately (and often at odds with one another) on their own uncoordinated, small-scale initiatives.

Still, if these groups are not working in unison when the change agent arrives on the scene, they are unlikely to begin doing so spontaneously, without his intervention. And this intervention is unlikely to be productive until the change agent is established as a credible source among the major stakeholders. Thus, the first order of business for the change agent entering the Relate stage is to establish such an image.

Havelock and Zlotolow speak of this process in terms of relating to the client system itself, and to the broader system(s) of which it is a part. In both discussions, the change agent is advised to become familiar with the norms and other characteristics of the system, and to strive to build a network of supporters who are likely to be most effective in aiding the change effort. Characteristics to look for in building this team are: opinion leadership (informal influence); formal authority; representation of major factions or vested interests; public relations ability; credibility and respectability; and compatibility with the change agent (Havelock & Zlotolow, 1995, p. 61).

Other aspects of the Relate stage that they discuss include tips for establishing or reestablishing relationships with the client; advantages and disadvantages associated with both internal and external change agents, guidelines for the initial approach to a new client; and characteristics of ideal and problematic client relationships. The authors observe that the best strategies may differ depending on whether the client has no prior experience with the change agent, a good prior experience, or a tenuous prior experience. They also discuss some special challenges associated with the change agent who arises from *within* the client system and must redefine his role within the organization (Havelock & Zlotolow, 1995, pp. 66-68). They note that the respective characteristics of internal and external change agents suggest that the internal initiator should consider collaborating with an external consultant. Likewise, the external initiator should consider seeking an internal partner to form a balanced change team (p. 70).

In discussing client approaches, Havelock and Zlotolow (1995) point out that in change agentry as in many other social endeavors, first impressions count for a great deal. Still, they reassure us, these first encounters can frequently be managed successfully simply by attending to four fundamental principles: "friendliness, familiarity, rewardingness, and responsiveness" (pp. 71-72). They are able to offer similar point-by-point checklists describing the ideal client relationship, as well as common danger signals that warn of a rough implementation ahead. The ideal relationship, the authors note, would exhibit the following characteristics (pp. 73-76):

- Reciprocity (two-way communication)
- Openness (to new ideas and to open, honest communication)
- Realistic expectations (not looking for miracles)
- Expectations of reward (reasonable optimism)
- Structure (both change agent and client understand what is expected)
- Equal power (neither party should be able to compel the other to do anything)
- Minimum threat
- Confrontation of differences (doesn't let suspicion build)
- Involvement of all relevant parties (does not exclude key stakeholders or interest groups).

Havelock and Zlotolow acknowledge that the change agent will rarely encounter optimal levels of all of these criteria together. They present them instead as indicators, which allow the change agent to estimate the extent to which the client system will predispose the effort toward success.

Likewise, the danger signals the authors cite are intended as indicators to help the change agent assess the predisposition of the client system toward implementation failure. Havelock and Zlotolow recognize that the change agent may not have the option of withdrawing from a project exhibiting several of these signals, but she will at least be forewarned. This will help the change agent to consider interventions to mitigate their effects, or–if success appears unlikely–to development an exit strategy, if possible. The authors (Havelock & Zlotolow, 1995, pp. 76-77) suggest that a client system is unlikely to approach change constructively if it:

- Has a long history of unresponsiveness to change
- Wants to use the change agent as a pawn
- Is already committed to a particular position
- Has no real power to effect change within itself
- Shows many signs of pathology or major incapacity
- Makes a negative response to a well-managed initial encounter with the change agent.

In summary, Relate stage activities are focused on getting to know the client, and helping the client to know you, in the most favorable light for ongoing collaboration. They also focus on diagnosing barriers within the client system that are likely to preclude successful change. Together with the activities in the preceding Care stage, when client and change agent develop an initial understanding of the concern(s) to be addressed, these activities lay the foundation for the analysis and action to follow.

Havelock and Zlotolow's stage two, Examine, is introduced as the step where you will "turn cares into problems you can solve; then go on to meaningful objectives." The authors caution that this stage is easily glossed over in a hasty attempt to seek solutions, uncritically accepting the need that galvanized you and the client to action in the care stage. Yet failure to study and understand the system in greater depth will most likely result in a misguided change effort and no significant improvement (Havelock & Zlotolow, 1995, p. 79).

The metaphor most central to, and explanatory of, the Examine stage is that of diagnosing a disease in the client system. For the change agent, the client system is very much like a patient. The concerns that brought the client to the Care stage, and that initiated the C-R-E-A-T-E-R cycle, are most likely not the disease, but only its symptoms. Havelock and Zlotolow are very clear about the importance of this stage: the change agent must work with members of the client system to help them "*articulate that need*: to describe the type of pain, to pinpoint its location, and to recall its origin" (1995, p. 79, emphasis in original). In short, a successful Examine stage must be a colla-borative effort involving open communication between change agent and client. The client most likely lacks the change process skills to make the diagnosis: this is probably a major part of his reason for involving a change agent. Yet the change agent (unless he is both an insider and either a formal or informal leader) most likely lacks the information that only the client can provide, upon which the diagnosis will be made. Once again, a true partner-ship among those on the change team is essential to its success (p. 86).

The authors present three perspectives from which a diagnosis may be pursued. They observe that each one is valid and can lead to accurate conclusions, but they recommend combining all three (Havelock & Zlotolow, 1995, p. 80). The first may initially be the most useful: identifying the problems. As we have already established, one or more problems probably caused the client to initiate the C-R-E-A-T-E-R process, and these are likely to be the easiest place to start (p. 80). However, the change agent may find it equally useful, once the problems have been identified, to also identify potential opportunities, or what is right with the client system (p. 81). (It is also possible that the change process was initiated because the client saw the potential to make things better, perhaps using a new technological or pedagogical tool. In this case these opportunities might be the first focus, with the change agent subsequently examining potential problems.) The final diagnostic perspective involves examining these strengths, weaknesses, obstacles, and opportunities in context within the client system, and seeking to understand their interrelationships (p. 82).

Once again, Havelock and Zlotolow also provide a useful look at common pitfalls in their discussion of the Examine stage. They identify five traps into which the unwary or inexperienced change agent is especially likely to stumble (Havelock & Zlotolow, 1995, pp. 86-88):

1. "Analysis paralysis": the change agent wants to spend too much time on diagnosis. She should get a good, holistic picture of the client's situation, then move on.

2. Avoidance or denial: the client wants to spend too much time on diagnosis as a means of putting off action.

3. Destructive confrontation: the change agent presents diagnosed problems in a way that demeans or threatens the client.

4. The "house diagnosis": the change agent has a specialty, which mysteriously appears as the major cause of trouble in every client system he examines.

5. Fire fighting: the change agent races from symptom to symptom as they are identified, without looking for more fundamental causes.

One of the most useful tools the authors provide in discussing this stage is a five-question outline of a *diagnostic inventory* that the change agent might use in gathering the information required to draw informed conclusions about the problems or opportunities facing the client system. While the reader is referred to pages 84-86 of Havelock & Zlotolow's *Change Agent's Guide* (1995) for a complete discussion (including helpful sub-questions), the basic diagnostic questions they suggest are:

1. What are the system's goals?
2. Is there adequate structure for achieving these goals?
3. Is there sufficient openness in communication?
4. Does the system possess the necessary capacities?
5. Do rewards exist for members who work toward system goals?

The authors recommend that the change agent use these questions as the core of a more specific inventory (Havelock & Zlotolow, 1995, pp. 84, 86). The sub-questions they offer in their book provide a good place to start, but they are unlikely to be sufficient by themselves for any given diagnosis. Nor will all of them be appropriate to a particular client system, although the areas represented by the five major questions listed above must be covered, as a minimum (p. 84). Armed with such a diagnostic inventory, and with an understanding of both effective approaches to diagnosis and likely pitfalls, the change agent is ready to proceed to the next stage.

Stage three in the C-R-E-A-T-E-R model is the Acquire stage. Havelock and Zlotolow subtitle this stage as "seeking and finding relevant resources, which may be as diverse as electronic or print materials, people, or products" (1995, p. 91). The authors begin with a discussion of the major purposes for acquiring resources in support of change. They list seven such purposes, which correspond roughly to the stages of C-R-E-A-T-E-R (p. 94) and to a lesser extent to the CBAM model discussed in Chapter 7. Represented as *D-A-E-T-E-I-M*, they are: (1) *diagnosis*, (2) *awareness*, (3) *evaluation-before-trial*, (4) *trial*, (5) *evaluation-after-trial*, (6) *installation*, and (7) *maintenance.*

These purposes serve the change agent as a useful reminder of the major points in the change process where some form of informational, human, or other resource input will be required–along with the change activities those resources will serve. The first two feed back into the stages we have already covered (and provide a good example of why C-R-E-A-T-E-R is not necessarily sequential). Resources for diagnosis help the change agent investigate the problems facing the client, while those for awareness help him identify the range of potential solutions available. The next three relate to the assessment of a potential innovation's fit to the client's needs. Evaluation-before-trial resources support judgments of validity, reliability, or effectiveness based on others' experience with the innovation. Resources for trial support the actual testing of the innovation in the client system (for example, an IC Component Checklist, discussed in Chapter 7, which offers a blueprint of what the innovation should look like in practice). Evaluation-after-trial resources will help with assessing the trial results and with making an informed decision on adoption. The final two purposes pertain to post-adoption stages: installation resources support implementation, and maintenance resources support continuance and institutionalization.

Havelock and Zlotolow's also describe a resource acquisition strategy serving these purposes. In this section, the process leading up to selecting a solution is used to organize potential information sources and information-gathering activities. The authors list the following possibilities for "acquiring an expanded awareness of who the client is and what the universe of concerns could be" (1995, pp. 96-98):

- Use the client representative who contacted you as a source.
- Use other key sources within the system, especially those representing key factions, perspectives, or interest groups.
- Interview an assembled group representing all key stakeholders. Note how they interact as well as what they say.
- Observe key stakeholders "in action" in the client system. Note what they do and how they interact in day-to-day activity.

In each of these activities, Havelock and Zlotolow recommend a three-step process: (1) *listen*, (2) *reflect*, and (3) *inquire*. Listening is exactly as it sounds: the change agent should say as little as possible to guide the discussion, allowing the client to provide the details–and only the details–they feel the change agent needs to know. Reflecting has two aspects: paraphrasing the source's key points back to them to check for understanding, and reflecting on that understanding and its implications once it is confirmed. Finally, inquiring allows use of focused questions to probe for additional information, especially to fill any gaps remaining after the first two steps (1995, p. 97).

Later, of course, the change agent will require more detail to arrive at a particular diagnosis. To acquire valid information for these purposes, Havelock and Zlotolow (1995, pp. 99-100) recommend:

- Observing and measuring system outputs (intended and unintended results, products and byproducts, etc.)
- Organizing a self-diagnostic workshop for representatives of all key stakeholders in the client system
- Engaging the services of an external diagnostic research team
- Using a collaborative internal/external team to design and conduct a contextual self-diagnosis

- Analyzing data from continuous diagnostic monitoring activities
  (such as quality assurance/quality control routines) within the
  client system.

Once a diagnosis has been made, the change agent's logistical task
becomes one of obtaining and "harvesting" resources on *searching for and
obtaining resources*, a process Havelock and Zlotolow refer to as building
"an adequate awareness of the resource universe" (1995, p. 101). Here, the
focus is on identifying the range of possible solutions for each of the
problems/opportunities identified during the diagnosis procedure. The
authors emphasize two parts of this process: *building awareness* and
maintaining awareness (pp. 101-102). The best source for building
awareness is, of course, experience. The change agent, who is already an
expert in the field in which she is operating, has accumulated a broad,
longitudinal awareness of it. For the inexperienced change agent, or one
consulting in a field for the first time, the authors recommend getting a
good overview by reading an introductory text or even taking an
introductory university course in that area. For maintaining awareness, they
suggest using periodicals and the mass media, as well as using information
systems to search services and databases.

When the full range of possible solutions has been identified, the change
agent must shift once again to narrowing the focus: what Havelock and
Zlotolow call "homing in" (1995, p. 102). They recommend a six-step
sequence for arriving at an implementation decision (pp. 102-105):
1. Obtain an overview of the problem(s) and solution(s) from a
   comprehensive, written source.
2. Obtain a similar overview from at least one person who has had
   direct experience with the problem(s) and/or solution(s).
3. Observe the innovation in a concrete or "live" form.
4. Obtain evaluative data from an objective source, if possible, or
   from at least two persons, representing different perspectives,
   who have had direct experience.

5. Obtain the innovation for trial.

6. Acquire or develop a framework for evaluating its results (i.e., a rubric for making the decision to implement or reject), before actually conducting the trial.

The authors close their discussion of the Acquire stage by making the case for what might be considered the logistical counterpart to the Renew stage: "building a permanent capacity for resource acquisition" (Havelock & Zlotolow, 1995, pp. 105-107). They argue that while the change agent must arrive on the scene with these competencies already well developed, she must not leave without beginning their development within the client system. To launch this process, they provide eight suggestions for building such a permanent capacity that the change agent can recommend to the client system (pp. 106-107):

1. Officially recognize the need for resource acquisition by providing time/money for the activities discussed above.

2. Support any good sharing and search norms that already exist, then encourage the others.

3. Take advantage of any creative practitioners or in-house experts within the organization.

4. Generate open, but realistic, expectations for the information sources that are available.

5. Evaluate the effect of past experience with use of informational, human, or other resources on attitudes toward these resources throughout the organization.

6. Obtain descriptions of successful cases of resource acquisition and use them to demonstrate payoff in relevant terms.

7. Structure the process to avoid gathering mountains of questionable information that will never be used.

8. Make resources that are acquired available locally throughout the organization (i.e., not from some distant central storehouse, but within easy reach of every participant who might need them).

Havelock and Zlotolow do offer a caution concerning resource acquisition
as well. They note that when deciding how much time and money to invest
in these endeavors, the change agent and the client should weigh the
expected benefits against the costs (1995, p. 107). Failure to make an
adequate investment in the Acquire stage could leave the change effort with
inadequate resources to make or implement a decision in later stages. Making
too much of an investment could expend resources needed more elsewhere,
and yield, not only what is needed, but mountains of trash, as well. They also
reiterate that, "in a knowledge universe which is expanding rapidly," the
change agent (and later, the client system) must strive for breadth rather than
depth of knowledge...plus the competencies required to tap the knowledge
base for depth whenever and wherever it is required (p. 107).

Havelock and Zlotolow use the tag "from knowledge to action" to introduce
their stage four, Try (1995, p. 109). The core of this stage is a six-step
process that is largely sequential (p. 109), although they acknowledge that
information or obstacles may be encountered during a particular step that
may require returning to an earlier one and beginning anew from there (p.
110). The steps are (p. 109-110):
1. Assemble and sort the relevant findings from the acquire stage.
2. Derive implications from the knowledge base that affect the client
   system and its objectives or circumstances.
3. Generate a range of solution ideas based on the possible solutions
   identified in previous stages and the unique needs, strengths, and
   limitations of this change effort in these circumstances.
4. Test feasibilities.
5. Adapt the remaining solution(s) to the unique characteristics and
   needs of the client system.
6. Act. (Choose one–or, in some cases, more than one–solution. Pilot
   test it, and evaluate the results to arrive at a decision.)

The first of these steps is largely a summary activity for the acquire stage.
The authors use it to sort the acquired resources into those that serve

diagnostic applications and those that serve solution-oriented applications. They present five subcategories of the former and six subcategories of the latter to help the change agent organize the knowledge and other resources obtained up to this point (Havelock & Zlotolow, 1995, p. 112).

The second step is largely interpretive. Much of what is obtained during the Acquire stage will be either highly generalized theory (not situated in any particular context) or highly specific research and its application (explicitly situated in a context different–at least in some respects–from that of the client system). In this step the change agent, ideally in collaboration with the client, must identify those differences and their impact on the resource's generalizability to this particular change effort and its environment. Havelock and Zlototlow caution that this step is not easy, and for this reason they devote three pages to walking the reader through a concrete example of the process they recommend. This process consists of four steps: retrieve, summarize (paraphrase), relate (to the client context), and derive (Havelock & Zlotolow, 1995, pp. 113-116).

The third step can be summarized in a single word: brainstorming. The active participation of the client is essential by this point. The authors lay out a particular brainstorming technique, consisting of preparing, stage setting, rule setting, and summarizing (Havelock & Zlotolow, 1995, pp. 117-118). They emphasize that at no point during these sub-steps should ideas be critiqued, by others in the group or even by the originator. The goal here is to create a "mind-stretching" experience that will generate ideas free from assumptions about feasibility (p. 116).

Feasibility does not stay absent for long, however: it is the domain of the fourth step in the Try stage. Once the full range of possible solutions have been identified, the change team's attention turns to comparing alternatives in order to find the one that is most likely to succeed and have the greatest benefit for the level of resource expenditure, such as time, money, and staff. Havelock and Zlotolow (1995, p.119) define feasibility as having three dimensions–*benefit, workability,* and *diffusibility*–each represented by a question:

1. Benefit represents the question, "How much good will the potential solution do if it works, and at what cost?"
2. Workability represents the question, "Is the potential solution really practical in this context, at this time?"
3. Diffusibility represents the question, "Will the solution be accepted by enough members and factions to last, given demonstrable benefit and workability?"

Havelock and Zlotolow also offer several sub-questions for each dimension (1995, pp. 119-120) and suggest that the change team should create a rubric (perhaps using these sub-questions as its core). This rubric can help ensure that each potential solution is evaluated on the same set of criteria and that no criteria are missed.

The fifth step offers the change team the opportunity to adapt, or "reinvent" the innovation(s) selected in the preceding steps. Recall our earlier discussion of reinvention in Chapter 3 for some cautions. The authors generally seem to recommend use of "off the shelf" innovations whenever possible, since reduced fidelity often leads to reduced effectiveness, and innovation redevelopment requires another set of skills which the team may lack. They emphasize that a good fit between the innovation and the specific requirements of the client system is essential, and that adaptation may offer the only feasible way to make use of an existing innovation (Havelock & Zlotolow, 1995, pp. 121-122).

The sixth and final step is where the proposed innovation is actually put to trial for the first time in the client's own system. Havelock and Zlotolow warn that this step may be more complex than it appears. They divide the trial into three phases (1995, pp. 122-124). First, the change team must determine if the potential innovation is minimally acceptable to the system's key stakeholders. (They pose this question in terms of the innovation's "label" or "package.") Next comes a very pragmatic test: can the innovation even be set up and tried outside the "lab," in the client's own system? Finally, the results of the trial are examined (according to the rubric recommended earlier, in the Acquire stage) and a decision is made: to implement or not to implement.

Stage five of the C-R-E-A-T-E-R model is Extend, defined as "gaining deeper and wider acceptance" (Havelock & Zlotolow, 1995, p. 125). It's treatment in *The Change Agent's Guide* is divided into five major sections: (1) how individuals accept innovations, (2) how groups accept innovations, (3) strategies for solidifying adoption, (4) strategies for diffusion to a wide audience, and (5) strategies for flexibility during implementation (p. 125).

The authors' discussion of the adoption process at the individual level is based heavily on Rogers' work (see Chapter 3). The major new contribution they make here is their suggestion of change agent activities that should be linked to each phase of the innovation-decision process (Havelock & Zlotolow, 1995, pp. 129-131). Figure 8 illustrates this linkage using their adaptation of Rogers' categories. Note that the suggested focus of change agent activities, in each case, not only supports the client's current stage in the adoption cycle, but also paves the way for his transition to the next.

As these stages progress, Havelock and Zlotolow also emphasize the importance of the change agent using her understanding of the adoption process to avoid common causes of failure. They note that here, unlike most other aspects of their model, each individual adopter must pass through all stages "in sequence without skipping any" (Havelock & Zlotolow, 1995, p. 131). A corollary point is that individual adopters will do so at varying rates (which is treated in greater depth in Chapter 7's discussion of the Stages of Concern).

In moving to consider how groups reach collective innovation decisions, the authors return to the language of social systems introduced earlier. We are reminded that human societies, as part of their mission, protect the system from "invasion" by undesirable outside influences (Havelock & Zlotolow, 1995, p. 133). One of the ways that this function is exercised is through the actions of members in key roles. Innovators serve as advocates who "sniff out" necessary changes. They are balanced by resisters, who defend the virtues of the status quo. Finally, leaders–who may be authority figures, opinion leaders, or gatekeepers (controlling access)–have various roles in judging the opposing arguments and making a decision, which generally starts the "rank and file" moving in the designated direction (pp. 133-134).

Next Havelock and Zlotolow offer some tips for extending adoption both deeper and wider. Extending deeper anchors the implementation at hand, making discontinuance less likely. Techniques for facilitating this include (1995, pp. 139-141):

- Continuing reward (benefits gained through innovation use)
- Practice and routine (making the innovation part of "the way things are done around here")

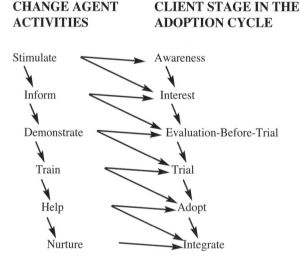

CHANGE AGENT ACTIVITIES

CLIENT STAGE IN THE ADOPTION CYCLE

Stimulate — Awareness
Inform — Interest
Demonstrate — Evaluation-Before-Trial
Train — Trial
Help — Adopt
Nurture — Integrate

Figure 8. Matching Change Agent Actions to the Client's Adoption Process. *Note.* From *The Change Agent's Guide* (p. 130), by R. G. Havelock and S. Zlotolow, 1995, Englewood Cliffs, NJ: Educational Technology Publications. Copyright © 1995 by Educational Technology Publications, Inc. Reprinted by permission.

- Structural integration into the system (provision of the necessary time and money to continue use)
- Continuing evaluation (provision of feedback ensuring the innovation continues to produce improved performance)
- Providing for continuing maintenance (in-house "technical support" to make sure deterioration of the innovation does not lead to failures, which can erode acceptance)
- Continuing adaptation capability (recognizing that the client system, its needs, and its environment will change, and building in the flexibility to adapt the innovation to these new circumstances).

Extending wider implies building on a successful implementation in this client system to diffuse the same innovation to other systems sharing similar concerns and circumstances. This discussion focuses on the strengths and limitations of media that the change agent can use to "spread the message," and how to effectively combine them into a successful multimedia strategy (pp. 142-145).

The authors conclude their discussion of the Extend stage with tips for staying flexible during implementation. They note that judicious further adaptation of the innovation may be necessary to adjust to environmental changes, or to address the concerns of key stakeholders. They observe that the client system may prove more or less receptive to change than originally anticipated, necessitating acceleration or slowing of the change process (Havelock & Zlotolow, 1995, pp. 146-147). Finally, they caution that an implementation strategy–like any other plan–may require modification as the effort encounters unforeseen obstacles, requirements, or political constraints. Each of these situations, they suggest, should be met in collaboration with the client system's key stakeholders (p. 148).

The final phase of Havelock and Zlotolow's C-R-E-A-T-E-R model, stage six, is Renew. The authors subtitle this stage *Renew, Re-C-R-E-A-T-E,*

Terminate, and place it in the center of the circle (recall Figure 7) in recognition that it is an ongoing function that should eventually launch another cycle of the model (Havelock & Zlotolow, 1995, p. 149). This should not, however, be interpreted as meaning that the change agent's work is done, that there is nothing left to do but say goodbye and make a graceful exit, or that renewal implies nothing more than "do it all again." While the change agent concluding a successful implementation may be able to take this view and walk away with a paycheck, the long-term survival of the innovation, the client system's ability to continue to evolve, and the change agent's enduring reputation with members of that system depend on much more.

Immediately upon emerging from the Extend stage, the change agent should first assemble the full change team, including all key stakeholder representatives, for an *after-action review* (AAR). This should be the minimal level of evaluation for any change effort: an organized review of the project's records, timelines, costs, and observed outcomes. Anecdotes supplied by project participants in the change team or throughout the client system (especially "end-users," such as teachers, students, and parents) may also be useful to the extent that they illustrate the effectiveness of the product or process. The scope of the evaluation should, however, expand in proportion to the scope of the change effort. For example, a large and comprehensive project funded by a substantial government grant will have a similarly large evaluation effort–with its own staff, director, and even budget–backed by up to ten percent of the project's resources (Havelock & Zlotolow, 1995, pp. 150-152).

One significant result of this evaluation should be a formalized reflection on the entire change cycle that has just completed. Havelock and Zlotolow suggest structuring this "change retrospective" according to the stages of the C-R-E-A-T-E-R model, answering five questions for each stage (1995, p. 152):

1. What resources (time, effort, money, people, etc.) were devoted to this stage?
2. Were these resources adequate? Were they too much?
3. Was this stage successful in meeting its stated objectives?
4. What could we have done to make it (more) successful?
5. Would a better plan or process have improved the outcome?

The authors further recommend that the results of the AAR then be used to redesign the change process for this particular client system, adapting it in light of the feedback just reviewed to make it more effective and/or efficient in subsequent rounds (Havelock & Zlotolow, 1995, p. 153). They also place a high value on adapting the process to reach out to a broader audience, becoming more inclusive and perhaps involving stakeholders of whom the change team was only marginally aware in this round (pp. 154-155).

As the change team looks ahead, the authors suggest that a crucial goal is to strengthen its internal members' ability to sustain support for the effort just completed and to build an overall sense that "something new and important is happening." This must include making it clear that change isn't going to end or become less important when the change agent leaves (Havelock & Zlotolow, 1995, p. 155). They recommend six possible ways to do this (pp. 155-156):

1. Bring new, internal members onto the change team.
2. Adapt to changes in the local environment.
3. Consider expanding your definition of who the client is.
4. Re-assess the nature of the concern in light of your experience.
5. Check for the availability of new knowledge or resources.
6. Be open to further adaptation or repackaging of the innovation.

These guidelines are, of course, paving the way for building a permanent, in-house capacity for change in the client system. The authors refer to this as enabling self-renewal, and list four key features that must be fostered (Havelock & Zlotolow, 1995, p. 156):

1. A positive attitude toward change and innovation
2. An internal subsystem focused explicitly on identifying and facilitating constructive change
3. A mindset that values seeking external information and other resources
4. A perspective that views the future as something that can and should be planned for.

They observe that complete integration of a self-renewal mechanism within the client system will be a gradual process–if, in fact, it occurs at all. They compare the stages of such a process to the stages of the C-R-E-A-T-E-R model, an observation that makes sense intuitively when one considers that the client is being asked to adopt and implement the innovation of self-renewal. Of course, like any other change effort, this process is prone to "fits and starts and random discontinuities" which may accelerate the process…or derail it (Havelock & Zlotolow, 1995, p. 158). During this time, the client system must make four key commitments to institutionalize the *self-renewal* process (pp. 159-162):

1. Regenerating/renewing the authority or sanction for the change process under internal "ownership"
2. Credible guarantees of continuing resources, eventually through the organization's own budget
3. Acceptance throughout the system of the new change agent roles
4. Acceptance of the interrelationships between the change subsystem and the rest of the client system (including other subsystems).

Havelock and Zlotolow caution that during this time the normal flow of organizational life goes on for the client system and the systems of which it is a part. There will be times of fiscal stringency when budget reductions and cost-cutting initiatives abound, which is when other organizational subsystems are likely to fight any effort to allocate funds to a self-renewal capability for fear that those funds could affect adversely their own budgets.

The authors advise that during such times, those in the fledgling internal change subsystem should bide their time, focusing on preserving what has already been secured. Such "belt-tightening" occurs in cycles as well. When it has run its course, the system's thoughts will likely turn to how it can reconfigure itself to take advantage of the upswing, and innovation will once again be in vogue (Havelock & Zlotolow, 1995, p. 163).

Once a robust capacity for self-renewal is installed within the client system and accepted as part of its way of life, these internal change facilitators may wish to consider more fundamental, transformational change. Havelock and Zlotolow refer to transforming the system in this manner as *system change*, a term applied to "more fundamental concerns" and sweeping projects, such as system-wide reengineering and reallocation of budget priorities. It may even include changing the organization's fundamental mission, or how it is pursued, in far-reaching ways (Havelock & Zlotolow, 1995, pp. 163-165). The reader should note that such system change, which Havelock and Zlotolow recommend only for organizations that have already developed a robust change subsystem, is distinct from *systemic change* as discussed in Chapter 9 (which is an orientation that should be applied to all change efforts).

In pursuing transformational, system change efforts, the change agent will need to explicitly define what constitutes "better" for the system in a way that can guide any redesign. The authors present five "a priori goods" to be considered in this process (Havelock & Zlotolow, 1995, pp. 166-167):

1. Positive growth (which does not necessarily refer to size; such growth can include serving more people, providing more products and services, or becoming more inclusive, for example)
2. Greater integration (e.g., strengthening interrelationships between subsystems, enhancing communication and collaboration)
3. More differentiation (which should be accompanied by greater integration and which includes more specialization of labor or accumulation of focused expertise)

4. More rewards (accruing to those who provide inputs to the system, work within it, or receive outputs from it)
5. Enhanced effectiveness in innovation and problem solving.

Finally, the original change agent must turn his attention to the questions of disengaging and moving on. While some change agents, especially those emerging from within the client organization, may find that success leads to an appointment to manage that organization (and thus may never leave), most will at some point have to move on to other clients, or other change efforts elsewhere within the same client system. Havelock and Zlotolow treat this issue in two parts: when and how.

They suggest three possible criteria for deciding when to disengage, which might be described as *problem-centered, innovation-centered,* and *system-centered.* A change agent following the problem-centered criterion would begin to consider moving on when he has solid evidence that the problem identified in the initial diagnosis is on its way to solution. One following the innovation-centered criterion would use acceptance of the selected solution by the client's leadership and the start of rapid diffusion throughout the system as the cue to begin disengagement. Finally, the system-centered criterion would initiate disengagement when there is enough evidence that the system is successfully generating a self-renewal capacity (Havelock & Zlotolow, 1995, p. 167). The authors note that, theoretically, the system-centered approach is superior, but they acknowledge that change agents with multiple clients or other competing demands may find this impractical (p. 168).

How to disengage is slightly more complicated. Havelock and Zlotolow (1995) recommend that the process should be gradual. This both protects the change agent's relationship with the client and allows for the internal members of the change team to build confidence in their ability to manage self-renewal on their own before they truly are on their own. The authors also suggest that continuing availability for emergency help, and even annual reunions (perhaps leading to follow-up contracts), may serve the change agent's best interests as well as those of the client system (p. 168).

Havelock and Zlotolow close their discussion of stage six with a final reminder that it "is not exactly a stage. It is an end point and a new beginning and a whole new series of stages all rolled into one" (1995, p. 168). This is a fitting way to conclude our discussion of the C-R-E-A-T-E-R model and the change process. As we shall see in greater detail in Chapter 9, the ultimate goal of the change agent should be removal of the institutional barriers that prevent the system from independently evolving in adaptation to its changing environment, which is a characteristic of all healthy, living systems.

Other Studies

While *The Change Agent's Guide* is in its second edition–and the first was itself a revision of an earlier book by Havelock–other valuable resources related to Havelock's model have not continued to be updated. Some of these have actually been incorporated into the *Guide* itself, but one which has not is *Training for Change Agents: A Guide to the Design of Training Programs in Education and Other Fields* (Havelock, 1971). Since the core of Havelock's model has remained sufficiently stable, this publication may still be of considerable use to those charged with schooling prospective change agents in its use. Personnel associated with state education departments, in particular, should review Part VI, which lays out a detailed model for change agent training in such agencies as an example.

Havelock's model has been validated and extended by other researchers and practitioners, as well. Some of the resulting publications have directly cited Havelock's findings, such as *Strategies for Change* (Lindquist, 1978). Lindquist analyzes six case studies of planned change in colleges and notes five factors associated with successful implementation, which are roughly congruent with Havelock's stages. In a similar, more recent study, Foley

(1997) examines a wider sample, this time among 36 K-12 schools that had succeeded in significant change. While her paper emphasizes the principal's role, her findings nonetheless outline a change process similar to the C-R-E-A-T-E-R model. Together, such studies suggest that this model can be used across settings and time.

Other studies of the principal's role have been less kind to theoretical models of the change process. For example, in "A Study of the Change Process Utilized by Colorado High School Principals," Jacobus (1997) found little correspondence between the process steps identified by principals and any of the classical change models examined. Respondents in this study indicated that the two most important and most commonly incorporated strategies were problem identification and marketing the need for change to stake-holders, but they suggested a general disdain for research, external change agents, and pilot programs. Their justification for these views was often rooted in their perceptions of the unique nature of their particular schools.

Three aspects of these findings are especially significant for the change agent. First, the principals in this study seem to have an intuitive grasp of some of the early stages of the change process, as evidenced by their emphasis on problem identification (Examine stage) and developing a shared vision for change (Care and Relate stages). Yet once the action begins, their understanding of change diverges from what studies of successful change in their own settings tell us about the process. Second, while the results of such prior research in comparable settings are available, principals often do not use them. This reflects one of the common errors Havelock & Zlotolow identify: assuming that the situation at hand is so unique that prior knowledge and knowledge from other systems is irrelevant (1995, p. 91). Third, as we shall see in the next chapter, the principal plays an exceptionally important role in successful change, so these misperceptions must be overcome (which can be a tricky process considering that telling the principal she has serious misperceptions will hardly help your case).

As we have gained more experience with the change process, one of the factors most frequently overlooked has been the criticalness of effective staff development. Havelock and Zlotolow reflect this in the C-R-E-A-T-E-R model, especially during the Extend and Renew stages. This has also been a common theme in subsequent research. Probably the most common approach to such studies is exemplified by Kalapothakos (1996) in her study of professional development in a P-8 setting aimed at developing the self-renewal capacity Havelock discusses. She found that a strong program, which included administrative support for the sort of "cosmopolitan" activities outside the local system that Havelock recommends, caused teachers' dissatisfaction to drop, and their involvement in and effectiveness at change activities to increase.

Freidus and Grose (1998) offer the perspective of the new change agent in their study of curriculum change. This paper reflects Havelock's discussion, during the Renew stage, of the process of becoming a change agent as an instance of the change process itself. The authors describe the professional development model used in the project they studied, its interplay with change agent concerns, and the effect of these factors on success of the overall change project. Interestingly, a more detailed consideration of this concept is offered by Hall, Newlove, George, Rutherford, and Hord (1991), who extended the Adopter Stages of Concern model (discussed in the next chapter) to include a corresponding model for change agents, as well.

Further crossover from other frameworks is seen in Rogers' (1995) chapter on the "innovation-decision process." Like Hall and associates, Rogers discusses the change process here from the adopter's perspective, but he also provides a good discussion of stages in this process and their relationship to communication channels as it progresses. Several of Rogers' other chapters (e.g., on the generation of innovations, diffusion networks, and innovation in organizations) also provide useful insights on the change process from a non-specific, "objective" standpoint.

A final consideration of the change process that is worth mentioning is Harvey and Wehmeyer's (1990) *Checklist for Change*. While many change researchers would argue that such a simple, systematic treatment of the change process glosses over its inherent complexity, this book is worthwhile for two reasons. First, for the "home grown" change effort with few resources and fewer "change experts." The straightforward approach to change it contains may cut through some of the more arcane details, and give change agents the confidence to proceed in the first place. Second, the sections in the *Checklist for Change* (which include analysis, planning, implementation, and evaluation) draw obvious parallels between the change process, which is still alien and unfamiliar to many educators, and the traditional process of Instructional Development.

Summary

One of the most important things to notice about the C-R-E-A-T-E-R model is the interrelationship between the phases. Repeatedly through this discussion, we have encountered instances where the nonlinear nature of the change process was highlighted. This is an important development in Havelock's model, as recent criticism of the original edition of *The Change Agent's Guide to Innovation in Education* (Havelock, 1973) has frequently centered on the problematic aspects of its linear approach to change. Linear models are, of course, easier to understand, but at the price of fidelity to what is, after all, a complex form of human interaction.

Havelock and Zlotolow have created a useful hybrid, which offers a convenient, superficially sequential depiction of the process–then infuses treatment of the model's non-linear aspects throughout the discussion. The C-R-E-A-T-E-R model presented in their *Change Agent's Guide* (1995) has seven stages:

- Stage 0: Care ("There's something wrong here, or something could be more right!")

- Stage 1: Relate ("Who and what make up this system? How are they interconnected?")
- Stage 2: Examine ("What is the true nature of the problems and opportunities at hand?")
- Stage 3: Acquire ("What information or other resources are available? How do I get them?")
- Stage 4: Try ("What solutions will really work here, and how might I need to adapt them?")
- Stage 5: Extend ("How do I solidify adoption or diffuse the change to other populations?")
- Stage 6: Renew ("How do I develop a capacity for self-renewal in the client system?")

Havelock's model has been refined over the decades since its first publication, and has been developed along a variety of dimensions by other researchers. Practitioners engaged in change efforts in these contexts are encouraged to explore these and related studies in greater detail. (Terms in italics are ERIC descriptors, with * indicating *major* descriptors–the primary subjects of the document or article.)

- Foley, J. (1997). *Success in restructuring: A step-by-step recipe.* Paper presented at the annual meeting of the Association for Supervision and Curriculum Development, Scottsdale, AZ. (ED 409 607)

  *Change Strategies; Computer Uses in Education; Cooperative Planning; *Educational Change; *Educational Technology; Elementary Education; *Leadership; Minimum Competencies; School Effectiveness; *School Restructuring*

- Freidus, H., & Grose, C. (1998). *Implementing curriculum change: Lessons from the field.* Paper presented at the annual meeting of the American Educational Research Association, San Diego, CA. (ED 422 606)

*Change Agents; Curriculum Design; *Curriculum Development; *Educational Change; Educational Cooperation; Educational Experience; Elementary Secondary Education; Literacy; *Outcomes of Education; *Teacher Characteristics*

- Hall, G., Newlove, B., George, A., Rutherford, W., & Hord, S. (1991). *Measuring change facilitator Stages of Concern: A manual for use of the CFSoC Questionnaire.* Greeley, CO: Center for Research on Teaching and Learning. (ED 353 307)

*Attitude Measures; *Change Agents; Educational Attitudes; *Educational Change; Educational Innovation; Elementary Secondary Education; *Questionnaires; *Rating Scales; Scoring; Teacher Attitudes; Test Interpretation; Test Manuals; *Test Use*

- Havelock, R. (1971). *Training for change agents: A guide to the design of training programs in education and other fields.* Ann Arbor, MI: Ann Arbor Institute for Social Research. (ED 056 259)

*Change Agents; Conferences; Educational Change; *Educational Programs; *Guides; *Models; Problem Solving; *Program Design; Role Theory; Skill Development; State Programs; Training Objectives*

- Jacobus, K. (1997). *A study of the change process utilized by Colorado High School principals: The concordance of practice and theory.* Paper presented at the annual meeting of the American Educational Research Association, Chicago, IL. (ED 407 742)

*Administrator Responsibility; *Change Strategies; *Educational Change; High Schools; Models; *Principals; Program Implementation; *Theory Practice Relationship*

• Kalapothakos, A. (1996). *Pre-kindergarten to eighth grade teachers become change agents through active participation in school reform.* Unpublished doctoral practicum, Nova Southeastern University, Fort Lauderdale, FL. (ED 401 014)

*Change Agents; *Educational Change; Elementary Education; *Elementary School Teachers; Observation; *Professional Development; School Organization; School Restructuring; Staff Development; Surveys; Teacher Attitudes*

• Lindquist, J. (1978). *Strategies for change.* Berkeley, CA: Pacific Soundings Press. (ED 200 113)

*Adoption (Ideas); Black Colleges; *Change Strategies; Church Related Colleges; *College Planning; Educational Change; *Educational Innovation; Futures (of Society); *Higher Education; *Long Range Planning; Organizational Change; *Organizational Development; Private Colleges; School Community Relationship; Small Colleges; State Universities*

The Intended Adopter

chapter 7

The innovation is ready. The client system environment is ready. The change agents are ready and trained, and a careful, collaborative plan has been generated. Representatives of all the key stakeholders have been involved throughout the process, and are satisfied that this change–and the way its implementation will be managed–is in the best interests of their organization. Appropriate resources have been identified and acquired, and the innovation has performed well in a trial for the change team. The hard part is over, right?

Many change agents have walked away at this point, with their fees collected and another "success" added to their resume. While all the milestones just mentioned in the previous paragraph do set up an ideal situation for change, the point where most innovations fail still lies ahead.

As you may recall from the previous chapter, innovations are adopted or rejected not only at the system level, but at the individual level, as well. Unfortunately for the change agent, no change team can ever be "representative enough" for the level of adoption described above to settle the matter. No client system can ever be autocratic enough for a "decision from the top" to suffice. Each user will try the innovation in his practice, and will make an independent adoption/rejection decision. If enough of these individual decisions go against an innovation, even in a system as centralized as the military, it will likely fail, even if only because it is plagued by a seemingly endless series of unexpected "glitches" (Ellsworth, 1998, p. 7). Understanding how these individual decisions operate, and addressing the motives and uncertainties underlying them, calls for a focus on the intended adopter within the context of the change effort as a whole.

Hall and Associates' Concerns-Based Adoption Model

Research along these lines to date has been led by Hall and various colleagues, beginning in the early to mid 1970s, with the Concerns-Based Adoption Model (CBAM). First proposed by Hall, Wallace, and Dossett (1973), CBAM recognizes that "the effective change facilitator [must] understand how his or her clients (e.g., teachers) perceive change and adjust what he or she does accordingly" (Hall & Hord, 1987, p. 5). By focusing on the adopter's perceived needs, CBAM seeks to prevent a common shortfall noted by the authors: "change facilitators [basing] their interventions (i.e., what they did) on their own needs and timelines rather than on their clients' needs and change progress" (Hall & Hord, 1987, p. 5).

One of the central assumptions underlying CBAM is that change is a process, not an event (Hall, 1978, p. 1). Another is that change facilitators can only offer strategies to support implementation if they have diagnostic tools to use. Consequently CBAM research has developed and validated three diagnostic dimensions: *Stages of Concern, Levels of Use,* and *Innovation Configurations* (Hall, 1978, p. 2). CBAM operates through the change facilitator's diagnostic probing on each of these dimensions. The change facilitator collects data using validated instruments designed for these purposes. She then uses those measurements to derive prescriptive strategies for interventions, drawing on information and other resources outside the user system as appropriate (Hall & Hord, 1987, p. 12). This process is depicted in Figure 9. Each instrument may be administered multiple times during an entire implementation effort, for example once a year for three years. This allows the change facilitator to observe trends in

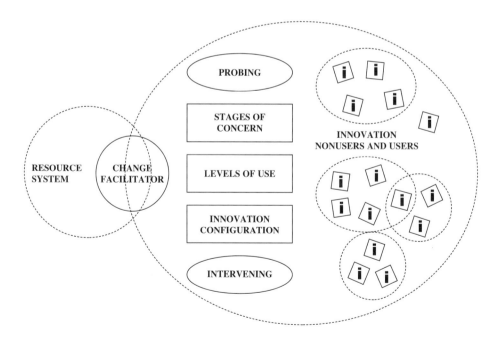

Figure 9. The Concerns-Based Adoption Model. Note. From *Change in Schools: Facilitating the Process (p. 12),* by G. Hall and S. Hord, 1987, Albany, N.Y.: State University of New York Press. Copyright 1987 by SUNY Pres. Reprinted with permission.

the diagnostic dimensions that these instruments measure–both to assess the implementation's progress (users advancing along each dimension individually or as a group) and to obtain feedback on the effectiveness of the interventions the facilitator is using.

Stages of Concern focuses on seven kinds of concerns, that an innovation's intended adopters may have as it is implemented. At stage 0 *(Awareness)* an individual may know the innovation exists, but has little concern or involvement with it. Stage 1 *(Informational)* concerns occur when individuals decide they would like to know more about the innovation. Stage 2 *(Personal)* concerns address prospective adopters' uncertainty about the demands of the innovation, their ability to meet them, and their role in relation to the innovation. Stage 3 *(Management)* concerns involve the administrative and logistical challenges of innovation use. Stage 4 *(Consequence)* concerns begin to ask how innovation use is affecting students. Stage 5 *(Collaboration)* concerns consider how the individual adopter can coordinate and cooperate with others in use of the innovation. Finally, stage 6 *(Refocusing)* concerns occur when the adopter begins to have ideas about replacing or improving on the innovation (Hall & Rutherford, 1983, p. 4).

This consideration of the time dimension of change is worthy of comment. It suggests that these concerns, and the most effective strategies for addressing them, will vary as implementation proceeds (Hall & Rutherford, 1983, pp. 7-8). In fact, CBAM specifies procedures in great detail for diagnosing where a given individual or group falls within the change process (Hall, George, & Rutherford, 1977; Hall, Loucks, Rutherford, & Newlove, 1975). This could be problematic in some settings, where administration of the diagnostic instruments is impractical or overly obtrusive. The pedagogic dividends expected from an innovation tend to appear as participants move into higher levels of concerns (Hord, Rutherford, Huling-Austin, & Hall, 1987, p. 74). Still, the authors caution, "Movement through the stages of concern cannot be forced, but, with appropriate support and assistance, it can be aided. At the same time, a lack of assistance or the wrong kind of support can interfere with developmental changes in concerns" (Hord, et al., 1987, p. 43).

While Stages of Concern focuses on the affective progress of the intended adopter during implementation, Levels of Use maps the adopter's behavioral progress in putting the innovation into practice. At level 0 *(Non-use)* the individual knows little or nothing about the innovation, is not involved with it in any way, and is doing nothing to become involved. Level I *(Orientation)* is marked by the first attempts to acquire information about the innovation, its associated philosophy, and what it requires from those who use it. Level II *(Preparation)* is the stage where individuals ready themselves to use the innovation for the first time. Level III *(Mechanical)* use is possibly where the innovation is at the greatest risk: users are focused exclusively on the short-term, rote details of use, with little time for reflection and less for any student-centered adaptation. Upon reaching level IVa *(Routine)* use, this crisis has passed: use of the innovation has stabilized, but little thought is being given to improving its effectiveness yet. This begins at level IVb *(Refinement)*, when the individual begins to adapt the innovation to enhance its short- and long-term benefits to those within the immediate sphere of influence. At level V *(Integration)* this adaptation begins to mass the effects of the individual's own use with the efforts of colleagues, to improve outcomes for those in their combined spheres of influence. Finally, at level VI *(Renewal)* the individual re-evaluates his innovation use and begins to consider major modifications, or new innovations that might work better (Hord, et al., 1987, p. 55).

At first glance, CBAM's Levels of Use (LoU) dimension might seem to be a model of the change process, similar to the C-R-E-A-T-E-R model discussed in the preceding chapter. On one level, this is accurate. However Havelock's model is, first and foremost, a model of the change process at the system level, while the LoU dimension describes that process at the level of the individual intended adopter. This, combined with its association with validated instruments for data collection, offers the change facilitator the unique ability to track the needs and progress of those who must actually make the innovation work.

Hall and his colleagues provide a classic example of this (and of the danger inherent in studying the larger system as the unit of adoption) in relation to studies showing no significant difference in academic achievement between schools using an innovation and non-user "control" schools (Hall & Hord, 1987, pp. 78-79):

> The general finding from the LoU data was that, in the so-called treatment schools, only 80 percent of the teachers were "users" of [the innovation]. In other words, 20 percent of the teachers in the experimental schools were not using [it]. In the comparison schools, 49 percent of the teachers were "users" of [the innovation]. In this case, the treatment and comparison groups were mixed; there was not a pure sample of users in one group and a pure sample of nonusers in the other group. It does not, then, seem surprising that the evaluation results found no significant differences between the two groups. By contrast, when all the LoU-identified users were compared with the nonusers (LoU 0, I, and II), large, statistically significant differences were identified in favor of [the innovation.]

The significance of this bears some elaboration. Historically, change has often been treated as an event rather than a process. Even with the aid of a clear process description (as Havelock and Zlotolow provided in the previous chapter), administrators and policymakers are frequently left without any empirical framework that will show whether, and to what extent, their policies have been implemented in the classroom. With its focus on actual classroom actions, the Levels of Use framework fills this gap, offering a rigorous way to describe the change process that answers decision makers' need for accountability (Hall & Hord, 1987, p. 103).

It should be clear from this discussion that there is a close relationship between the first two dimensions of CBAM. Stages of Concern describes feelings and affect, and Levels of Use describes behavior and action. Yet both provide metrics for the same change process across time, and therefore must be interrelated. Hord, et al. (1987, p.55) hint at this by weaving the intended adopter's "decision points" in with a depiction of advancing Levels of Use. This makes it possible to construct an illustration loosely relating the two time-indexed dimensions to one another (Figure 10), although these relationships will not always hold.

The third diagnostic dimension of CBAM, Innovation Configurations, does not relate directly to time. Veteran change facilitators will recall situations where concerns, focused on educational outcomes and teachers, appeared to use the innovation with those goals in mind. Yet it was obvious from observing teachers in the classroom that their understanding of what the innovation was differed dramatically from the facilitator or developers' understanding!

This reflects no malicious intent or lack of ability on the teacher's part: in most cases no one ever showed them what innovation use was supposed to look like in practice. Such an omission again is not malicious: innovation developers are simply more likely to describe innovation use in terms of the broader, philosophical goals that it serves than in terms of observable behavior (Hall & Hord, 1987, p. 123). This serves their commitment to those goals, which probably led to development of the innovation in the first place. It also serves their need to secure the approval of system-level leaders before implementation can proceed. These leaders, in turn, may be responding to public pressure (which is almost by definition expressed in broad terms, such as "back to basics"), and be no more able than the developers to articulate the tactics of classroom implementation.

This has important implications for the success or failure of the entire change process. As Hall and Hord observe, "When one is at a Mechanical use with intense personal and management concerns, it is extremely difficult to think reflectively about an innovation's philosophy. The consequence frequently is increased ambiguity and feelings of uncertainty about what should be happening in the classroom" (1987, pp. 112-113). Of course, this is the last thing the change facilitator wants to happen at that stage, as prolonged periods of a Mechanical Level of Use are likely to lead the adopter to question the innovation's benefits, which in turn may lead to "convenience adaptation" destructive to learning outcomes, or even to outright discontinuance (p. 100).

For these reasons, Hall and his associates stress the importance of developing Innovation Configuration (IC) Component Checklists prior to implementation. Failure to do so often results in the innovation's earliest adopters being told that their use is "out of compliance" with subsequently-developed guidelines (Hall & Hord, 1987, pp. 119-120).

The IC Component Checklist is actually a table. The column at the left contains the innovation's key components (e.g., technology, pedagogy, group processes, classroom management), and the next column contains the innovation developer's ideal implementation of each component. Successive columns to the right of the "ideal" column describe increasingly "flawed" implementations, most of which may still be acceptable because all critical components are adequately implemented (Hall & Hord, 1987, pp. 129-130). The last columns at the right, however, may contain unacceptable adaptations in which one or more of the critical components are implemented in a way that cripples the innovation's design (for example, using "mastery learning" to describe when students are tested only once or twice and then moved on regardless of their performance).

Several comments regarding the use of IC Component Checklists are especially important. First, a separate checklist for each type of adopter (e.g., administrators or teachers) is required, because the checklist must describe concrete, observable behaviors (Hall & Hord, 1987, p. 135). This is not as complicated as it sounds, since many classroom innovations have only one type of adopter (which is usually the teacher). However, for some innovations, such as site-based management, the active adoption by several types of stakeholders may be required for successful implementation. Second, the effectiveness of IC Component Checklists is supported by the experience of the National Diffusion Network (NDN). According to Hall and Hord, later editions of *Educational Programs that Work*, NDN's catalog of empirically validated innovative programs, included IC Component listings in recognition of their value to potential adopters (p. 114).

In undertaking the checklist development process, Hall's group echoes Havelock's emphasis on collaboration. An innovation's developers must clearly play a central role in defining what implementation should look like. However, given their philosophical tendencies and their inclination to believe the innovation will work best in any setting, if implemented exactly as they designed it, it is best that they not do so in isolation. It is neither practical nor necessary for every stakeholder group to participate in this process, but participation by the following groups is strongly encouraged (Hall & Hord, 1987, p. 125):

- Change facilitators (to ensure that they can use it to advise teachers and administrators)
- Administrators (to ensure that the innovation as defined is consistent with their vision)
- Teachers (to ensure that they understand what implementation is supposed to look like in their classrooms)
- Evaluators (to ensure that they understand what they are supposed to be looking for when assessing implementation).

Hall and his colleagues have subsequently focused on development of pragmatic tools for translating CBAM's theory into practice. They developed guidebooks to help practitioners apply its prescriptive strategies to facilitate implementation (Hall & Hord, 1987; Hord, et al. 1987). They also validated the CBAM framework in specific contexts, such as mediation of staff development programs (Marsh, Pelland, Melle, & Cooke, 1985) and facilitation of cultural adaptation in schools in response to change (Stiegelbauer, 1982).

Other Studies

Research by others outside the original group has contributed to these areas as well. Kember and Mezger (1990), pursuing the staff development focus in a distance education organization, used CBAM principles to structure a course team approach to developing instructional design skills in subject-matter experts. Horsley and colleagues (Horsley, Terry, Hergert, & Loucks-Horsley, 1991) produced a reference book targeted toward facilitation of change in rural schools. This book is especially valuable as an integration of CBAM's focus on the intended adopter, with a change process focus similar to that discussed in the previous chapter.

Applications of CBAM to the implementation of other specific innovations have often focused on computer technology. Two studies that are especially illustrative of the model's operation in practice are Hope (1995) and Wesley and Franks (1996). Hope investigated the integration of teacher workstations in a Florida elementary school. He administered the Stages of Concern Questionnaire (SoCQ) three times during the one-year period of his study. His results showed the typical movement of concerns from the early, self-focused stages (Informational and Personal) through the task-focused (Management) concerns, to the higher-level impact (Consequence, Collaboration, and Refocusing) concerns by the end of the observation period. By the time his study concluded, 80% of the teachers had reached Level of Use IVA (Routine). Wesley and Franks (1996) examined the implementation of two computer technologies: networked Computer-Assisted Instruction and desktop multimedia. Their study was supported by qualitative analysis, which offers some interesting insights into teachers' voluntary individual and collaborative activities as their involvement with the innovations grew.

Sevilla and Marsh (1992) provide a final case study of CBAM in a specific change effort. They studied the implementation of Project SEED, a practice-oriented science curriculum at the elementary level. This paper is an outstanding example of a phenomenon which Hall calls "tailing up," when high levels of self-focused (especially Personal) concerns are accompanied by high levels of Refocusing concerns, and actual use is only at the Mechanical level. This reflects a situation when the intended adopter feels swamped by the rote aspects of making the innovation work while having to attend to all the other duties of her position (e.g., teaching), which in turn leads simultaneously to concerns about personal adequacy and consequence. This may lead directly to a discomfort-inspired search for alternatives, resulting in Refocusing concerns before the innovation has even been truly implemented. This is a common, but important, danger signal to the change facilitator. (This is also a good example of why the relationships between Stages of Concern and Levels of Use, illustrated in Figure 10, do not always hold.) Finally, the authors' discovery that the program's simpler aspects were implemented in isolation, bypassing its more demanding aspects, highlights the IC Component Checklist's value. Its value is in making such a determination possible, as well as in explaining to teachers why this weakens the innovation's effectiveness.

Mitchell (1988) wrote a more general paper of interest to the evaluation community. She studied the use of CBAM as a program evaluation tool, assessing the effectiveness of three implementation efforts in an Oregon school district. She focuses on formative uses, such as defining program elements (IC Component Checklist), interpreting related concerns (SoC), monitoring innovation use (LoU), and designing practical interventions. Yet aspects of her discussion suggest possible summative applications, as well. For example, use of the IC Component Checklist method obviously applies to evaluation planning and conduct. She also mentions CBAM's utility for linking outcomes with innovation use.

Other recent CBAM research has focused on replication and validation of the model itself. A classic example is the 1992 Bailey and Palsha study, which examined CBAM's validity in a study of professionals who received

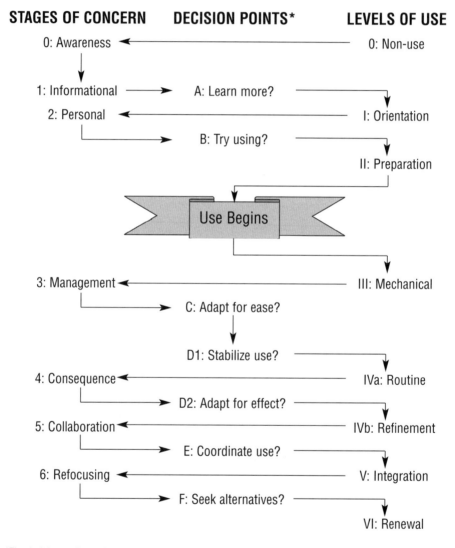

*The decision to discontinue use can be made at any time.

Figure 10. Relationship Between Stages of Concern and Levels of Use Dimensions

training in early childhood intervention. The researchers found that the overall CBAM philosophy was supported, but suggested that a reformulated model using an abbreviated and restructured questionnaire might be more valid. They proposed two revised questionnaires based on a shortened, five-stage model: one with 35 items and one with 15. A follow-up study was conducted by Shotsberger and Crawford (1996), which computed reliability estimates and ran a factor analysis on data gathered from algebra teachers using the original SoCQ and each of the two Bailey and Palsha questionnaires. This study ultimately arrived at a five-factor, 27-item questionnaire having consistently higher reliability estimates than a confirmatory study using another group of algebra teachers. These studies are significant because the intrusiveness of the original 35-item SoCQ is often cited as a limitation. The ability to obtain similar reliability with a significantly shorter instrument would be an important advantage.

Similar to several other classical models, CBAM has been validated internationally. In 1993 van den Berg reported on a study conducted in the Netherlands, Belgium, and the United Kingdom, which focused on the validity of its underlying theory. He found that the model held in these settings and represented a useful way to help schools deal with change (van den Berg, 1993).

It is also worth noting that Rogers (1995) contains a chapter describing his seminal work on adopter categories and their effect on innovativeness. Hall and his associates offer the best framework for describing what is important to intended adopters and helping them through change. Yet Rogers is widely considered authoritative in his theoretical categorization of adopters and their characteristics, which may be of considerable use in understanding why certain adopters progress through CBAM's stages and levels at different rates.

Summary

The Concerns-Based Adoption Model (CBAM) is a powerful framework for assessing and tracking change's progress at the level of the individual adopter, where success is ultimately determined. It offers tools for spotting and addressing concerns before they mushroom; assessing the extent to which the innovation is actually being used in practice; defining what "use in practice" should look like; and determining what adaptations can be made without reducing its effectiveness. This is crucial for today's change agent, who must maintain the innovation's philosophical rigor, satisfying the adopter's need for guidance and the policymaker's need for accountability. These points are supported by a growing body of research that uses CBAM as a tool for guiding implementation of particular innovations, and as a tool for evaluating such efforts. The CBAM framework consists of three diagnostic dimensions. Two of these are linked to the change timeline, allowing the facilitator to prescribe interventions that address concerns when they are most likely to arise. The CBAM framework is outlined below:

1. Stages of Concern (SoC) (Which affective issues is the adopter focused on?)

    Stage 0: Awareness ("I am not concerned about the innovation.")

    Stage 1: Informational ("I would like to know more about it.")

    Stage 2: Personal ("How will using it affect me?")

    Stage 3: Management ("Just using it is taking all of my time!")

    Stage 4: Consequence ("What effect is my using it having on students' learning?")

    Stage 5: Collaboration ("How might I integrate my use with other teachers' use?")

    Stage 6: Refocusing ("I have some ideas about something that might work even better!")

2. Levels of Use (LoU) (What is the adopter actually doing regarding the innovation?)

 Level 0: Non-use (neither using it nor taking any action to get involved)

 Level I: Orientation (learning what the innovation is all about)

 Level II: Preparation (getting ready to use the innovation for the first time)

 Level III: Mechanical (focused on the rote aspects of use, driven by own convenience)

 Level IVa: Routine (use has stabilized and few if any changes are considered)

 Level IVb: Refinement (changes are considered and made to improve learning outcomes)

 Level V: Integration (use is coordinated with colleagues to improve learning outcomes)

 Level VI: Renewal (use is reevaluated and new innovations examined for better options)

3. Innovation Configuration (IC) Component Checklist (What does "use" look like?)

 a) A table listing the innovation's key components (such as technology, pedagogy, and behavior).

 b) Next column to the right describes ideal implementation of each component.

 c) Successive columns represent increasingly flawed implementations.

 d) Many may still be "acceptable" if they satisfactorily implement critical components.

 e) Last column or two at right may represent common unacceptable implementations.

Hall and associates' CBAM framework has been applied to change research and practice in a wide range of settings. Practitioners engaged in change efforts in these contexts are encouraged to explore these and related studies in greater detail. (Terms in italics are ERIC descriptors, with * indicating *major* descriptors–the primary subjects of the document or article.)

- Bailey, D., & Palsha, S. (1992). Qualities of the Stages of Concern Questionnaire and implications for educational innovations. *Journal of Educational Research*, 85(4), 226-232. (EJ 447 952)

  *Attitude Measures; Change Strategies; Disabilities; Early Intervention; *Educational Innovation; Infants; Inservice Teacher Education; Models; Preschool Education; Questionnaires; *Teacher Attitudes; Toddlers*

- Horsley, D., Terry, W., Hergert, L., & Loucks-Horsley, S. (1991). *Managing change in rural schools: An action guide.* Andover, MA: Regional Laboratory for Educational Improvement of the Northeast & Islands. (ED 340 553)

  *Adoption (Ideas); Change Agents; *Change Strategies; *Educational Change; *Educational Improvement; *Educational Planning; Elementary Secondary Education; Improvement Programs; Program Implementation; Rural Education; *Rural Schools*

- Kember, D., & Mezger, R. (1990). The instructional designer as a staff developer: A course team approach consistent with a Concerns-Based Adoption Model. *Distance Education*, 11(1), 50-70. (EJ 415 316)

  *Adoption (Ideas); Change Strategies; Contingency Management; Cooperative Planning; *Distance Education; *Instructional Design; Literature Reviews; Models; *Staff Development; Teamwork*

- Mitchell, S. (1988). *Applications of the Concerns-Based Adoption*

Model in program evaluation. Paper presented at the annual meeting of the American Education Research Association, New Orleans, LA. (ED 301 940)

*Adoption (Ideas); Change Strategies; *Educational Assessment; *Educational Diagnosis; Elementary Secondary Education; Evaluation Methods; *Formative Evaluation; Information Utilization; Inservice Teacher Education; *Program Evaluation; Program Implementation*

• Sevilla, J., & Marsh, D. (1992). *Inquiry-oriented science programs: New perspectives on the implementation process.* Paper presented at the annual meeting of the American Educational Research Association, San Francisco, CA. (ED 381 371)

*Elementary Education; Elementary School Teachers; *Inquiry; Longitudinal Studies; *Program Implementation; Science Curriculum; Science Education; *Science Programs*

• Shotsberger, P., & Crawford, A. (1996). *An analysis of the validity and reliability of the Concerns Based Adoption Model for teacher concerns in education reform.* Paper presented at the annual meeting of the American Educational Research Association, New York, NY. (ED 400 278)

*Algebra; *Educational Change; *Reliability; School Restructuring; Secondary Education; *Secondary School Teachers; *Teacher Attitudes; *Validity*

• van den Berg, R. (1993). The Concerns-Based Adoption Model in the Netherlands, Flanders and the United Kingdom: State of the art and perspective. *Studies in Educational Evaluation, 19*(1), 51-63. (EJ 461 978)

*Child Development; *Educational Change; Educational Innovation; Educational Research; Foreign Countries; *Measures (Individuals); Models; *Organizational Change; *Technical Assistance; Test Construction; Theories; *Validity*

- Wesley, M., & Franks, M. (1996). *Advanced adoption of computer technology in the classroom and teachers' participation in voluntary innovation adoption activities.* Paper presented at the annual meeting of the Mid-South Educational Research Association, Tuscaloosa, AL. (ED 402 907)

*Adoption (Ideas); Case Studies; *Computer Assisted Instruction; Computer Attitudes; Computer Literacy; Computer Networks; Educational Technology; Elementary Education; Magnet Schools; Microcomputers; *Multimedia Instruction; Multimedia Materials; Questionnaires; Teacher Attitudes; Teacher Collaboration; Teacher Response; *Teaching Methods; Technological Advancement*

The Resistance to Change

 chapter 8

Change, by definition, disturbs the status quo. This simple statement has profound implications for the change agent: even those who approve of an innovation are likely to find some aspect of their cultural or social identity challenged, and some professional or psychological comfort zone intruded upon. Rogers makes this point by beginning his book, *Diffusion of Innovations*, with a quote by Machiavelli: "Whenever his enemies have the ability to attack the innovator they do so with the passion of partisans, while the others defend him sluggishly, so that the innovator and his party alike are vulnerable" (Rogers, 1995, p. 1).

This resistance can be especially frustrating when it does not come from the innovation's intended adopters, or even from inside what the change agent understood to be the client system. Opponents of change can sometimes be highly adept at mobilizing support from groups outside the community who wouldn't normally be seen as stakeholders in a local effort. These factors make it crucial for the change agent to understand the causes of resistance.

Despite the negative connotations associated with resistance, a careful examination of its causes can be a powerful tool for the change facilitator. While most studies of resistance focus on techniques for overcoming it, a few, like Field's (1988) handbook on curriculum change, also note that resistance is sometimes an indicator that the *change effort* is off course (Part D, p. 1). This point is often overlooked due to the pro-innovation bias of much diffusion research noted by Rogers (1995, pp. 100-113). Even when its proponents conclude that their reforms are on target, "[Resistance] forces advocates to rethink, reformulate, and restate why they put so much faith in the program under attack." (Mitchell, 1995, p. 1). In short, it constitutes a valuable form of feedback that helps change agents know how they are doing, and how well the intended users see the innovation as fitting their needs (Corbett, Firestone, & Rossman, 1987).

Zaltman and Duncan's *Strategies for Planned Change*

What Rogers is to innovation attributes promoting adoption, Zaltman and Duncan are to attributes and conditions hindering it. Their 1977 classic book, *Strategies for Planned Change*, includes an entire chapter on *resistance factors*. They identify eighteen such factors, comprising four major categories of barriers focused on increasingly smaller social units: *cultural, social, organizational,* and *psychological* (p. 61). Some factors describe clashes between innovation characteristics and these categories, while others concern incompatibilities between environmental conditions and the categories. An opposite relationship to one of Rogers' or Ely's factors is often clear: "Incompatibility of a cultural trait with change," a cultural barrier, obviously decreases Rogers' "compatibility." "Technological barriers for resistance," an organizational barrier, implies an absence of Ely's requirement that "knowledge and skills exist."

In other cases, such as "group insight" or "rejection of outsiders," there is little obvious relationship, however. There also may be no clear parallel with the process issues highlighted by Havelock or the more "internal" or "subjective" concerns noted by Hall. This is why resistance is presented as the "interference" component of the change communication model in Figure 2. It can operate independently from the skills of the sender (change agent), the attributes of the message (innovation), the effectiveness of the medium (change process), or even the readiness of the environment and the receptiveness of the receiver (intended adopter) to disrupt or even block communication of the innovation.

Zaltman and Duncan open their discussion with an overview of resistance that alludes to its value as feedback for the change agent, as mentioned in this chapter's introduction. Relating their resistance chapter to the rest of their book, the authors make an observation that applies equally to the other chapters of my book as well. While resistance may also emerge from other sources, "violation [of] or insensitivity to" principles associated with other components of the change communication model "is a potential source of resistance *caused by the change agent.*" (Zaltman & Duncan, 1977, p. 62, emphasis added). Needless to say, implementing change is difficult enough for reasons outside the change agent's direct control. We can scarcely afford to make it more so by failing to attend to signals that our actions may not be having the desired effect. Resistance is one of those signals; the effective change agent must be able to interpret its causes and adjust the implementation strategy accordingly.

The first major category of resistance that the authors discuss is the cultural barrier to change. These obstacles are rooted in the traditions and values of the client system. Broadly speaking, these barriers are the other side of Rogers' compatibility attribute, discussed in Chapter 3. Zaltman and Duncan identify four examples of cultural barriers: *values and beliefs*; *cultural ethnocentrism*; *saving face*; and *incompatibility of a cultural trait with change* (1977, pp. 68-72).

Values and beliefs are often religious, but may also include secular issues, such as work ethic, competitiveness, or fatalism (Zaltman & Duncan, 1977, pp. 68-69). For example, such resistance would be in American public schools if a values education program, based heavily on a particular religious morality, were introduced. In higher education, an example would be an accountability proposal involving the abolishment of tenure. The change agent detecting such resistance would be able to consider "repositioning" the innovation in a way that would appear less threatening to cultural norms. For example, the values education program could espouse principles common to most major religions and use secular language emphasizing their contribution to a safe, productive society. The accountability proposal might reduce resistance while achieving the same ends by retaining tenure at a "livable" base salary, then providing bonuses for excellence in teaching certified by a "master teacher" program.

Cultural ethnocentrism can operate in either of two directions. The change agent who believes his own culture to be superior to that of the client system will project this belief, consciously or unconsciously, which will frequently provoke resistance from the client. Alternatively, some clients will approach an innovation from the perspective that their culture is superior, and will project that nothing from the change agent's world could be of use (Zaltman & Duncan, 1977, p. 69). This barrier has obvious implications for international change efforts, and perhaps less obvious lessons for change agents operating across regional (e.g., northern vs. southern United States) or urban/rural boundaries. However, these barriers can also be observed in the same physical community, such as in an industrial client resisting an "ivory tower" academic innovation, or a university faculty resisting a pragmatic adaptation to theory suggested by a practitioner. Since much of this resistance is caused by a perception that the innovation and its advocates are "alien," one strategy for responding to (or averting) this type of resistance is the involvement of client system personnel throughout the change process, as suggested by Havelock and Zlotolow in the previous chapter. More will also be said on this matter in Chapter 9, which explores systemic change.

Saving face is a form of culture-based resistance that reminds us, in Rogers' terms, that relative advantage may be perceived in different terms by members of different systems. Zaltman and Duncan note that innovations are often perceived as carrying an implicit assumption that the tool or practice they replace is inferior. In fact, change agents frequently reinforce this perception by stressing the negative consequences that the individual can avoid by adopting (Zaltman & Duncan, 1977, p. 70). In this fashion, current practices are stigmatized as "wrong" or "bad," and adoption becomes seen as an admission of this. Even those who desire the benefits of adoption may refuse to adopt for this reason. Saving face may also express itself in an even more incongruous manner: the intended adopter may freely admit to the change agent that he would like to adopt, yet refuse to do so because the innovation's benefits may remove a face-saving excuse for some other circumstance (p. 71). For example, a technology-savvy teacher who might want to learn more about instructional technology may resist attending courses in this subject because her lack of formal training lets her avoid "technology coordinator" duties that would take her out of the classroom. Saving face, as a cultural barrier, carries two main lessons for the change agent. The first is to highlight the "enhanced" benefits of adoption and thereby avoiding overemphasis on direct comparison between the innovation and current practice that attaches a negative stigma to past behavior. The second is to take the time to identify the root causes of resistance, because they may reveal misunderstandings of the client value system embedded in the implementation plan.

The authors cite their final cultural barrier, incompatibility of a cultural trait with change, as one of the most common causes of resistance (Zaltman & Duncan, 1977, p. 72). An example of such a barrier operating in an education setting would be encountering resistance to diffusion of the 12-month school calendar. The nine-month calendar characteristic of American schools carries numerous direct and indirect obstacles to such a proposal, even if the intended adopters acknowledge the general merit of the innovation. Likewise, certain innovations aimed at correcting educational inequity are largely hamstrung by the traditional, property-tax-based funding system for American public schools. Changing the cultural trait is outside the power of virtually any change agent. In cases like this, the incompatibility is often with the fundamental purpose of the innovation, rendering significant adaptation impractical. If such an innovation must be implemented in spite of these adverse conditions, the change agent will need to make judicious use of incentives to make adoption worthwhile, or devise strategies for circumventing the incompatible trait. Taking year-round schooling as an example, a strategy using incentives could involve substantial bonuses for teachers and administrators who agree to work in the summer. A strategy circumventing the incompatible trait might involve giving those employees three months off during another portion of the school year. In cases like this, various strategies might even be combined.

Zaltman and Duncan consider social barriers to change next. These obstacles represent characteristics of how individual intended adopters react as members of a social system (as opposed to cultural barriers, which focus on characteristics of the social system itself). The authors identify five examples of such barriers: *group solidarity; rejection of outsiders; conformity to norms; conflict;* and *group introspection* (Zaltman & Duncan, 1977, pp. 72-75).

In its most obvious form, group solidarity arises as an obstacle to change when adopting an innovation would result in hardship for other members of the same group, or members of a group important to the intended adopter (Zaltman & Duncan, 1977, pp. 72-73). For example, out of concern for the impact on her faculty, the chair of an instructional technology department might resist implementing a curriculum-infused approach to teaching use of emerging technologies to pre-service teachers. However, group solidarity may also reflect interdependence between components of a larger system (p. 72). One example of this sort of barrier in operation is resistance from schools asked to abandon traditional letter grades for alternative forms of assessment. Innovative grading practices may be rejected because of concern for their impact on admission to higher levels of education, where letter grades are perceived as expected. Probably the most important countermeasure the change agent can take to reduce this sort of barrier is to identify all affected groups and provide targeted support addressing the needs of those groups. In the first example, perhaps team teaching could be introduced as a co-innovation to ensure that instructional technology faculty receive credit for maintaining their teaching load as the location of that teaching moves into methods courses. In the second example, the schools receiving forms of assessment other than letter grades may be surveyed to identify their admissions needs, and the alternative assessment framework may be adapted to provide the necessary information.

Rejection of outsiders is a barrier related to cultural ethnocentrism, discussed in the previous section. However, rather than representing a belief that the client system's culture as a whole is generically superior, rejection of outsiders is often expressed as a belief that no one outside the client system could understand it well enough to produce an innovation of value to it. Obviously, the change agent may reduce this barrier by actively involving client system personnel throughout the change process (as discussed for cultural ethnocentrism). The authors also suggest that rejection of outsiders may sometimes be diffused by focusing on dissemination of an innovation that creates the conditions for successful implementation of the desired change (Zaltman & Duncan, 1977, p. 73). For example, a principal interested in implementing a constructivist pedagogy in his school might focus on providing opportunities for graduate professional study: learning the history and rationale underlying various instructional methods is likely to result in greater openness to innovative educational theories like constructivism.

Social systems are, by one definition, collections of individuals who accept a common set of rules or norms in exchange for the benefits of membership. Thus, conformity to norms can be a powerful barrier to changes encouraging or requiring behavior outside their bounds (Zaltman & Duncan, 1977, p. 74). Similar in some respects to the effects of contrary cultural values and beliefs, or to incompatible cultural traits (both discussed in the preceding section), conformity to norms may exert an even stronger influence on the adoption decision, as the reference group is smaller. The rules may also be more explicitly codified, with specific penalties assigned to nonconformance. For example, implementation of cross-disciplinary collaboration may suffer in colleges where discipline-based programs are seen as competing for a fixed pool of resources. System norms reward those who help their own discipline "get ahead." Zaltman and Duncan observe that, "the critical question for a change agent to ask is, 'Why do people participate in this norm?' Knowing the answer to this question may enable a change agent to modify his change to meet the need satisfied by the norm" (p. 74). In our collaboration example, this might involve allocating resources based, in part, on the extent and effectiveness of the desired behavior. Another strategy might emphasize the ability of collaboration to yield synergies that effectively expand the pool of available resources, enabling each academic discipline to receive more.

Conflict within a social system can also be an important barrier to change. Effective change involves the coordinated movement of a "critical mass" of system components in a unified direction representing adoption, as we shall see in detail in the next chapter. Thus a system divided by conflict that is pulling factions in different directions is an unlikely candidate for meaningful change. In such a situation, the authors observe, an innovation supported by any one faction is likely to cause suspicion, if not outright rejection, of it among all the others (Zaltman & Duncan, 1977, p. 74). For example, in some settings, if the teachers' union backs a change, the district administrators will almost reflexively oppose it (and vice versa). Even change agents who possess the formal authority to order change may find themselves obstructed by conflict, should they fail to attend to its root causes. The head of a corporate human resource development unit, who attempts to change her operation using a human performance improvement model, may be stymied if this change is perceived as devaluating training rather than as augmenting training with other strategies. The change agent is generally advised to strike a neutral or moderate stance between factions by involving representatives of all influential groups throughout the change process. (If their being involved in decisions would immobilize the change team, due to the conflict among them, these representatives may serve as advisors or liaisons rather than members who participate fully.) This will, at a minimum, ensure that all concerns are aired and may even enhance support by promoting a sense of ownership within the factions.

The final type of social barrier, group insight, might be better understood as group *introspection* or "self-awareness." Zaltman and Duncan (citing Lippitt, Watson, & Westley, 1958, p. 181) describe this source of resistance as "the members' imperfect awareness of their own interpersonal processes and their lack of a frame of reference in which to judge their performances and their possibilities for improvement" (1997, p. 75). This type of barrier can be summed up with the metaphor of not being able to "see the forest for the trees." Such resistance occurs when members of the client system, caught up in the "insider perspective," subconsciously provide rationalizations for why change cannot or should not occur. For example, the teachers and administrators at a particular school may resist a creative thinking and problem-solving curriculum, even though they agree "in theory" that these skills are valuable. Subconsciously, the decision to resist may be based on a long-ago judgment that there was a strong relationship between the adequacy of the curriculum and scores on a particular standardized test. Within the system, no one is even consciously aware anymore that this assumption is being made. This highlights the importance of having both "insiders" and "outsiders" on the change team: to balance the fresh perspective necessary to detect (and question) such assumptions with the "inside information" (and respect of other insiders) necessary to defeat cultural ethnocentrism or rejection of outsiders.

The next major category of resistance introduced is the organizational barriers to change. These types of resistance arise when characteristics of the client system itself (as opposed to the characteristics of the broader social system or of individual adopters as members of that system) conflict with the demands of change. The authors cite five examples of this type of barrier: (1) *threat to power and influence,* (2) *organizational structure,* (3) *behavior of top-level administrators,* (4) *climate for change in the organization,* and (5) *technological barriers for resistance* (Zaltman & Duncan, 1977, pp. 75-81).

Threat to power and influence may be one of the most important barriers to understand. Real change isn't as simple as introducing a new tool or method. If some parts of the organization are to use the change–or use it more visibly–while others are not, this creates a new "difference" between them. It may affect the way they interact with each other, or even with others outside the organization. Such disturbances to the traditional power dynamics of the organization add to the discomfort of the change, and may create the impression of "winners" and "losers" resulting from implementation. The authors cite a decision making innovation that allowed for more input from teachers. Principals strongly resisted at first, feeling that allowing teachers such input reduced their authority to manage their schools (Zaltman & Duncan, 1977, p. 76). Perhaps one of the most effective strategies for minimizing such resistance is to align those in key positions in implementation with those in key positions of influence or respect in the current system. This may involve providing them with information or training (in a form convenient for them) that allows them to start out as sources of information or advice for the groups over which they have traditionally exercised influence.

Sometimes the organizational structure itself is a source of resistance. An innovation may require extensive communication–or even collaboration–between subunits or individuals who previously operated independently. Block scheduling, for example, presents several challenges for a school organized into traditional departments. Modern organizations also tend to seek economies of scale through specialization of labor (Zaltman & Duncan, 1977, p. 77). If adopting the innovation requires redefinition of these roles, employees who have become adept at one set of processes may be reluctant to accept a role in new ones with which they are unfamiliar. Consider the transition from a training department to a performance improvement organization: experts at designing training interventions may balk when asked to consider changes in equipment, procedures, or compensation, for example, as part of a solution package to improve workforce performance. The best approach for the change agent under these circumstances depends on the nature of the change. If the innovation is a minor tool to help the organization be more efficient at what it already does well, the change agent should try to adapt the innovation or its marketing to the existing organizational structure (see Chapter 3). If, however, the innovation represents a fundamental change with far-reaching implications throughout the organization, the change agent should consider reengineering the organizational structure as part of a coordinated innovation package to better align the entire client system with the needs of its environment (see Chapter 9).

Another source of organizational resistance, which is often overlooked, is the behavior of top-level administrators. Summed up in its positive aspect, this is called "leadership by example." Zaltman and Duncan explain the resistance issue as "Why should I really go through the effort of trying to change my behavior if the people at the top don't change theirs" (1977, p. 78). If district administrators direct sweeping changes in classroom technology or methods–yet fail to change their budget practices to provide the necessary equipment or inservice training–teachers may interpret this as tacit permission to ignore the change. When the importance of this is recognized, the solution is fairly straightforward: the change agent must emphasize the importance of policies and actions (including funding) that send an unequivocal and consistent message of support in initial discussions with the client system leadership. If those in authority are unwilling, or unable, to do so, the change agent has little reason to trust their commitment to the implementation's success.

Another important, potential source of resistance is the overall climate for change in the organization. Zaltman and Duncan emphasize three dimensions of the climate for change: need for change, openness to change, and potential for change. Need for change refers to the extent to which organization members perceive that change is necessary. Openness to change describes the extent to which these individuals see their organization as willing to consider change. Finally, potential for change expresses the perceived ability of the organization to successfully cope with change (Zaltman & Duncan, 1977, pp. 78-79). An important irony for the change agent to understand regarding these dimensions is that there is some evidence that need for change is negatively correlated with the other two dimensions. In other words, the greater the perceived need for change, the less likely are members of the client system to see their organization as open to or capable of effective change (pp. 79-80). The schools in the worst shape (in the eyes of their faculty) are usually those with long histories of poor response by faculty to previous efforts to introduce innovation (including poor support during implementation). The authors observe that in such cases, the change agent must build confidence among members of the client system that they have the necessary competencies for a successful effort, and that with adequate motivation and support their organization is capable of effective, lasting change (p. 80). It is equally important to consider the opposite extreme: in organizations already confident in their openness and ability to change, change agents may need to place extra emphasis on the benefit of continuous improvement, as these clients are less likely to perceive a need for change (p. 79).

Technological barriers to change illustrate the final example of an organizational barrier. Technology, considered broadly here, is the application of science to the solution of problems. These barriers arise when the client system lacks the institutional knowledge to understand, accept, or apply the innovation (Zaltman & Duncan, 1977, p. 80). As already noted, this corresponds roughly to the absence of Ely's condition requiring that "the people who will ultimately implement any innovation must possess sufficient knowledge and skills to do the job," discussed in Chapter 4. This may be one of the most difficult barriers to overcome, as possession of these competencies may be unrelated–or even inversely related–to content expertise. Those who have the greatest content expertise may be the least likely to seek help with the technology, finding resistance an easier course. For example, the most experienced faculty, and one would hope the most accomplished, are usually the oldest. Not only may they be less familiar with emerging technologies, but they may have built long and successful careers without them. The challenge for the change agent is thus to target specific interventions that provide at least a baseline of technological expertise in a way that does not threaten or diminish the professional standing of the individual. One way of doing this is to thoroughly research each individual's professional interests, and design "participatory demonstrations" focusing on use of the innovation to support those activities.

The final major category of resistance that Zaltman and Duncan discuss is the psychological barriers to change. This category exists solely within the individual, and therefore may be the most difficult to detect in operation. The authors identify four such barriers: *perception; homeostasis; conformity and commitment;* and *personality factors* (pp. 81-88).

Perception has several variants. Selective perception causes individuals to note or retain only certain facts about the innovation, usually supporting a view they already hold (Zaltman & Duncan, 1977, p. 81). For example, those opposing Internet access in schools because of the inappropriate content available may discount (or be unaware of) even the most successful positive applications (and vice versa). Perception may also be a barrier when the change agent and client disagree on which problems are most important, and therefore cannot agree on the best solutions (p. 82). For example, both advocates and opponents of bilingual education agree that Limited English Proficient (LEP) students are at risk in American schools, but they are diametrically opposed in their plans for reducing that risk. Perception of the meaning of the innovation and its use is another form of this obstacle highlighted in the previous chapter's discussion of the IC Component Checklist. Block scheduling is an example of an innovation that is understood in widely differing ways in different school systems. Perception may also provoke resistance when change agents act in ways the client sees as inappropriate (p. 82). For example, a college may resist if a consultant, hired to research a problem independently, starts implementing a particular solution. In each of these circumstances, the key to the change agent's success is delivery of a clear, understandable message that markets the innovation in terms that are relevant to the adopter. Ironically, a final variant of this barrier can arise when help is offered too freely. The common association of price with quality may cause donated resources to be devalued (p. 83). In these cases, change agents may wish to specify a market value "cost" which will be offset by a corresponding "grant" from the supplier.

Homeostasis is quite simply the natural desire to maintain a comfortable level of stability. Living systems do adapt in order to survive and flourish; however many innovations force the systems in which they are introduced to adapt in ways that are far from comfortable (Zaltman & Duncan, 1977, p. 83). Today's teachers generally accept inservice training and other continuing education as requirements of a dynamic profession, yet the seemingly endless procession of "panacea du jour" fads may numb them to being open to any sort of change. Overcoming this resistance is much more complex than this simple explanation might suggest. Perhaps the best recommendation is to review CBAM's Stages of Concern in the preceding chapter. Understanding the issues that the intended adopter is facing at each stage of implementation, and targeting the right concerns at the right time, will go a long way toward containing the discomfort that can lead to homeostatic resistance.

Conformity and commitment are overlapping, but distinct, issues. Conformity drives the cultural and social resistance forms involving values and beliefs or their expression in behavioral norms. Commitment may express itself in relation to an organization or social unit, but is also seen in a client's reluctance to abandon tools or practices in which significant resources have been invested (Zaltman & Duncan, 1977, p. 83). Another form of commitment results from professional education or experience (p. 84). For example, teachers and administrators may support or resist an innovation based on commitment to their concept of their professional role, and these reactions may well not be in concert. In the former case, the authors recommend incentives as a means to "create alternative investments in the advocated change" (p. 83). In the latter, communication and collaborative problem solving may help dissenting stakeholder groups arrive at common ground.

The final example of psychological barriers to resistance is personality factors. This broad category represents those specific personality charac-teristics–possessed by some individuals but not by others–which have been shown to promote resistance to change. (This distinguishes these factors from the other psychological barriers discussed above.) Examples include low empathetic ability or high dogmatism; inability to deal with abstractions; fatalism; low achievement motivation; lack of conceptual or inquiring skills; lack of creativity; and inability to tolerate ambiguity. Risk tolerance is also specifically cited as important (Zaltman & Duncan, 1977, p. 86).

Interested readers are referred to Zaltman and Duncan's eighteen "general principles" with which the authors close their chapter on resistance (1977, pp. 88-89). These principles are offered as their summary of the chapter, and while they do not correspond one-for-one to the eighteen specific barriers discussed above, they do provide a comprehensive set of guidelines for minimizing or addressing these causes of resistance.

Other Studies

Other studies offer additional support for considering the dissemination problem from the perspective of resistance to change. A particularly interesting treatment reinforcing the concept of resistance as constructive feedback is Johnson's (1969) paper arguing that resistance is actually necessary for change to occur. Her argument resembles that of Hall and associates' in discussing Stages of Concern: resistance is an indicator that the adopter population has become aware of the innovation and learned enough about it to experience personal concerns (which are an inevitable part of implementation). Another study drawing an even more explicit parallel to Stages of Concern was reported by Gjerde (1983), who developed an interactional resistance model suggesting relationships between stage of implementation and the sources and manifestations of resistance. A more recent study emphasizing the feedback aspects of resistance is found in Theron and van der Westhuizen's paper, "The Management of Resistance to Change and Polarity in Educational Organisations" (1996). This paper may be especially useful to those seeking specific strategies for dealing effectively with resistance during implementation.

Many investigations of resistance to change have examined the recent influx of emerging technologies into educational settings. In discussing the limited extent to which computer technology in higher education has lived up to the grandiose predictions of the early '80s, Waldrop and Adams (1988) point to unexpected resistance (and ineffective strategies for dealing with it) as a major cause (pp. 4-6). They cite several examples of technological innovations that failed in order to derive four primary reasons people resist change: the perception that the innovation threatens their self-interest; a misunderstanding of the innovation and its implications; a belief that the innovation doesn't make sense for the organization; and an individual's low tolerance for change. In another study of educational technologies, Rose (1982) reached similar conclusions, noting that innovations are sometimes perceived as a direct threat, viewed as requiring more effort than they are worth, or are not understood by their intended users. Furthermore, Rose notes that effective innovation use by some may result in loss of influence by others, that change agents may alienate clients with pressure tactics, and even that early adopters may become discouraged if they see the rest of the organization as not contributing to implementation (pp. 12-15).

Schieman and Fiordo (1990), in a study of this same issue, are even more focused. Higher education, they suggest, has resisted instructional technology because it poses a direct threat to institutionalized power (p. 4). Much lies behind this simple statement, however. What these authors are in fact noting is that these technologies–or more accurately, common perceptions of them among faculty–challenge a number of fundamental assumptions about the nature of teaching and learning, and the respective parts played by faculty and students in this process (p. 4). In effect, they are suggesting that resistance has resulted from the turmoil into which instructional technology has thrown faculty notions of self and role.

Change agents working in physically or philosophically isolated communities may wish to consult Hillery's (1972) examination of the causes of resistance in Navajo native American communities and in Trappist Roman Catholic Monasteries. While most properly in the rural sociology tradition of change research, this paper offers an insightful look at the cultural and social barriers Zaltman and Duncan discuss, which may inform educational change efforts in these contexts as well.

A final study focusing on resistance that is worthy of mention is Poole's (1991) review of the resistance literature. This meta-study represents one of the few recent attempts to integrate the findings of diverse inquiries in this area. From a sample of 32 studies, Poole identifies seven major categories of resistance factors: (1) *personality and psychological factors*, (2) *innovation attributes*, (3) *the type of innovation decision*, (4) *problems during the implementation phase*, (5) *schools as organizational or social systems*, (6) *communications networks*, and (7) *the faculty culture*.

The "personality and psychological factors" category examines the characteristics of the user who is expected to adopt the change (p. 2). The "innovation attributes" category looks at the nature of the change itself (pp. 2-3). The "type of innovation decision" category considers the source of the change, as well as whether the decision to adopt is made individually, collectively by consensus, or collectively by authority (pp. 3-4). The "problems during the implementation phase" category describes the marketing of or support for the change (pp. 4-5). The "schools as organizational or social systems" category concerns the social structure or hierarchy into which the change is being introduced (pp. 5-6). The "communications networks" category involves the interpersonal connections via which information and perceptions of the change diffuse (pp. 6-8). The "faculty culture" category considers the beliefs, values, and norms that interact with the change (pp. 8-10). It is safe to assume that culture is an important category in non-school settings as well (p. 9).

Finally, Poole notes that systemic influences outside the unit of analysis can also impact resistance (p. 10). She also offers support for my book's integrative approach in noting that "It is no longer acceptable to blame resistance on any one of the forces that influence the innovation process...several, or even all of these factors may play a part..." (pp. 10-11).

While most of these subsequent studies do not identify resistance factors with the specificity of Zaltman and Duncan, they do offer support for this approach, as well as additional insights that would not be available from the other perspectives alone. Their findings serve to validate the notion that the perceived reasons to reject an innovation is often more important to potential adopters than the reasons to accept it. It is also worth noting that the categories identified in these studies, like those of Zaltman and Duncan, include some which have no clear counterpart in the "pro-change" frameworks of Rogers and Ely. Likewise these categories show an approach to the issue from a perspective distinct from that of Hall, or of Havelock and Zlotolow.

Summary

Resistance to change is a topic many change agents would like to ignore. Most others might prefer to deal with the adoption what facilitating practices covered in the preceding chapters, and trust this to avoid resistance. These approaches overlook two important facts. First, while resistance can be provoked when the change agent fails to take such positive actions, this is not its only cause. Resistance operates as the "interference" component in the change communication model presented in Figure 2, and may result from cultural traits and values, social norms, organizational characteristics, or individual psychological factors. It may come from sources inside or outside the change agent sees as the client system. Whatever its origins, it can prevent or inhibit implementation just as surely as a poorly designed innovation, an unprepared environment, an ineffective change agent, or a bad change strategy. Second, although resistance may oppose the initial change strategy, it can be an important source of constructive feedback as well, alerting the change team to issues that must be addressed or modifications to the innovation that should be made if lasting, meaningful change is to occur. The resistance framework that Zaltman and Duncan present offers the change agent a diagnostic tool for identifying resistance's root causes and designing interventions–or adapting the innovation itself–to address the issues at its core. The authors identify 18 issues in four major categories of barriers to change:

Cultural barriers to change (traditions and values conflicting with the innovation)
1. Cultural values and beliefs ("The innovation is wrong.")
2. Cultural ethnocentrism ("My culture is superior–or the change agent thinks his is.")
3. Saving face ("I can't do that; I'd never live it down.")
4. Incompatibility of a cultural trait with change ("It just won't work here because…")

Social barriers to change (group psychology factors inhibiting implementation)
5. Group solidarity ("I can't do this because it would be a hardship for my coworkers.")
6. Rejection of outsiders ("Nobody who isn't 'one of us' could create something of value.")
7. Conformity to norms (If I participated in this, I would be ostracized.")
8. Conflict ("There are too many factions here pulling in different directions.")
9. Group introspection ("I'm too much a part of this group to see its problems objectively.")

Organizational barriers to change (client system characteristics opposing change)
10. Threat to power and influence ("If we do this, I won't be as important anymore.")
11. Organizational structure ("This cuts across department lines and intrudes on their turf.")
12. Behavior of top-level administrators ("The boss isn't doing it; why should I?")

13. Climate for change in organization ("We don't need to change, or couldn't if we tried.")

14. Technological barriers for resistance ("I can't understand this or apply it to my work.")

Psychological barriers to change (individual traits and reactions discouraging adoption)

15. Perception ("My mind is made up: I just don't see it the way you do.")

16. Homeostasis ("All this change is just too uncomfortable.")

17. Conformity and commitment ("This just isn't the way people in my profession do things.")

18. Personality factors ("I can't do this; it just isn't right for who I am.")

Other researchers in a variety of settings have reached similar conclusions about resistance, often independently of Zaltman and Duncan's original framework. Some of their studies have focused on particular types of resistance, while others have comprehensively examined the resistance literature. Practitioners engaged in change efforts in these contexts are encouraged to explore these and related studies in greater detail. (Terms in italics are ERIC descriptors, with * indicating major descriptors–the primary subjects of the document or article.)

- Gjerde, P. (1983). *An interactional model for resistance to change in educational institutions.* Paper presented at the annual meeting of the American Psychological Association, Anaheim, CA. (ED 234 917)

  *Educational Change; Educational Innovation; Elementary Secondary Education; Institutional Characteristics; *Institutional Environment; *Models; *Organizational Change; Personnel; Problems; Program Implementation*

• Hillery, G. (1972). *Social structure and resistance to change.* Paper presented at the Third World Congress for Rural Sociology, Baton Rouge, LA. (ED 068 245)

   *American Indian Culture; *Attitude Change; Catholics; Community Study; *Comparative Analysis; Cross Cultural Studies; *Religious Cultural Groups; Rural Population; Social Structure*

• Johnson, R. (1969). *Resistance: A precondition for change.* (ED 027 898)

   *Educational Psychology; *Learning Processes; *Rejection (Psychology); *Teaching Methods; *Two Year Colleges*

• Poole, W. (1991). *Resistance to change in education: Themes in the literature.* Unpublished manuscript, Syracuse University. (ED 330 307)

   *Adoption (Ideas); Communication (Thought Transfer); Decision Making; *Educational Change; Educational Innovation; Elementary Secondary Education; Literature Reviews; Program Implementation; *Psychological Studies; *Resistance to Change; Teacher Administrator Relationship*

• Schieman, E., & Fiordo, R. (1990). *Barriers to adoption of instructional communications technology in higher education.* Paper presented at the Australian Communications Conference, Melbourne, Australia. (ED 329 244)

   *Adoption (Ideas); Bureaucracy; Compliance (Psychology); Educational Change; Educational Technology; Foreign Countries; Higher Education; *Instructional Innovation; *Resistance to Change*

• Theron, A., & van der Westhuizen, P. (1996). *The management of resistance to change and polarity in educational organizations.* Paper presented at the annual meeting of the American Educational Research Association, New York, NY. (ED 396 394)

*Change Strategies; Conflict Resolution; Educational Change; Elementary Secondary Education; *Organizational Change; Organizational Communication; *Principals; *Resistance to Change; School Administration; Teacher Administrator Relationship*

• Waldrop, P., & Adams, T. (1988). *Overcoming resistance to the use of instructional computing in higher education.* (ED 296 656)

*Attitude Change; *College Instruction; Computer Literacy; *Computer Uses in Education; *Educational Change; Educational Innovation; Faculty Development; Higher Education; Improvement*

The System

It was noted in Chapter 1 that the change communication model is a representation of a system, which was defined as "a set or arrangement of things so related or connected as to form a unity or organic whole" (Webster's, 1979, p. 1853). Likewise, the point has been made repeatedly that understanding change as a system, as well as understanding the operation of the model's individual components, is essential to a complete understanding of how change works. Thus it is appropriate, having explored each part of the change communication model, to conclude its coverage with a discussion of the research tradition that considers it as an "organic whole."

While our examination of the model's individual components in the preceding chapters has occasionally reminded us of change's systemic nature, this chapter is not going to be a mere redrawing of those connections. Nor is it a summary of what has already been stated. The cliché about the whole being greater than the sum of its parts is one of the defining characteristics of a system, and the emphasis here will be on exposing those parts of change that have not been revealed in the classical models to greater scrutiny.

In the first chapter of *Systems Design of Education*, the book that thrust systemic change into the limelight of education, Banathy (1991) relates how piecemeal efforts or failure to integrate the lessons of the classical models into a blueprint for educational transformation have hobbled our reform efforts (p. 11). He argues that successful educational change must instead consider "the educational problem situation" in light of its integrated, interdependent parts and, based on this, must design a system of integrated, interdependent solutions, i.e., changes (pp. 12-13). Succeeding in this–or, in fact, in creating any lasting change–requires a focus on the system that unites the tactics addressing particular components of the change communication model.

Reigeluth and Garfinkle's *Systemic Change in Education*

While Banathy (1973) introduced educators to the systems thinking paradigm, it was Reigeluth and Garfinkle who gave it the "critical mass" to attain its current prominence more than 20 years later with their edited book, Systemic Change in Education (1994). Significantly, their success can be attributed in part to their treatment of the systemic model as an *innovation* and their application of a systemic strategy to its implementation. For example, because their book is an edited volume, involving 20 other scholars or practitioners who wrote chapters covering a wide variety of cases, it ensures a broad-based initiative. Banathy encapsulated his original work in an early chapter of their volume, providing a link to the movement's theoretical foundation. Perhaps most importantly, Reigeluth concurrently founded a division for systemic change in the Association for Educational Communications and Technology (AECT), a well-known and respected professional association. He also secured a Presidential Session at the annual AECT conference for Banathy to speak on systemic change. Such ties to an established and influential group in the field added to the fledgling movement's credibility by making it less alien to the education community.

Reigeluth and Garfinkle present the *systemic change model* using the metaphor of an architect designing and building a house. Systems design theory is compared to architecture as the essential body of knowledge informing the process. Models articulating this theory provide the equivalent of blueprints. Deconstructing these models in order to analyze key components and their interrelationships is compared to analyzing subsystems such as plumbing and wiring. Finally, examples of practice are presented as analogous to the actual process of building (Reigeluth & Garfinkle, 1994b, p. vi).

In Section One, the editors have assembled perspectives on systems design theory from four noted scholars, including Banathy. This section offers the change agent a quick course in systemic thinking as an essential first step in undertaking change. While each author examines this theory through a different lens, several major commonalities are seen throughout. Probably the most important is that effective change must consider all members and components of the system, their interrelationships, and their relationships to other systems, as well as the relationship of the system as a whole to larger systems of which it is a part or with which it interacts. For example, systemic design of a new school must consider stakeholders (teachers, administrators, parents, students, and school board members), physical plant (buildings, electrical and plumbing systems, computer networks), technology (computers, printers, projection devices, audio/video devices,

SmartBoards™), pedagogy, methods, and legal or regulatory requirements. Staff and faculty development training, sources of funding, support personnel, and other resources are also key issues that must be part of an integrated effort.

When they are part of the same system, each of these issues and components is likely to be related. For example, a "simple" innovation like using the Internet for research may require new equipment, connectivity, support personnel, pedagogy (which may in turn require an inservice program), and an acceptable use policy (which may require school board approval), to name just a few. Such relationships will also extend outside the system: pressure to adopt this innovation may be exerted by employers hiring the school's graduates, by colleges admitting them, through its adoption by competitors, or by a broader society captivated by emerging information technologies. Likewise, stakeholders within the system may be influenced or aided in supporting or resisting the innovation by related groups in other systems.

This widespread and varied stakeholder influence leads in turn to one of the other commonalities in the systemic change literature: stakeholder involvement. A mechanical system may consist of a complex set of interrelated pulleys, gears, and cams: if any one breaks, the entire system will cease to function, or develop significant problems. Likewise, if any stakeholder group in an organizational system resists implementation, the change effort as a whole is likely to fail or be significantly obstructed.

Where each author focuses on either of these dimensions differentiates their major contributions to this section. Two authors, Banathy and Morgan, provide contrasting arguments in the debate over centralized vs. distributed leadership for systemic change. The other two authors, Hutchins and Jenks, explore change itself as a system, examining the interrelationships between its functional or process components.

Banathy (1994) offers the distributed view, based on his earlier writings. In his model, design is a collaborative activity undertaken jointly by stakeholders at all levels (p. 29), to replace the system when its own fundamental design has become the problem (p. 27). Banathy's model is explicitly nonlinear: he doesn't even speak of stages or phases, preferring the term "spaces." Each space overlaps and interacts with those adjacent to it. For example, the second space, Organized Knowledge, is accessed by and informs actions in the first space (Genesis, Exploration, Visioning, and Image Creation), the third space (the Design Solution), and the fourth space (Testing Design Alternatives). Banathy also offers five "organizing perspectives" for systemic change, which do not receive the same emphasis in the other models. The first, the importance of broad stakeholder participation throughout the change process, has already been mentioned. The second is that the change "architect" must be committed to *idealized design*: in order to break free of the creative limitations inherent in the structure of what currently exists, constraints of "practicality" or even "possibility" should come into play only after the best conceivable (ideal) design has been crafted. The third and fourth are interwoven: design is learning, and it never ends. A learning organization is one that continually redesigns itself to adapt to the changing world of which it is a part. Finally, because design takes place within the context of the "suprasystem" of human society, it must be guided by a commitment to improving the human condition (pp. 32-33).

Morgan (1994) presents what Reigeluth describes as "an interesting counterpoint to Banathy's approach" (p. 13). Morgan concedes that all levels of stakeholders must be involved in the process of change (noting that "the authority and responsibility for public education is so diffuse that no one is in control"). Yet he argues that successful systemic change has resulted not from collaborative design but from strong leadership at each level, faithfully implementing solid designs crafted by instructional systems professionals and under the coordination of national or regional leadership (p. 45). In fact, Morgan asserts that effective change must be both systemic and systematic (p. 49). The model of change he describes is essentially the classic Instructional Systems Development (ISD) model (Branson, 1975) used to guide the creation of instructional materials, with the evaluation phase moved up before implementation to a more formative role. This application of a traditional instructional development model to guide the change process is especially significant for two reasons. First, the ability to apply a model generally used to develop relatively small "instructional systems," such as a course or a lesson, to the systematic design of an entire educational system reinforces the concept that certain characteristics are true of systems in general. Second, it provides a solid example of the use of a familiar construct to represent an unfamiliar process in a way that reduces its strangeness or incompatibility. See also the discussion of Harvey and Wehmeyer's (1990) *Checklist for Change* at the end of Chapter 6.

Hutchins' (1994) chapter provides a convenient philosophical transition by approaching the second dimension–the interrelationship between system or process components–from the perspective of the state education system. Hutchins outlines a framework for state-level leadership of systemic change based on the primary functions of this level of stakeholder. The functions discussed include operational policies (such as laws and regulations); financing; school organization (by area and size); management and administration; school approval and accountability; and personnel training and certification (pp. 16-22). This is not, however, a prescriptive model; each part of the chapter discussing these functions is devoted to examples of systemic relationships in action (often action which disrupted the best-laid plans of the change agent). The reader is also cautioned not to try to equate the functions with particular organizations. While one organization may appear to "have the lead" in a given function, interactions among other stakeholders exert considerable influence, and these are often the cause of the disruptions noted in the sections (p. 16).

While Hutchins illustrates the operation of systemic interdependence with dysfunctional examples, it is equally important to note that such relationships can be leveraged to facilitate change as well. This is the perspective adopted by Jenks (1994), who presents a systemic evaluation model structured around the systematic instructional design process. Jenks' chapter is not the last in Reigeluth and Garfinkle's Section One. It is discussed last here because, having considered frameworks emphasizing the breadth and complexity of systemic change in the other three chapters, Jenks allows us to integrate this knowledge under a more comfortably structured set of guidelines. In this framework, the process of change is divided into three broad phases: design, development/implementation, and evaluation. Within design, Jenks lists five subprocesses: identification of core values; establishment of organizational purposes and learner goals; defining the functions supporting those goals and purposes; designing the idealized system; and describing the necessary support system (pp. 37-40). Within each of these subprocesses, and within the development/ implementation and evaluation phases, Jenks provides "evaluation questions." This may be this chapter's most significant contribution: here alone are criteria that can help the change agent assess the health of the change effort that is explicitly systemic. These questions highlight the interdependence of the phases and their relationships to broader societal factors outside the client system. They are intended to help ensure that the stakeholders' ideal vision does not become increasingly distorted with each step toward implementation.

To summarize these four chapters, I would have to say first and foremost, that there are few easy prescriptions here. Rather, there are word pictures illustrating how the development stages or stakeholder groups that we have tried to treat as discrete are, in fact, intricately interwoven. There are contrasting images of leadership for change as general practices or in consideration of each specific situation, which one may choose between or intermingle in some likewise fixed or variable proportion. The astute reader will emerge from Section One with an extended appreciation for why change must be approached systemically, and a notion of how to begin deconstructing a client system to understand its nature and needs.

In Section Two, the editors bring together four models (and one "metamodel") that "put some structure on the foundations of the theoretical articles presented in Section One" (Reigeluth & Garfinkle, 1994b, p. 51). These "blueprints" offer the change agent examples of how to put what we know about systemic change into practice, while still leaving plenty of room for "alterations" to better fit the client system. The metamodel is the New American Schools Development Corporation (NASDC) grant competition to encourage partnerships of teachers, education scholars, community leaders, and industry executives to redesign K-12 (really *birth*-12) education "from the ground up." Two of the models presented next were designed in response to NASDC's call for proposals, weaving new pedagogy, technology, and other "building blocks" into truly revolutionary concepts of schools as community partnerships. The other two models represent attempts to draw a new paradigm for public schooling from systems that already exist–private schools and corporate training–while still retaining the essential characteristics of a public system. The editors note that these models are not presented as prescriptive, but rather as illustrative of what a "break-the-mold" school design might look like. That is, they are offered to stimulate broader thinking about new designs, not to stake out new boundaries by claiming to be "optimal" (p. 59).

The NASDC design team competition resulted in funding of 11 proposals for new school designs that, while unique on several critical dimensions, shared certain common characteristics. Traditional grade levels were replaced by ability- or achievement-based grouping. Formerly isolated academic disciplines were integrated into a curriculum designed around authentic experiences. Technology was infused throughout all aspects of the curriculum as a tool, rather than as a new discipline, and used to connect students to databases and other resources around the world. Preschool and "school readiness" programs were integrated within the school itself. Alternative assessment strategies, such as portfolios, replaced traditional report cards. Teachers received governance authority (and performance accountability) within their own schools. Finally, health and social services agencies were brought onto school grounds, making schools true centers of human growth and development from birth through 12th grade (Rundell, 1994, p. 57). Still, the truly revolutionary concept uniting all these features is the community-based partnership underlying every NASDC proposal, many of which were implemented even if their design team was not selected for funding (p. 56). This is a defining feature of the systemic change movement: all stakeholder groups are interrelated around the child. Schools are in partnership with parents in raising and educating children. Education scholars at universities train new teachers and administrators, and equip experienced ones with new tools. Businesses hire schools' graduates, and therefore have a stake in their competence.

Bringing each of these stakeholders–and others–together to reinvent education was the underlying objective of NASDC's design team competition, and partnerships from across America responded. Reigeluth and Garfinkle were themselves involved in one such effort; their design, LearningSphere 2000, is the first of two profiled in this section. It is framed around 16 features including the common traits discussed in the preceding paragraph. Central to the LearningSphere 2000 concept is the notion that opening schools to market forces will stimulate quality. The basic unit, rather than being a "school" (too big) or a "classroom" (too small) becomes a "cluster" of four to ten "guides" (teachers) who operate independently to a large extent. Parents request guides for their children on an order-of-preference list; students are assigned to guides using an algorithm maximizing first choices, district-wide. A "consumer aid agency" offers parents information on the performance of each guide in "delivering" the contracted-for learning outcomes for her students. Barring an appeal for a change (from parents, students, or guides), students remain with the selected guide for "an average of four years, building a long-term, caring relationship" (Reigeluth & Garfinkle, 1994a, p. 61). To avoid competition, clusters–not individuals–are rewarded for frequent top choice requests for their guides with a percentage bonus to their base budget, which is determined by how many students they serve. Specialized "learning centers" (likewise budgeted based on how many students they serve) provide instructional support services (pp. 63-64). With market control replacing bureaucratic control, local administration is freed to focus on supporting clusters and learning centers (pp. 68-69).

The second NASDC model discussed is the Cooperative Networked Educational Community of Tomorrow, or CoNECT School. While CoNECT schools share many of the same structural characteristics of LearningSphere 2000, as well as the traits common to all NASDC designs, the focus of this chapter (Collins, Morrison, and Newman, 1994) is on the technology infrastructure supporting this model. The CoNECT infrastructure was designed on the precept that NASDC programs use a project-based curriculum because it is most authentic, and this requires an institutional information systems structure that is equally authentic. In other words, it must be assumed that schools will share the same technology requirements as any other professional workplace. These include: unlimited access to computers for all users, including students: a local network linked to the Internet access to a full suite of software tools and video resources, and local management of technology (p. 75). Perhaps most importantly, reflecting the systemic orientation, the authors emphasize that if this technology infrastructure is to be effective, it must be supported by parallel initiatives shaping all aspects of the school, such as "governance, technology, physical structure, curriculum, assessment, and teaching practice" (p. 81).

Moving into lessons drawn from existing models in other contexts, the next chapter (Williams, 1994) discusses the charter school movement as a model for public education that incorporates some of the strengths of private schools, while retaining the essential characteristics of a public education system (p. 92). Charter schools, Williams states, are based on three "foundational assumptions." First, change is inhibited by the "exclusive franchise" of local school boards to create, and in most cases dissolve, public schools. Second, if these barriers were removed, there are teachers who are willing and prepared to innovate. Finally, the contracted partnership that exists between a charter school and its sponsor will drive new levels of accountability (pp. 86-88). Williams also notes that the charter school concept can be implemented in conjunction with the sort of model promoted by NASDC. For example this can be done by creating partnerships with students, parents, and other stakeholders (p. 90) and by making publicly funded education accountable through marketplace forces (p. 91).

The final model discussed (Bowsher, 1994) is that of business training. Bowsher cites the absence of inflexible and bureaucratic regulation as an important reason why corporate and military trainers are often ahead in systemic change (p. 96). This, coupled with an absolute need to remain competitive, facilitates system-wide reform: they can change (lack of restrictive regulation) and they must change (or be overcome by adversaries). Yet the reason their change efforts are successful, Bowsher argues, is because they have adopted an integrated package of philosophical innovations. First, mastery learning has become the norm. For example, workers train until they get it right; dropouts or failures are unacceptable. Training has been linked to business requirements: it is only funded if it can be shown to benefit organizational objectives. Instructional design and development are recognized as activities requiring skills distinct from one another and distinct from teaching. Emerging technologies have been integrated to provide more training at the worksite, often "just-in-time," in the form of Electronic Performance Support Systems (EPSS). Instructional programs are evaluated on all four Kirkpatrick (1994) levels: learner reaction, competency acquisition, transfer of learning to the job, and impact on business results. A systematic process is governing the translation of business requirements into performance requirements, from that into learning requirements, and from that into training programs. Finally, senior executives, often including a corporate chief training officer, are establishing training as a priority (pp. 96-98). Bowsher asserts that these innovations must also be adopted in our educational settings, and that business itself–not just business practices–should be brought into our schools and colleges as a partner in the educational system (p. 99).

With these chapters, Section Two builds on the theoretical framework presented in the first section by offering examples of systemic change models, both new and adapted from other settings. While each model comes from a complete system, it is often easy to see how their precepts could be combined, perhaps with adaptations, to form an original model best suited to the needs of a given client system. LearningSphere 2000 builds on the common characteristics of the NASDC models with an example of a particular governance structure. The CoNECT School offers a look at how emerging technologies can be harnessed to the service of a "break-the-mold" school. The charter school concept illustrates one way such revolutionary concepts could be implemented, free from the restrictions of regulations instituted to govern the Industrial Age education system. Finally, adopting the market-driven and performance-focused principles of corporate and military training is one way for a newly-competitive education "business" to learn from the experience of those who have trained in a competitive environment for some time. Perhaps a picture of what education could look like–should look like–in your setting is beginning to emerge at this point. What would you add (or subtract, or change) to make it complete?

To help guide your thoughts as you consider this, Section Three examines some key components (subsystems) of any educational structure we might build from the blueprints we have seen and/or constructed. One of the dangers to keep in mind when seeking to adopt the best parts of several systemic models is that what you'll get–similar to the mixed pieces of several puzzles–will not work together as a complete system. By focusing at the subsystem level, this section begins the process of inspecting the components you may have collected to avoid this pitfall. Expressly considered here are the subsystems of finance, local and state governance, and student assessment (p. 101). The finance and local governance chapters take a contrary view, discussing subsystems seen as likely obstacles to systemic change and then presenting possible solutions. The state governance and student assessment chapters propose subsystem-level reforms to align these functions with systemic change. Together, these perspectives illustrate the range of possibilities for ensuring that the blueprints you start to build from will yield a workable structure.

In discussing the finance system, Pipho (1994) observes that state control over education funding, coupled with the proportion of state budgets allocated to education, makes true revolutionary reform of the education finance subsystem very difficult. To overcome this barrier, an incremental approach is proposed, using pilot studies of alternative finance models already enjoying significant constituencies to test and perfect a finance subsystem that supports the other components of systemic reform (p. 108). As a baseline, Pipho suggests a site-based approach to finance, with state moneys being allocated directly to the school. The school then "contracts" with the district office for whatever central services are desired. For the pilot, innovative districts could be encouraged to adopt this model, or the "academic bankruptcy" provisions requiring state takeover of districts that fail to meet standards could couple such a model with other system changes in districts under state "trusteeship" (p. 106). Pipho recommends combining this site-based approach with a voucher system to send each student's "share" of state funding directly to the school educating that student, perhaps piloted to fund supplemental summer instruction to allow the concept to be tested outside the regular school year and budget cycle (pp. 106-107). A final possibility Pipho suggests is reforming existing laws governing categorical monies (e.g., Title I) to allow phase-in of incentives paid to classrooms adopting innovative and effective ways of achieving those programs' goals (pp. 107-108). In essence, they could be phased in to replace the existing system with minimal resistance-provoking disturbance, since such pilot tests demonstrated which forms of alternative finance appeared to best promote desired systemic reforms (p. 108).

Another subsystem already mentioned as a potential obstacle to systemic reform is local governance. Brock (1994) addresses this issue as a complete subsystem, observing that the basic characteristics of the local governance system make it an unlikely leader for cutting-edge education reform (pp. 120-121). Electing the lay public to serve on school boards makes it likely that their awareness of cutting-edge developments will be limited to what is reported in the mass media. Such awareness often reinforces this obstacle, as the mass media's market dynamics reward casting stories in a sensational or controversial light. Coupled with board members' desire be reelected, this often ensures opposition to all but the tamest reforms. Brock maintains that there is an inherent conflict of interest in expecting those who have benefited from the existing system to lead, or even permit, its destruction (p. 122). Even board members, who understand the crisis and support meaningful reform, can fall victim to backlash from the electorate who put them there (p. 123). She sees the charter school concept discussed earlier as essentially the only viable way to construct a self-governing system of education professionals in partnership with the stakeholders they serve (p. 124).

Such a strategy is very much in line with radical reform: discarding the existing system in its entirety and starting over. Still, this approach may promote a needless adversarial relationship as the change effort begins. Smith, O'Day, and Fuhrman (1994) propose an alternative strategy to combine "both top-down and bottom-up reform in a supportive *state* policy structure that would provide direction and a strong infrastructure for sustained *school-level* reform" (p. 110, italics in original). These authors argue that while the state also has a vested interest in the current system, it must respond to concerns about the economy and business productivity (two of the factors driving systemic reform), and is therefore a potential ally for the change agent. They observe that the state's central role in American public education gives it considerable influence, and also that it has a guiding role over state providers of another critical system component: teacher and administrator education and credentialing (p. 110). The authors see three key components to a state-level policy: a unifying vision and goals developed cooperatively with other stakeholders; a clear system offering consistent instructional guidance to districts, schools, and teacher education programs; and a reengineered governance system focused on support to schools and teachers (pp. 111-117). They detail four subcomponents within the instructional guidance system they envision: a state-level core curriculum framework; locally developed or selected curricular materials adapting that framework to community needs; a professional development program empowering teachers to implement those materials; and a performance-based assessment system to provide feedback and accountability (pp. 111-115).

In the final chapter in this section, Mitchell (1994) focuses on this last area–an assessment framework to help drive systemic reform. Presented as a fictional "retrospective," it opens with a story of a student preparing for a graduation exercise that lasts a year and that will certify her as ready for adult citizenship. This exercise has many components. Projects which must display her ability to work with others; her capacity to conduct research; her community service; her participation in the fine arts; her analysis of a major social issue; her autobiography and future goals; and her evaluation of her educational experiences (pp. 127-128). Mitchell goes on to describe the advances in organization design, cognitive psychology, assessment, and the business environment that contributed to the evolution of such a system. While presented as a look backwards from an undefined future point, this description (pp. 129-133) shows how assessment initiatives of the late 1980s and early 90s might converge to drive systemic reform. It is often a compelling picture. However some of its confident predictions have already gone down in flames amidst lawsuits (a powerful statement about systemic interdependencies in itself), rather than laying the hoped-for foundation for future reform. Mitchell concludes with a presentation of the Community of Learners model (pp. 131-133). The central feature of this model is in all stakeholders collaborating to apply resources toward learning in a system where assessment is entirely formative until standards for "completion" are met.

In their final section, Reigeluth and Garfinkle offer examples of successful systemic change. Two of the three chapters in this section are descriptions of actual broad-spectrum reforms that are sometimes even more dramatic than the fictionalized example illustrating the model just discussed. Vaguely reminiscent of Ely's model discussed in earlier in my book, the third chapter extrapolates "conditions for systemic change" from the author's experience with individual successful examples. Alike in their scope, each of these chapters views change from a different angle. One emphasizes the wide range of services and stakeholders that may emerge as part of the Information Age "school" when it is defined systemically. Another focuses on the importance of community involvement and support through all stages of the change process. Yet another offers loose prescriptions for "setting the stage" for systemic reform (p. 137). Together, they represent the culmination of the editors' objective for this final section: to help the reader see what a systemic change effort might look like when all the pieces are pulled together, drawing on the knowledge and imagery presented earlier in the book.

The first concrete example is the Independence (Missouri) School District, as described by Caccamo and Levitt (1994). This district, with a long history of innovative, integrative programs (p. 140), voluntarily embarked on "a philosophical shift to viewing *families*, not just children, as clients" (p. 139, italics in original). This was driven by a realization that readiness for learning has many components, including physical and mental health, stable family life, and even routine nutrition. At the heart of the shift was an organizational attitude: existing funding streams can sometimes be used in innovative ways to more effectively provide the targeted services (p. 140). The resulting system integrates an astounding variety of programs under the umbrella of the "school," including referrals to community services, adult parenting education, literacy education and vocational training, childcare, services for children with special needs, and even health care (pp. 140-144). Illustrating the systemic concepts discussed throughout this book, one of the most dramatic effects of these programs (some of which have been operating together for almost a decade) has been the way that various community members have come together to address the requirements of learning from a holistic perspective. Parents with a greater understanding of growth and development, who associate the school with sources of help, were more likely to be actively involved with their children's education (p. 142). The presence of health care and daycare services on-site often enabled early detection and treatment of physical or mental difficulties that would have interfered with learning had they gone untreated (p. 144). Reading this chapter offers an outstanding look at how synergies between subsystems can be used to the system's advantage–and to the advantage of the children it serves.

While the Independence School District example highlighted integration of services, the next example–Gosport (Indiana) Elementary–emphasizes the stakeholder collaboration that is both necessary and empowering to the change effort. In this chapter, Wiggam (1994) describes the creation of a systemic design by a school that had searched unsuccessfully for an "off-the-shelf" solution that would meet their local needs. One side effect of this search was the staff's discovery that many programs implemented elsewhere had quickly been discontinued, despite obvious potential. A common characteristic in each failed case was lack of community understanding or support (p. 155). To avoid this pitfall, Gosport mobilized participation early, including community representation equal to staff representation beginning at the Design stage (p. 156). While the impact of this policy on community support was likely considerable, public participation at routine meetings dwindled steadily. A survey conducted to identify the cause of this suggested it may have reflected a dissatisfaction with the plan (p. 157). This is worthy of note because resistance can grow just as quickly, and be just as devastating, with ignorance at its root as with an actual disagreement. Stakeholders who are not kept informed are likely to believe the worst. Other lessons mentioned include the importance of taking the time to reach a community consensus on objectives (i.e., analysis) rather than bringing representatives in with goals already defined.

The decline in public participation also suggested that election of delegates, who would participate throughout the process, might facilitate broader input (p. 159).

While Miller's chapter (1994) is in the middle of this section, it is treated last here because of its summary nature. The author has consulted on several successful change efforts similar to the two examples just discussed, and she uses this experience to distill a set of loosely prescriptive "conditions" for systemic change in her chapter. While similar in concept to Ely's Conditions described in Chapter 4, Miller asserts that all must be present together for effective systemic change. Like the design team at Gosport Elementary, she concludes that consensus among stakeholders on a common vision is the essential foundation. Like Ely's requirement for dissatisfaction wit the status quo (see Chapter 4), Miller's conditions call for agreement that the existing system can no longer succeed. This in turn must lead to design of a new system, and then to development of an implementation plan that equips all stakeholders for success in their new roles. Two final conditions are specified, which are probably essential throughout the effort: clear and unequivocal support from all major stakeholders, and pressure to proceed either from these stakeholders or from a "traumatic event" in the system's environment (p. 148). Miller also reinforces the importance of broad, consistent stakeholder involvement to ensure that those who must build and operate the new system "are able to spend more professional energies paving new paths for learning rather than in waging battles for survival" (p. 154).

One could easily come away from the preceding discussion concluding that the systems view is not so much a model of change as a prescription for undertaking specific changes. This would be a mistake. Instead the systemic change literature has typically adopted the phenomenological outlook that the model is best understood through situated examples that illustrate subsystems and their interrelationships, rather than through decontextualized description. The crucial point for the change agent to take away is that all "givens" are subject to inspection and challenge. When integrating and applying the models from the preceding chapters, you may find a simple solution to the client system's troubles in merely questioning a premise of its Industrial Age design, or even in questioning the design itself.

In his introduction to *Systemic Change in Education*, Reigeluth (1994) presents this as a core tenet of the systemic model, noting that "systemic change, often called paradigm shift...entails replacing the whole thing," i.e., creating an entirely new education system to meet the needs of information-based society (p. 3). This conviction was natural, given the impetus for the movement's launch. Where industrial society expected schools to sort children into vast numbers of workers, smaller numbers of managers, and still smaller numbers of thinkers, information-based society demands critical thinking and problem-solving skills of all (p. 7). Systemic change rose on the growing realization that such profoundly different societal needs require a profoundly different educational system to meet them.

Gradually, though, it became clear that a systems view is crucial to the success of any change, not just such radical change. If implementation results in a conflicting "foreign body" (the innovation) within the system, rejection is likely. Above all, the systemic paradigm teaches us that the result of the change agent's efforts must still be a viable system–whether one or 100 percent of it is new–where inter-component relationships and dependencies reinforce rather than constrain one another (Brethower & Dams, 1999; Ellsworth, 1997; Hirumi, 1995).

Other Studies

Following the publication of *Systemic Change in Education*, the volume of research conducted and reported in this area grew dramatically, with one hundred ERIC-indexed studies being published in 1995 alone. The scope and attention associated with research in this area has lead to an incredibly broad knowledge base of use to the practitioner in planning and guiding systemic reform initiatives. Kemp (1996) offers a concise look at why school reform is needed and what it is, aimed at K-12 school personnel. Honig (1994) expands this basic philosophy using lessons learned from the experience of 1980s school reformers to derive four guiding principles for systemic school change. Extending the paradigm outside traditional schools, Slotnik (1993) presents a similar analysis based on his experience with Boston's Community Training and Assistance Center: he emphasizes the need for coordinated top-down and bottom-up initiation and offers three alternative reform strategies.

This "how-to" orientation is also adopted by other authors, and may be of particular use to the practitioner for obvious reasons. Hawley (1997) offers an overview emphasizing the basic phases of a systemic change effort: planning/preparing, building the core team to lead the effort, transforming vision into systems design, making the transition to implementation, evaluation, and closure. Carr (1997a) takes a different view, offering an outstanding orientation to specific methods and techniques helpful in implementing systemic change, such as stakeholder involvement, ethnographic field methods, and a range of design strategies. Finally, the Education Department's Office of Educational Research and Improvement (1994) has published a brochure that offers stakeholders "intermediate benchmarks" that may be particularly useful in providing accountability, while acknowledging that years may pass before specific reforms result in measurable learning effects.

Another interesting perspective comes from papers exploring the goals and objectives associated with effective systemic change efforts. Thompson (1994) presents a good synthesis of some of the cultural and educational imperatives driving radical reform, including key outcomes considered essential for citizens of an Information Age society, such as problem-solving and critical thinking. Reform tactics for achieving these objectives are derived from a study of five Coalition of Essential Schools member institutions by Wasley, Hampel, and Clark (1997). These include: continuously refining the plan; planning for interconnected "packages" of initiatives; directly addressing controversy; encouraging feedback; and viewing reform from multiple dimensions.

Operationally, of course, school reform is often closely tied to federal and state legislation or regulatory guidance, and systemic change is no exception. Goals 2000 and related education agendas are explored by Stephens (1994) in a paper focused on school change and the rural community. Stephens maintains that state and federal government interest in systemic reform in the United States has five areas of emphasis (the first being adoption of Goals 2000). He observes that linking student learning to federal funding through a rigorous accountability system emphasizing student performance is another major emphasis, as is use of reforms uniting standards, curriculum, assessment, governance, professional development, finance, and other subsystems in an integrated "package" of innovations. Stephens also notes government emphasis on implementing a national technology policy and addressing the requirements of diversity as other important objectives.

The importance of local governance in facilitating (and sometimes resisting) systemic reform is a repeated theme in Reigeluth and Garfinkle's book, and it is often accorded the same attention in other research. Brock (1994) identified local school boards as a likely inhibitor of serious change; Danzberger, Kirst, and Usdan (1992) provide important additional detail on some of the reasons for this, as well as some of the actions that state or local stakeholders can take to encourage governance reforms. At the building level, Poole (whose solid meta-analysis of the resistance literature was mentioned in the previous chapter) offers another contribution in the systemic arena. Her paper (Poole, 1995) presents a case study of a central New York school district's efforts to institute a more collegial relationship between teachers and administrators.

Outside the school, community participation and commitment are no less essential to meaningful change. Carr (1997b) provides an important resource for the principal desiring to facilitate reform, advocating adoption and modeling of transformational and participative leadership styles. Thompson (1998) reinforces another crucial understanding: that community stakeholders must be invited into the change process at the beginning, before an agenda of goals and objectives has been set. Knowing which stakeholders to involve is equally critical. Some authors have considered this from a functional perspective: Minnesota's Information Infrastructure Working Group (1996), in the section titled "Education and Lifelong Learning," identifies curriculum developers, instructors, resident students, distance learners, parents and guardians, educational researchers, administrators, internal evaluators, and external evaluators. Others, like Hutchins (1994), emphasize organizational categories: elected executives (e.g., mayors, governors, presidents), legislatures, courts, education agencies, health and human services agencies, service agencies or cooperatives, accreditation agencies, teacher- and administrator training institutions, professional associations and lobbying groups, and the public at large. All play important roles, and entrenched, unified opposition from any one can grind change to a halt.

Another important area for the prospective change agent to explore in greater detail is the role of various non-instructional subsystems in contributing to lasting change (and strategies for configuring them do so). Hirth (1996) offers such a look at the finance subsystem, presenting a superb model that uncovers the interrelationships among policymaking bodies, systemic reforms, and finance system components. Darling-Hammond (1997) looks at the connections between school organization, professional knowledge, and the teacher education and development subsystem; her other works are some of the best literature on the Holmes Group's Professional Development School (PDS) partnership concept, Grant, and Wasser (1998) explore the subsystem of emerging technologies in their consideration of technology's relationships with other components of the instructional system, such as curriculum, infrastructure, and professional development.

Those actually seeking to implement systemic reforms are also generally interested in applying these reforms to produce benefits in certain content areas or for certain populations. The National Science Foundation's Directorate for Education and Human Resources (1994) offers a concise, but comprehensive, guide to successful programs supporting specific curricular reforms that, together, can provide a blueprint for the content component of systemic change. Some research has addressed particular pedagogical or methodological innovations, such as service learning (Bhaerman, Cordell, & Gomez, 1995). Other authors have addressed transforming schools to better serve particular student subpopulations, such as at-risk students (Thornton & Spiesberger, 1994) or learners with disabilities (Blumberg Center, 1989).

A final area of systemic change for the change agent to consider is evaluation and assessment. Barley and Jenness (1994) provide an evaluation study of particular use. Based on their work with the Michigan Statewide Systemic Initiative (MSSI), the authors approach evaluation from a perspective incorporating the collaborative, stakeholder-based approach used throughout the systemic paradigm. Perhaps most significantly for the practitioner, they constructed and validated seven evaluation instruments allowing school districts to compare their efforts to those of similar districts. In the assessment arena, Jorgensen (1993) offers guidelines for using alternative assessments to evaluate student learning within the new, performance- and problem-based curricula required for Information Age schools.

Summary

Chapter 3 through Chapter 8 considered the components of the change communication model (Figure 2) individually, to guide the change agent in intervening at each of these specific points. Nevertheless, it is just as critical to remember that these interventions, and even the changes they support, do not occur in isolation. Because change is uncomfortable, it is generally only initiated due to pressure from some outside source: a directive from a higher authority, agitation from stakeholders, or antecedent changes to surrounding systems. Thus, before embarking on a change effort (and during the effort, and after the effort!) the change agent should ensure as thorough an understanding as possible of the members, components, and goals of the client system, as well as the relationships that interconnect them. Failure to keep an eye on the whole picture while working on the individual pieces can defeat even the best piecemeal implementations, as related subsystems are unable to interact effectively, and may even actively conflict with one another.

The systemic change paradigm in education, pioneered by Banathy and popularized by Reigeluth, offers a metaphor for understanding the complex, nested interdependencies among system components that allow the system to function as more than the sum of its parts, or leave it unable to function at all. While each of the authors contributing to Reigeluth and Garfinkle's edited volume explores a different though related perspective on the issues surrounding systemic reform, they share several key underpinnings, including:

- *Ensuring stakeholder involvement* (ensuring that everyone affected has input and can participate)
    - Coordinate efforts (as opposed to uncoordinated efforts pulling in different directions)
    - Work as a team (avoiding "us vs. them" or "not invented here" syndromes)
- *Designing for the ideal* (challenging old assumptions)
    - Reexamine obstacles (do old barriers still exist?)
    - Research solutions (have new tools or techniques become available?)

- *Understanding interrelationships* (planning for systemic ripple effects)

  Minimize conflict (be alert for dissonance between new and existing subsystems)

  Maximize synergy (seek ways for new and existing subsystems to reinforce one another)

- *(Re-) Creating a viable system* (making sure that the end result works as a coherent whole)

  Remove barriers (that might inhibit continuous adaptation to the changing environment)

  Reengineer the organization (to support the new set of processes).

Other researchers have explored these and other issues that illustrate the systemic change paradigm in ways that can guide the change agent seeking to maintain a focus on the change communication model as a whole, while designing and conducting the specific interventions that target its individual parts. Some of their studies emphasize the philosophy of comprehensive school change and factors contributing to its rise. Some focus on levels of our educational systems, while others focus on particular subsystems at a given level. Practitioners engaged in change efforts in these contexts are encouraged to explore these and related studies in greater detail. (Terms in italics are ERIC descriptors, with * indicating *major* descriptors–the primary subjects of the document or article.)

- Barley, Z., & Jenness, M. (1994). *The role of evaluation in systemic change in education.* Paper presented at the annual meeting of the American Educational Research Association, New Orleans, LA. (ED 375 175)

  *Access to Education; Comparative Analysis; Constructivism (Learning); Cooperation; *Educational Change; Elementary Secondary Education; Evaluation Needs; *Evaluation Utilization;*

*Local Issues; Mathematics; Outcomes of Education; *School Districts; School Restructuring; Science Education; *Standards; Test Construction*

- Bhaerman, R., Cordell, K., & Gomez, B. (1995). *Service-learning as a component of systemic reform in rural schools and communities*. Philadelphia, PA: Research for Better Schools, Inc. (ED 391 614)

*Curriculum Development; Education Work Relationship; *Educational Benefits; *Educational Change; Educational Objectives; Educational Policy; Educational Principles; Elementary Secondary Education; Program Descriptions; Program Implementation; Rural Areas; Rural Education; *Rural Schools; *School Community Programs; School Community Relationship; *Service Learning; Teacher Attitudes; Teacher Education*

- Blumberg Center for Interdisciplinary Studies in Special Education. (1989). *Guidelines for integration of learners with severe handicaps. Derived from experiences of Indiana's Federal Statewide Systems Change Project.* Terre Haute, IN: Indiana State University. (ED 319 173)

*Delivery Systems; Educational Change; *Educational Improvement; Educational Philosophy; *Educational Practices; Elementary Education; Inservice Teacher Education; *Mainstreaming; Preschool Education; Program Administration; *Severe Disabilities; Social Integration; Special Education; Student Evaluation; Teaching Methods*

- Carr, A. (1997a). User-design in the creation of human learning systems. *Educational Technology Research and Development, 45*(3), 5-22. (EJ 552 523)

*Action Research; Cooperation; Decision Making; Ethnography; Guidelines; *Instructional Design; Leadership; *Performance Technology*

- Carr, A. (1997b). Leadership and community participation: Four case studies. *Journal of Curriculum and Supervision, 12*(2), 152-168. (EJ 535 751)

  *Community Involvement; Intermediate Grades; *Leadership Styles; Middle Schools; *Parent Participation; *Participative Decision Making; *Principals*

- Danzberger, J., Kirst, M., & Usdan, M. (1992). *Governing public schools: New times, new requirements.* Washington, DC: Institute for Educational Leadership. (ED 353 654)

  *Boards of Education; Comparative Analysis; Educational Policy; Elementary Secondary Education; Foreign Countries; *Governance; *Governing Boards; *Public Schools; School Administration; School District Autonomy; *School Restructuring; State Action; *State School District Relationship*

- Darling-Hammond, L. (1997). School reform at the crossroads: Confronting the central issues of teaching. *Educational Policy, 11*(2), 151-166. (EJ 547 270)

  *Diversity (Student); *Educational Change; *Educational Policy; Elementary Secondary Education; *Instructional Improvement; *School Organization; *School Restructuring; *Standards; Teaching Conditions; Work Environment*

- Directorate for Education and Human Resources. (1994). *Foundation for the future.* Washington, DC: National Science Foundation. (ED 370 808)

  *Braille; Demonstration Programs; Elementary Secondary Education; Higher Education; *Mathematics Education; Program Descriptions; Science Education; *Science Programs*

- Hawley, C. (1997). Systemic change in education: A road map. *Educational Technology, 37*(6), 57-64. (EJ 555 776)

  *Design Requirements; *Educational Change; *Educational Development; Evaluation; Guidelines; Instructional Design; Program Development; Program Evaluation; Program Implementation; Strategic Planning; *Systems Approach; Teamwork*

- Hirth, M. (1996). Systemic reform, equity, and school finance reform: Essential policy linkages. *Educational Policy, 10*(4), 468-479. (EJ 535 730)

  *Educational Equity (Finance); *Educational Policy; Elementary Secondary Education; *Finance Reform; *Linking Agents; *Models*

- Honig, B. (1994). How can Horace best be helped? *Phi Delta Kappan, 75*(10), 790-796. (EJ 486 337)

  *Curriculum Development; *Educational Change; Elementary Secondary Education; *Guidelines; *Networks; Outcomes of Education; State Action*

- Jorgensen, M. (1993). The promise of alternative assessment. *School Administrator, 50*(11), 17-23. (EJ 475 772)

*Administrator Responsibility; Elementary Secondary Education; *Program Implementation; *Staff Development; *Student Evaluation; *Teacher Made Tests*

• Kemp, J. (1996). School restructuring: Your school can do it! *TechTrends, 41*(1), 12-15. (EJ 518 403)

*Adoption (Ideas); *Change Strategies; Cultural Pluralism; Educational Finance; Educational Innovation; Educational Technology; Elementary Secondary Education; Instructional Design; *School Restructuring; Student Characteristics*

• McNamara, E., Grant, C., & Wasser, J. (1998). Putting it all together. *Hands On, 21*(1), 10-13. (EJ 566 728)

*Computers; *Educational Change; *Educational Technology; Elementary Secondary Education; *Professional Development; Technology Education*

• Office of Educational Research and Improvement. (1994). *Intermediate benchmarks for systemic reform in mathematics and science education.* Washington, DC: U.S. Department of Education. (ED 405 177)

*Educational Change; Elementary Secondary Education; Guidelines; Mathematics Curriculum; *Mathematics Education; Science Curriculum; *Science Education; Student Evaluation*

• Poole, W. (1995). Reconstructing the teacher-administrator relationship to achieve systemic change. *Journal of School Leadership, 5*(6), 595-596. (EJ 516 001)

*Accountability; *Collegiality; Elementary Secondary Education; Models; Professional Development; *Self Evaluation (Individuals); *Teacher Administrator Relationship; *Teacher Evaluation; *Teacher Responsibility; *Teacher Supervision*

- Slotnik, W. (1993). Core concepts of reform. *Executive Educator, 15*(12), 32-34. (EJ 474 263)

  *Educational Change; Elementary Secondary Education; *Guidelines; *Remedial Programs; *School Based Management; *School Restructuring*

- Stephens, E. (1994). The "new" federal and state education agenda. In G. Karim & N. Weate (Eds.), *Toward the 21st century: A rural education anthology, Vol. 1.* Oak Brook, IL: North Central Regional Education Lab. (ED 401 076)

  *Accountability; Diversity (Institutional); *Educational Change; *Educational Legislation; Educational Objectives; *Educational Policy; Educational Technology; Elementary Secondary Education; Federal Government; Federal Legislation; *Government Role; *Rural Education; Rural Schools; *School Role; Standards; State Government*

- Thompson, J. (1994). Systemic education reform. [On-line]. *ERIC Digest Number 90.* Available: http://www.ed.gov/databases/ERIC_Digests/ed370178.html (ED 370 178)

  *Administrator Role; *Educational Change; *Educational Improvement; Elementary Secondary Education; *Leadership Responsibility; Partnerships in Education; Principals; School Based Management; *School Restructuring; Socioeconomic Influences; Superintendents; *Systems Approach*

• Thompson, S. (1998). Moving from publicity to engagement. *Educational Leadership, 55*(8), 54-57. (EJ 565 131)

*Agenda Setting; *Democratic Values; *Participative Decision Making; *Publicity*

• Thornton, S., & Spiesberger, B. (1994). *Transforming schools: Finding success for students at risk through systemic change.* Sacramento, CA: Resources in Special Education. (ED 383 156)

*Change Agents; *Change Strategies; *Educational Change; Educational Quality; Educational Trends; Elementary Secondary Education; High Risk Students; *Models; Organizational Change; Program Development; Program Implementation; *School Based Management; School Restructuring; *Special Needs Students*

• Wasley, P., Hampel, R., & Clark, R. (1997). The puzzle of whole-school change. *Phi Delta Kappan, 78*(9), 690-697. (EJ 544 328)

• *Change Strategies; *Curriculum Development; *Educational Change; High Schools; *Institutional Mission; Parent Participation; School Restructuring; *Teacher Improvement*

Contributions from Outside Educational Change

While it is easy–even in this interconnected age–to assume that the most valuable resources in one's professional endeavors will come from within one's own field, this is seldom entirely true. Just as the general communication model shown in Figure 1 describes the communication process in any setting, so too it would appear that the change communication model and its components illuminate the change process in any setting.

Specific interventions and concerns may vary from field to field, but much can be learned from the general principles and techniques. The most dramatic example we have seen thus far is Rogers' model, discussed in Chapter 3. Rogers is actually a scholar and professor of communication, not education–yet his work is a classic among theorists and practitioners of educational change.

Rogers is not alone, however–far from it. This may not come as such a surprise after the preceding chapter, which illustrated the connections and interdependence of systems (and their components) throughout our world. The changes in education that we are experiencing, and the changes we must still undertake, are as much driven by the society (of which our educational institutions are a part) as they are driven by advances in pedagogy and teaching tools. The critical thinking and problem-solving skills demanded of our graduates have become so vital because they are demanded for citizenship and professional competence in an information-based society. Because business, politics, and education are all subsystems within this new society, they are all being drawn through similar journeys as they adapt to changes in it–and, where they interact, in each other. In industry, if workers on the shop floor are not able (or not allowed) to spot product defects and halt the production process, millions of dollars can be wasted while the system waits for information to flow up the hierarchy to someone who can. In politics, ideological wars are now being waged on the uncensored battlefield of the Internet, with millions of votes as the spoils.

As educators, information-based society hands us some challenges and opportunities directly, such as the ability to bring the world to the school (and vice versa) in new ways, and the demand for multicultural awareness in a world where our graduates are virtually guaranteed to interact with citizens of other nations. But other requirements come from the direct changes this society calls for in other systems as well. Since our graduates become industry's employees, we must teach them different skills that enable them to gather information, make complex judgments, and act decisively within the scope of their own duties. Since they are tomorrow's citizens, we must develop their ability to gather and validate information from Internet and traditional sources; to compare opinions in light of their biases; to analyze direct and indirect consequences of legislation or candidate policies; and to reach conclusions that shape their voting and citizenship.

With these (and other) interrelationships with other systems and professions outside education, it is reasonable to expect that there are scholars and practitioners in other fields and environments grappling with similar issues concerning change. The work of other writers who are in education, but who are not focusing on change per se, may be useful in guiding the change agent. This chapter focuses on bringing these resources to bear on the educational change effort.

Major Contributing Domains

Because the changes now required of our educational systems are linked to corresponding changes in society, much useful basic theory comes from philosophical discussion of societal, community, and self-renewal transformation. Such work is particularly recommended to those seeking a deeper understanding of psychological and sociological strategies for guiding and supporting meaningful change. This understanding represents an important foundation for all that follows, as it helps illuminate the connections discussed in Chapter 9 and may enable identification of potential pitfalls or synergies.

Armed with this background, you will be ready to consider blueprints for change practice from other settings. By far the richest source of this information outside education itself comes from business and industry. Existing in an environment where complacency leads to both non-competitiveness and extinction with brutal efficiency, the corporate sector has led the way in change not because it is more comfortable with the process, but merely because to do otherwise is to go out of business. While this research has led to some useful contributions to basic theory, its best-known product is probably the discipline of reengineering. A subset of this research worth considering is that of the Total Quality movement, especially when defining what success should look like for the reengineered institution. Change literature from public or social service contexts outside education can also be useful, as can education literature focusing on policy or other areas besides change, per se. Such readings may be a useful capstone, bringing principles in the business literature closer to our own settings. Others may prefer to read the social research first to clarify what is most relevant to non-commercial organizations, and then proceed to the business literature to learn about tools facilitating those changes.

Once these models are explored, it is useful to delve deeper, examining specific components of education/change systems. Research of this type focuses on subsystems like curriculum, libraries, or technology. It may also focus on tools and techniques for change, both in communications and planning (e.g., creating a customer feedback system to inform continuous improvement) and in execution (e.g., benchmarking, breakpoints, and best practices).

Finally, we will look at some concrete examples of change "cultures" (paradigms with associated support systems) from instructional settings outside traditional education. One of these is the field of Performance Improvement, where the Human Performance Technology (HPT) model represents a systemic change from the traditional training paradigm. The HPT model encourages the organization to consider the full range of potential solutions when its performance falls below desired levels, rather than automatically gravitating to a training solution. Because HPT can be applied to the organizational learning system as a whole, as well as to specific performance problems, the model can serve as a framework for systemic change. A significant amount of Performance Improvement research explicitly focuses on this use. A closely related field is Human Resource Development (HRD), where employee training is explicitly the mission. The HRD literature may be particularly helpful in considering the training and performance support needs of staff and faculty in an institution undertaking meaningful change.

It is no coincidence that this "tour" of outside literature follows a pattern similar to that in Reigeluth and Garfinkle's exploration of systemic change. In both cases, the knowledge to be gained is less a fixed sequence of steps or elements than a "way of thinking" about the changes that you wish to undertake. Recall the metaphor of the blind men and the elephant used in the Introduction: while Chapter 3 through Chapter 8 focused on each part crucial to understanding their strengths and limitations, Chapter 9 and this chapter consider "the whole elephant," an endeavor best understood through this different structure.

Foundations: Other Research on Basic Change Theory

Some of the best-known foundational literature for understanding the broad social changes driving education reform comes from one source: Alvin Toffler. Both *The Third Wave* (Toffler, 1980) and the more recent *War and Anti-War: Survival at the Dawn of the Twenty-first Century* (Toffler & Toffler, 1993) are excellent introductions to the challenges of information-based society. Other resources at the global/societal level include general discussions, such as *Changing Consciousness: Exploring the Hidden Source of the Social, Political, and Environmental Crises Facing Our World* (Bohm & Edwards, 1991) and *The Information Revolution: Current and Future Consequences* (Porter & Read, 1998). More focused treatments, such as *Future Edge: Discovering the New Paradigms of Success* (Barker, 1992), may also be useful.

Other literature focuses on building a sense of community and shared purpose in support of change. A good introduction to the overall concept is *The Spirit of Community: Rights, Responsibilities, and the Communitarian Agenda* (Etzioni, 1993). Further introduction to the concept's value, and guidance in achieving these ends, is offered by the American Institute for Research in two publications: *The Importance of Community* (Gardner, 1994) and *Building Community* (Gardner, 1991). Anchoring the concept of community to an organizational context is *Building Community: the Human Side of Work* (Manning, Curtis, & McMillen, 1996).

Organizational change is explored explicitly in books such as *Changing the Game: Organizational Transformations of the First, Second, and Third Kinds* (Flamholtz & Randle, 1998). The authors describe three kinds of transformations: the transition of young, innovative organizations to mature, stable ones; revitalization of aging or "stuck" organizations; and the type of "re-visioning" we have called systemic change. Another corporate treatment recognizing the shared lineage of systems and chaos theory is seen in *Competing on the Edge: Strategy as Structured Chaos* (Brown & Eisenhardt, 1998).

At the individual level, Donald Schön provides a good foundation in *The Reflective Practitioner: How Professionals Think in Action* (Schön, 1983), which explores the psychology of continuous self-improvement. A related concept, self-renewal, is examined in publications such as *Learned Optimism* (Seligman, 1991) and *Managing Transitions: Making the Most of Change* (Bridges, 1991). Also worth a look are group techniques such as the focus group, discussed by Krueger (1994), which can facilitate disclosure of individual needs and priorities so they can be brought into the open and addressed in defining the change effort's objectives.

Blueprints: Other Models of Change in Practice

As mentioned earlier, the largest volume of recent organizational change literature falls under the domain of reengineering. Pioneered in *Reengineering the Corporation: A Manifesto for Business Revolution*

(Hammer & Champy, 1993), this is essentially a systemic approach to business change. Hammer and Champy begin with the "crisis" introduced, in part, by both the societal changes to which education is also responding and by the rigid and bureaucratic structure characteristic of mature Industrial Age organizations. They then introduce a process based on identifying fundamental business goals, and then aligning processes within the organization to support them in the most efficient manner possible. One of reengineering's core principles is that every requirement for one organization to pass an action to another for completion introduces delay, expense, and opportunity for error. (An obvious example of this in education is shuttling students from one room to another, several times a day, to learn about different subjects–in isolation–from different instructors.) Reengineering alters the organization in order to minimize the number of different subsystems that must interact for a given process to be successfully completed. Four case studies are provided to illustrate reengineering principles in practice.

Hammer returns to this topic with *Beyond Reengineering: How the Process-centered Organization is Changing Our Work and Our Lives* (Hammer, 1996). This book explores the gains offered by a process focus, bringing more recent lessons to bear. It also emphasizes the need for commitment at all levels, from executives and process owners (managers) to workers (who must see themselves as professionals and be treated as such). This model is also revisited with updated case studies in *Beyond the Basics of Reengineering: Survival Tactics for the '90s* (Quality Resources/The Kraus Organization, 1994). An even more current and comprehensive resource is *Business Process Engineering: Advancing the State of the Art* (Elzinga, Gulledge, & Lee, 1999), an edited volume combining chapters by leading experts into what may be the best single text on process-driven change. Another useful resource emphasizing proven techniques in this area is *Best Practices in Reengineering: What Works and What Doesn't in the Reengineering Process* (Carr & Johansson, 1995). This volume may be especially useful to the practitioner.

Much related research has occurred under the more general heading of organizational transformation. A particularly informative resource is *Corporate Transformation* (Bhambri & Sinatra, 1997), an edited compendium that explores systemic corporate change from an international perspective. The role of HRD in organizational transformation is explored in *HR to the Rescue: Case Studies of HR Solutions to Business Challenges* (Mone & London, 1998). Closely tied to systemic change, reengineering, and organizational transformation is the concept of the "learning organization," described in *The Fifth Discipline: the Art and Practice of the Learning Organization* (Senge, 1990). This notion has been taken up by other writers as well, for example Watkins and Marsick (1993), in *Sculpting the Learning Organization: Lessons in the Art and Science of Systemic Change*. Senge has also returned to the topic in *The Dance of Change: The Challenges to Sustaining Momentum in Learning Organizations* (Senge, et al., 1999). This is a particularly crucial area for the change agent: building the type of internal capacity for and disposition toward continuous growth (discussed under Havelock's model in Chapter 6) that is critical to the survival of real change beyond the thrill of implementation.

One corporate example of these concepts that is especially useful as an example for educators is *The Infinite Resource: Creating and Leading the Knowledge Enterprise* (Halal & Smith, 1998). Many educational institutions not funded by taxes truly are knowledge enterprises: businesses whose "product" is effectively communicated information, and whose survival depends on how well that product satisfies the institution's "customers." The authors in this edited book provide an insightful look at systemic change and organizational transformation in this type of market. Many other resources in this area are even more explicitly "how-to" guides for translating these principles into practice. Price Waterhouse's Change Integration Group (1995) offers a look at validated techniques in *Better Change: Best Practices for Transforming Your Organization*. A guide to another strategy for support of systemic change is seen in *Changing Organizations: Practicing Action Training and Research* (Bruce & Wyman, 1998).

While the language of reengineering and organizational transformation has largely supplanted references to a predecessor–Total Quality Management (TQM)–in the literature, a couple of TQM resources are worth mentioning in this context. From the corporate sector, *Building the Invisible Quality Corporation: the Executive Guide to Transcending TQM* (Maromonte, 1996) argues that a fundamental commitment to quality (that so permeates all levels of the corporate culture that it is "invisible") is essential for TQM to have the promised impact. *Quality Management for Educational Technology Services* (Richie, 1994) explores principles and techniques for implementing a quality culture in an explicitly instructional setting, and is of particular use for change agents in media and technology organizations.

A final set of models that you may wish to review concerns systemic change and organizational transformation in government and public (i.e., non-commercial) contexts. Bellamy and Taylor (1998) introduce this topic in *Governing in the Information Age*, which addresses government's need for change and its processes of reengineering. It also offers a model that includes components of philosophy, infrastructure, and policy (with some obvious implications for public education). This book also contains a good discussion of citizenship in an Information Age democracy, illuminating some of the new requirements for civics education in our schools. Sims (1998) offers a related discussion in *Accountability and Radical Change in Public Organizations*, an edited collection of papers that includes several case studies (including one on higher education), as well as other discussions on public education and public-sector training. A treatment of public administration reform with an international flavor can be found in *Beyond the New Public Management: Changing Ideas and Practices in Governance* (Minogue, Polidano, & Hulme, 1998). Finally, a model of a reengineered school is described in *The Process-centered School: Sustaining a Renaissance Community* (Costa & Liebmann, 1997).

Deconstruction: Other Explorations of the Subsystems of Change

Also useful are publications focusing on particular subsystems, or on tools or techniques in support of these broader efforts. Other writers in Rogers' field of communications have continued to offer valuable insights. D'Aprix (1996) offers a design for a feedback subsystem linking the organization with the needs and priorities of its customers, in *Communicating for Change: Connecting the Workplace With the Marketplace*. Within the organization, the changed world of corporate communication is explored by Marlow and Wilson (1997) in *The Breakdown of Hierarchy: Communicating in the Evolving Workplace*, which emphasizes the impact of electronic media on the pace of competition, and the resulting pressure toward flattened decision structures. The dissemination problem itself is tackled in such publications as *Network Models of the Diffusion of Innovations* (Valente, 1995), which explores the interpersonal communication links by which it occurs. The communication perspective on innovation is also presented in *Innovation: the Communication of Change in Ideas, Practices and Products* (Spence, 1994). Perhaps more closely approximating the environment in which educational innovations must diffuse, Chatterjee (1990) considers change in social services contexts in *The Transferability of Social Technology: Explorations in the Knowledge Structures of the Helping Professions and their Transfer.*

Other literature exploring specific techniques focused on one subsystem (e.g., content, technology, or libraries) includes examinations of curriculum, pedagogy, and assessment reform, such as *Curriculum Leadership: Rethinking Schools for the 21st Century* (Bernhardt, 1998). Explorations of "human factors" in information systems design, such as that presented by Rubinstein, Hersh, and Ledgard (1984), also fall into this category. This book, which proclaims on its front cover to be a guide in "Designing Computer Systems FOR PEOPLE," necessarily deals with factors which make a technology attractive (or unattractive) to its intended users. Since the technologies being introduced in educational settings are a subset of this population of information technologies (i.e., computer-based systems used in instruction), many of the same considerations may be expected to apply, such as adapting to users' conceptual models or language, or the interaction between systems' interface styles and users' cognitive styles.

Obviously the focus of such literature is on design of the device itself. Generally it also contains a discussion of needs assessment, implementation, and evaluation strategies to encourage user commitment to a new device. However, some publications of this type, such as Shneiderman's *Designing the User Interface* (1987), go beyond such developmental principles to discuss factors that more properly apply to implementation strategy. While most of his book follows the traditional pattern, Shneiderman's last three chapters are particularly useful for the change agent. Chapter 9 addresses post-implementation support, specifically documentation and on-line help, and emphasizes the importance of offering training to users. Chapter 10 discusses testing and evaluation, and is most useful as an illustration of the value of involving users throughout the process to pick up errors and misconceptions early, while they are still relatively easy to correct. Chapter 11 concludes the text with an excellent look at "hopes and dreams" and "fears and nightmares" about technology, much of which is just as applicable to a training environment as to any other.

Change agents working with libraries as a component of change in school or university settings may also want to consider *Finding Common Ground: Creating the Library of the Future Without Diminishing the Library of the Past* (LaGuardia & Mitchell, 1998). This volume is a key resource for adapting the library to the needs of Information Age education without sacrificing the underpinnings of its historical strengths, or inviting resistance from their defenders.

Contributions discussing specific tools can also be useful. Many come from business, and address tools for reengineering and quality initiatives. One such book is *Breakpoints: How Managers Exploit Radical Business Change* (Strebel, 1992). Another is *Benchmarking: a Tool for Continuous Improvement* (Leibfried & McNair, 1992), which explores the use of exemplary practice to set desired performance levels (thereby encouraging the organization to always strive for enhanced effectiveness). A final resource of this type, especially for those active in international settings, is *Decision Support in Organizational Transformation* (Humphreys, 1997), an exploration of techniques for harnessing information technologies in service of systemic change. Still other authors, within education but from outside diffusion research, offer further substantive or procedural guidance that may be useful in planning and designing change. For example, Garland, in Anglin's edited volume *Instructional Technology: Past, Present, and Future* (1991), presents a useful list of major stakeholders, along with brief summaries of the types of factors with which each would typically be most concerned.

Examples: The Practice of Change in Settings Outside Traditional Education

The final outside resources considered here are complete frameworks for systemic change, cultures of continuous improvement that offer both an architecture for building entirely new systems and a philosophy for transforming existing ones. In both examples, in addition to an extensive body of literature and an established community of practice, a national or international professional association exists which ties research to practice in business and industrial training settings. These examples were selected because the explicitly instructional nature of their contexts should apply to other educational settings.

The first of these frameworks is Human Performance Technology (HPT). Represented in instructional settings by the International Society for Performance Improvement (ISPI) at http://www.ispi.org/, this framework consists of three fundamental processes: performance analysis, cause analysis, and intervention selection. As already mentioned, this framework can be applied to entire organizational learning systems as well as individual performance problems, so HPT literature frequently has clear implications for change practice. The best single resource on this framework is the *Handbook of Human Performance Technology: A Comprehensive Guide for Analyzing and Solving Performance Problems in Organizations* (Stolovitch & Keeps, 1999). Several chapters in this edited volume deal explicitly with change or transformation in the sense we have discussed here. Others cover the design, development, or implementation of HPT interventions–which are, essentially, innovations. The strategies may also be useful in addressing other types of innovations in instructional settings.

Change issues are frequently discussed in other HPT literature as well. The broader issues of the link between organizations and wider society are explored by Kaufman, Watkins, Triner, and Smith (1998) in "The Changing Corporate Mind: Organizations, Visions, Mission, Purposes, and Indicators on the Move Toward Societal Payoff." The counterproductive, subtle lessons conveyed by many of our Industrial Age education and training systems are the subject of "Learned Disabilities: How to Re-invent Your Training System and Revise Its Real Lessons" (Gayeski, 1999). Brethower and Dams (1999) review research on "Systems Thinking (and Systems Doing)" that does not often appear in the systemic change literature. Finally, "Implementation: the Glue of Organizational Change" (Addison & Lloyd, 1999) presents a concise set of guidelines for developing an implementation plan.

The second framework suggested is Human Resource Development (HRD). Represented in instructional contexts by the American Society for Training and Development (ASTD) at http://www.astd.org/, this framework focuses on the needs of workplace learning from the human resources perspective. This framework also has a single, comprehensive resource: *The ASTD Training and Development Handbook: A Guide to Human Resource Development* (Craig, 1996). This book, another edited volume, devotes some attention to creating a "learning organization" (one with the "built-in" capacity for change Havelock advocates) but is strongest in offering specific tools, techniques, and interventions that are part of an effective HRD system design (e.g., benchmarking, metrics).

Further resources are also available in other HRD literature. Some are equally specific: Kramlinger (1998) presents guidelines for effective communication in support of change, in "How to Deliver a Change Message." Brody and Davidson (1998) explore the HRD perspective in an explicitly educational context in *Professional Development for Cooperative Learning: Issues and Approaches*. Some writers present case studies, such as Hebard (1998) in "A Story of Real Change," which outlines the transformation of a small bank into a learning organization. Others are more philosophical, while still addressing a focused topic: "The Teaching Organization" (Tichy & Cohen, 1998) asserts that building a learning organization is not enough–leaders must see it as their responsibility to pass their competencies on to others. Some HRD authors also examine broader issues: Juechter, Fisher, and Alford (1998) have derived another loose parallel to Ely's Conditions of Change in their "Five Conditions for High-Performance Cultures." (The five conditions are: a relevant focus; a process driven from the top but fueled throughout the organization; leaders' commitment; comprehensive involvement; and external coaches).

Summary

Unlike the preceding chapters, this discussion has not gone into detail in describing each publication: there are simply too many, and they cover too broad a spectrum. Rather, its purpose is to ensure that no reader finishes this book unaware of the vast resources available outside the educational change literature–even outside education altogether–that can be useful to the scholar or practitioner of educational change.

Unfortunately, it is easy for communities of practice to become and remain isolated: we are educators, so it would seem self-evident that the most useful publications for us to read (and publish in) are about education. Yet as we have seen in this chapter and in Chapter 9, the world is not a loose collection of unconnected entities: we are all part of the suprasystem of human society, and we are interdependent with members of other societal subsystems throughout that larger community. Researchers and practitioners in those other subsystems are often working on the same issues; sometimes, because of competitive pressures or greater systemic proximity to the root causes of change, they are substantially farther along in resolving them. Unfortunately, if they are managers, for example, they are probably equally certain that the venues they have to publish in, and read, are about management.

This chapter has been devoted to breaking through that isolation. Hopefully, you have seen at least some resources or topics that have sparked your interest. Start by investigating them; you will likely find references to still other resources that might be helpful. Gradually, the external community of practice related to what you're trying to accomplish should start to take shape. You'll begin to know the "buzzwords" that will drive successful literature searches in other fields, and then the world of solutions those disciplines have pioneered will open up for you.

Of course, communication is a two-way process. Not only can educators benefit from work done in other fields, but managers may also be able to benefit from work done in educational change, particularly where Performance Improvement or HRD are concerned. If you begin to see the names of certain journals in outside domains cropping up again and again with papers related to what you are doing, consider submitting a paper to them reporting on your efforts. In this way, both domains will become increasingly aware of one another, and the communications channels linking them will become wider and more commonly used, facilitating the flow of solutions (and questions) from each to the other. To paraphrase an old axiom on problem solving, two (fields') minds work better than one!

Conclusion

chapter 11

When I sat down to write this book, it was just going to be a review of the existing literature. I knew that over their decades of independent change scholarship, the authors of the major models I've described had given us some powerful tools. I realized, too, that these are tools we must use in reforming our educational systems so our nation will no longer be "at risk." As one of the founders of AECT's Council on Systemic Change, I also knew that we had bridged a major chasm.

We finally understood that lasting, successful change cannot wear blinders: it must recognize the interdependence of all members and all components of the system being changed, and unite them to transcend that system's limitations.

Yet in our enthusiasm for this crucial discovery, we almost (to reverse a metaphor used earlier) lost sight of the trees on account of the forest blocking our view! So I set out to help us refresh our collective memory: to aid the practitioner trying to make change happen in applying the lessons, techniques, and tools from classical change research to the problems we face. I hoped to unite this knowledge with the strategic guidance offered by systems thinking, so we might avoid repeating the mistakes of our history when "a change" was undertaken in isolation, as though social systems could be operated on *in situ*.

But then something really exciting happened. As I tried to figure out how I was going to organize this review and to sketch out a table of contents, I had to think about what each of the classical authors represents. I had to decide how I was going to express the circumstances under which each way of looking at change might be most useful. Rogers has the best focus on the innovation, Ely has the best treatment of the environment, and so on. And then, while skimming through Rogers, I found his statement (Rogers, 1995, pp. 5-6) that planned change is a specialized instance of the general communication model, and…"Voilá! The elephant!"

Pulling It All Together

At that point, I realized that the classical change models, together, comprised a comprehensive model of change communication. Yet due to the isolation of the various schools of change thought described in Chapter 1, their relationship to one another within this model has never been made explicit. This became my new, overriding goal for this book: to illustrate how the decades of knowledge accumulated by each of these "invisible colleges" can be integrated by the practitioner, within a systemic strategy grounded in his specific context, to improve education and learning in the Information Age.

I hope I have succeeded, in some small measure. Much has been learned from these models. It is of scant benefit, however, if those who must make change work are unaware of them or are confused about how to apply the multiplicity of frameworks, which, on the surface, are seemingly unconnected. Bertrand Russell once observed, "In science, the successors stand upon the shoulders of their predecessors; where one man of supreme genius has invented a method, a thousand lesser men can apply it." As one of these "lesser men," I am pleased to set before you the work of the geniuses of our field, with the hope that, borne upon their shoulders, we may see farther than ever before.

This section comprises the largest part of this chapter, and seeks to leave you with an example–greatly simplified, but still illustrative–of what application of the models in the fashion I have outlined might look like. In the same fashion as the overarching systemic strategy explored in Chapter 9, these are not intended as "school solutions" or prescriptions. Rather I hope for them to spark in you your own ideas, in your own setting, of how you might do "something like this" to help (or stop) a change effort with which you are, or would like to be, involved. As you read about the models, bear in mind the central theme I have stressed, which might be summarized as follows: We must strive to guide all of our change efforts with a systemic understanding of the context in which we undertake them. Nevertheless, it may be best to focus interventions on a particular component of the change communication model at a given point in time, depending on the circumstance in which the change facilitator finds herself, or as the implementation effort progresses.

We begin, of course, where you are. Are you a teacher, or a principal, or a student? Are you a district administrator? Are you a consultant? Are you an innovation developer, or even a school reform professional? Are you a parent, or a community leader concerned with improving your schools? Are you government representative charged with safeguarding equity and quality? Whatever your role, you can look to Chapter 5 to help decide where to start, what to do, or who to see to move your change forward (or to obstruct a poorly-conceived change).

From there, you might go to Chapter 9, to consider your relationship within the system being changed. You'll want to lay all your assumptions about the nature of that system—what its purpose is, who its members are, how it works, what constraints govern it, and others—on the table. You'll want to question those assumptions, to see whether they still hold true. But you mustn't stop there. You'll need to look inside the system, seeking the best possible understanding of its subsystems, stakeholders, and other components, and how they relate to one another and to the system as a whole. And you'll need to look outside the system as well, to understand how other, coequal systems (like business or higher education) are interrelated with it, and how it (and these other systems) in turn relate to the larger systems of community, nation, or human society. The understanding you gain will illuminate your goals for the innovation you are advocating, or your concerns for the change you are resisting, and will show you where issues relating to these sub- and suprasystems must be addressed.

Ultimately, this understanding is one of your most important tools for diagnosing the change needs of your system, and how a given innovation serves or impedes them. At this point, you are unquestionably embarked upon your change journey. In fact, you are probably somewhere between the Relate and Examine stages of the C-R-E-A-T-E-R model. The discussion of that model in Chapter 6 will guide you as you plan your efforts. It will serve as the outline for a checklist, to ensure that you consider and acquire the right resources at the proper time. It will help you design, conduct, and report on the results of your trial, or "test drive" of the innovation, in a way that is relevant and understandable to other stakeholders. It will help you extend implementation both wider and deeper in and around your system. It will help you prepare others to recognize when it is time to change again.

Still, at some point you must commit to a plan, and act. Chapter 7 gives you tools to "keep your finger on the pulse" of change as it meets its intended adopters. CBAM's validated instruments enable you to collect the information you'll need. The theory and guidelines it offers will help you understand the concerns that teachers, or other stakeholders, are experiencing as implementation progresses. This, in turn, will help ensure that you design and put into effect the appropriate types of interventions at the times when they will do the most to address the concerns most salient at each stage.

Even the most effective innovation, or the most informed implementation, will probably encounter some obstacles. Chapter 8 can help you narrow down the cause(s) of that resistance. Maybe you find that some stakeholders see the innovation as eroding their importance or influence in some key way. Possibly others would like to adopt the innovation, but feel they lack the knowledge or skills to do so. Some opposition may be grounded in well-entrenched values and beliefs, while other barriers may stem from lack of confidence that the system is capable of successful change.

You may find it easiest to approach certain of these obstacles by modifying the innovation's attributes. Perhaps, if you're the innovation's developer, or if its nature permits easy and effective adaptation to the needs of your context, you can actually change the attributes themselves. If you can't alter the actual innovation, though, you may be able to change its perceptions among the concerned groups. For example, instead of competing with those groups, perhaps the innovation is more appropriately seen as a tool they can use to enhance their effectiveness. Whether you are modifying the attributes themselves or merely their perceptions, Chapter 3 lays out the ones that are most influential, and will help you decide on your approach.

Other obstacles may owe their origins to the environment in which implementation occurs. Chapter 4 will help you identify which, if any, of the conditions for successful change are lacking, and perhaps suggest some ideas for addressing those deficiencies. Possibly a clearer, unequivocal statement of commitment by top leaders (or more evident leadership by example) is called for. Or maybe increased funding for and provision of adequate professional development is required, to help the stakeholders learn how to use their new tool(s).

Of course, this is not a fixed sequence. Your initial involvement in a change may come when you notice the first signs of resistance to an innovation you favor. In such a case, you might begin by focusing on resistance as discussed in Chapter 8, returning to Chapter 9 to help you identify the root causes of that resistance within the system or its interrelationships with its components, members, or other systems. If you're an innovation developer, you may begin with the innovation as discussed in Chapter 3, using the systemic diagnosis informed by Chapter 9 to guide your initial selection of the attributes you want your innovation to have. The professional change agent may begin with the change process in Chapter 6 as she plans her overall implementation approach.

The chapters are also frequently interrelated, like the components of any other system. When modifying innovation attributes pursuant to Chapter 3, you may wish to obtain an IC Component Checklist discussed in Chapter 7 to ensure you don't inadvertently eliminate or degrade a critical part of the innovation. When assessing the presence or absence of conditions for change, you may want to verify that the systemic conditions for change mentioned in Chapter 9 are present as well. While using Chapter 7 to design interventions for stakeholders at a particular level of use or stage of concern, you might find yourself addressing the psychological barriers to change presented in Chapter 8. As you first become involved in a particular change effort, you may also find it helpful to consult Figure 2. This visual depiction of the change communication model may aid you in identifying current or potential "trouble spots" or determining the easiest place to "get hold of the process" and influence it in the desired direction. As you do this, the most powerful interrelationships affecting your context should become clearer as well.

Reaching Out, Reaching Across

We have seen that the educational change literature is vast: I hope that the preceding discussion has mapped the territory to make it a little less intimidating. Yet as Chapter 10 showed, much useful knowledge of the change process has been gained in other fields as well, particularly the business-inspired domains of HPT and HRD. I encourage you not to neglect these other knowledge bases as your involvement with educational change grows.

My own background has highlighted the benefit of such non-parochialism. My masters degree is in business administration; my doctorate is in education. My daily work is in military training. My scholarship is in K-12 and higher education. These eclectic combinations have brought me face to face with the connections and possible synergies between these environments–connections I might have missed had I been purely of one camp or the other. In fact, I was first encouraged to write this book because my philosophical roots as a student of the classical models combined similarly with my leadership role in the systemic movement to give me a chance at reconciling the old tactics with a new strategy to form a unified whole.

I encourage you to seek out this type of opportunity as well. If you are a schoolteacher, knowledge of business changes may help you understand the environment your graduates will face, and the skills you must help them build. If you are a corporate trainer, understanding the changes happening in higher education may allow you to adapt more quickly to the changing backgrounds of the graduates you must hire and train. If you are a school board member, awareness of the new competencies required of citizens in an information-based society may give you a better appreciation for the financial and pedagogical reforms needed to prepare the children your constituents entrusted to your oversight. If you are a parent or a voter–in other words, whoever you are–understanding the factors shaping each of these domains and the larger societal changes driving them will help you make the decisions on which all of our futures depend.

Reach out to other disciplines, to share your experience with others as well as to benefit from the knowledge they have gained. Reach across to other stakeholders, to build the sense of community and shared purpose demanded for the changes that must lie ahead. The road won't always be easy, and you won't always know which path to take when it forks. But we can get where we need to go with mutual respect, honest work, and the understanding that we all have to live with the results. I hope that the knowledge bases made accessible to you through this book will help.

Succeeding Systemically

This brings us to a sort of "systems synthesis," drawing together some of the most important ideas I have tried to convey. The lessons of the classical change models are as valid today, and just as essential for the change agent to master, as they have ever been. Yet a single innovation (such as a new technology or a new teaching philosophy) that is foreign to the rest of the system will be rejected, just as an incompatible organ transplant is rejected by a living system. Success depends on a coordinated "bundle" of innovations, generally involving multiple stakeholders, that leaves a coherent system after implementation.

Rest assured, that despite some early rash statements, systemic change is not always radical change, and it does not ask you to discard your experience. If you are a principal, a teacher, or a district administrator with decades of experience in your school or district, that background is what makes you an expert. Use it! Yet the world has changed around us, and many of the restrictions and limitations that experience taught us may no longer hold. Conversely, new relationships or interdependencies–and new opportunities for collaboration–may have emerged. Before rejecting (or embracing) a new innovation, a systemic strategy merely asks you to recheck your assumptions about what is possible. You might be pleasantly surprised!

This brings us to one of the most important points for me to reinforce: that you are not alone! The news media, professional literature, and political campaigns bring us daily reports of all the people working diligently for educational reform: why would you think there aren't a few in your vicinity? We are far enough into the Information Age to understand that serious change is a necessity, not just an option. Yet many of us are still working in isolation, trying to improve our own classroom or our own library or our own district office. We don't realize that just down the hall or just across town are others, who also think they're alone, working just as hard toward the same goal in their immediate domains. In Chapter 5, we saw that this lack of communication is both demoralizing and inefficient. We would have taken a very big step into the future if administrators in every school and district made time every month for teachers and staff (and students? parents?) to share problems, ideas, and best practices and to identify and embark upon collaborative solutions.

We must also remember that those with whom you would like to collaborate are also busy professionals, just like you. They are unlikely to buy in to your team with their time just because you say you've got a similar idea. Another theme running throughout this book has been that merely having a great idea isn't enough. Rogers (1995, pp. 7-8) notes that it took almost 200 years after the value of lemon juice in preventing scurvy was first experimentally demonstrated in the British navy before it adopted citrus for use at sea. (It took an additional 70 years before this innovation was adopted for use in the British merchant fleet! Great ideas must also be communicated effectively and persuasively (i.e., the change communication model must be used successfully) for them to take hold. Talk with your potential collaborators. Ensure that they understand why what they're doing is important to you, how their efforts will impact your programs, and whether anything you're doing can similarly complement their efforts.

Finally, as you go out to apply what you have learned here (and what you learn from other resources to which this book may have introduced you), bear in mind that you are operating on–and within–a system of systems. Just as the changes you must pursue are made necessary by changes in society, the changes you make will cause ripples in your organization's own subsystems (employees, budgets, equipment, etc.) as well. These ripples of change may in turn spread to adjacent systems throughout the organization and even to the community. Consequently, the changes you implement must not merely be internally coherent as a system unto themselves (that is a necessary, but not sufficient, condition for success). They must also be externally viable as positive contributions to the overall curriculum, the organization as a whole, and to society. (For a terrific discussion of the ripples of that requirement in the evaluation of change efforts, and other programs, see Watkins, Leigh, Foshay, & Kaufman, 1998.)

These are exciting–and challenging–times to be a part of education. The transformation we must undertake is a dramatic one: we are, quite literally, called upon to equip the citizens and the workforce of the Information Age with the knowledge tools they will require to drive and maintain the engines of progress. Such watershed events as we shall witness–and perhaps cause–are not experienced without conflict. But conflict, as the Chinese know, is what we make of it. The Chinese ideogram for "conflict" contains two characters: one represents "danger," and the other "hidden opportunity." We get to choose which aspect of conflict–and of change–we emphasize.

I leave you on this positive note.

References

Addison, R., & Lloyd, C. (1999). Implementation: The glue of organizational change. *Performance Improvement, 38*(6), 8-11.

Aoki, T., Langford, C., Williams, D., & Wilson, D. (1977). *British Columbia social studies assessment* (Vols. 1-3). Victoria, British Columbia, Canada: British Columbia Ministry of Education. (ED 152 638)

Bailey, D., & Palsha, S. (1992). Qualities of the Stages of Concern Questionnaire and implications for educational innovations. *Journal of Educational Research, 85*(4), 226-232. (EJ 447 952)

Banathy, B. (1973). *Developing a systems view of education.* Salinas, CA: Intersystems Publications.

Banathy, B. (1988). Systems inquiry in education. *Systems Practice, 1,* 193-212.

Banathy, B. (1991). *Systems design of education.* Englewood Cliffs, NJ: Educational Technology Publications.

Banathy, B. (1994). Designing educational systems: Creating our future in a changing world. In C. Reigeluth & R. Garfinkle (Eds.), *Systemic change in education* (pp. 27-34). Englewood Cliffs, NJ: Educational Technology Publications.

Barker, J. (1992). *Future edge: Discovering the new paradigms of success.* New York, NY: Morrow. Barley, Z. & Jenness, M. (1994). *The role of evaluation in systemic change in education.* Paper presented at the annual meeting of the American Educational Research Association, New Orleans, LA. (ED 375 175)

Bauder, D. (1993). Computer integration in K-12 schools: Conditions related to adoption and implementation. *Dissertation Abstracts International, 54*(08), 2991A. (University Microfilms No. AAI94-01653)

Bellamy, C., & Taylor, J. (1998). *Governing in the Information Age.* Bristol, PA: Open University Press.

Berman, P., & Pauly, E. (1975). *Federal programs supporting educational change: Vol. 2. Factors affecting change agent projects.* Santa Monica, CA: Rand Corporation. (ED 108 324)

Bernhardt, R. (1998). *Curriculum leadership: Rethinking schools for the 21st century.* Cresskill, NJ: Hampton Press.

Bhaerman, R., Cordell, K., & Gomez, B. (1995). *Service-learning as a component of systemic reform in rural schools and communities.* Philadelphia, PA: Research for Better Schools, Inc. (ED 391 614)

Bhambri, A., & Sinatra, A. (1997). *Corporate transformation.* Norwell, MA: Kluwer Academic Publishers.

Blumberg Center for Interdisciplinary Studies in Special Education. (1989). *Guidelines for integration of learners with severe handicaps. Derived from experiences of Indiana's federal statewide systems change project.* Terre Haute, IN: Indiana State University. (ED 319 173)

Bogdan, R., & Biklen, S. (1992). *Qualitative research for education.* Needham Heights, MA: Allyn and Bacon.

Bohm, D., & Edwards, M. (1991). *Changing consciousness: Exploring the hidden source of the social, political, and environmental crises facing our world.* San Francisco, CA: Harper.

Bowsher, J. (1994). What can we learn from corporate education about systemic change? In C. Reigeluth & R. Garfinkle (Eds.), *Systemic change in education* (pp. 95-100). Englewood Cliffs, NJ: Educational Technology Publications. (ED 367 055)

Boyd, W. (1978). The changing politics of curriculum policy making for American schools. *Review of Educational Research, 48*(4), 577-628.

Branson, R. (1975). *Interservice procedures for instructional systems development: Executive summary and model.* Fort Monroe, VA: U.S. Army Training and Doctrine Command. (ED 122 022)

Brethower, D., & Dams, P. (1999). Systems thinking (and systems doing). *Performance Improvement, 38*(1), 37-52.

Bridges, W. (1991). *Managing transitions: Making the most of change.* Reading, MA: Addison-Wesley.

Brock, I. (1994). You're not likely to get there from here. In C. Reigeluth & R. Garfinkle (Eds.), *Systemic change in education* (pp. 119-125). Englewood Cliffs, NJ: Educational Technology Publications. (ED 367 055)

Brody, C., & Davidson, N. (1998). *Professional development for cooperative learning: Issues and approaches.* Albany, NY: State University of New York Press.

Brown, S., & Eisenhardt, K. (1998). *Competing on the edge: Strategy as structured chaos.* Boston, MA: Harvard Business School Press.

Bruce, R., & Wyman, S. (1998). *Changing organizations: Practicing action training and research.* Thousand Oaks, CA: Sage Publications.

Burkman, E. (1987). Factors affecting utilization. In R. Gagné (Ed.), *Instructional technology: Foundations,* (pp. 429-455). Hillsdale, NJ: Lawrence Erlbaum Associates, Incorporated.

Caccamo, J., & Levitt, D. (1994). Integration of social services in education: A process of development. In C. Reigeluth & R. Garfinkle (Eds.), *Systemic change in education* (pp. 139-145). Englewood Cliffs, NJ: Educational Technology Publications. (ED 367 055)

Carr, A. (1997a). User-design in the creation of human learning systems. *Educational Technology Research and Development, 45*(3), 5-22. (EJ 552 523)

Carr, A. (1997b). Leadership and community participation: Four case studies. *Journal of Curriculum and Supervision, 12*(2), 152-168. (EJ 535 751)

Carr, D., & Johansson, H. (1995). *Best practices in reengineering: What works and what doesn't in the reengineering process.* New York, NY: McGraw-Hill.

Chatterjee, P. (1990). *The transferability of social technology: Explorations in the knowledge structures of the helping professions and their transfer.* Lewiston, NY: E. Mellen Press.

Churchman, C. (1968). *The systems approach*. New York, NY: Delacorte Press.

Clinton, A. (1973). *A study of the attributes of educational innovations as factors in diffusion*. Unpublished doctoral dissertation, University of Toronto.

Collins, A., Morrison, D., & Newman, D. (1994). Putting technology to work for school reform. In C. Reigeluth & R. Garfinkle (Eds.), *Systemic change in education* (pp. 71-82). Englewood Cliffs, NJ: Educational Technology Publications. (ED 367 055)

Corbett, H., Dawson, J., & Firestone, W. (1984). *School context and school change*. New York, NY: Teachers College Press.

Corbett, H., Firestone, W., & Rossman, G. (1987). Resistance to planned change and the sacred in school cultures. *Educational Administration Quarterly, 23*, 36-59. (EJ 363 388)

Costa, A., & Liebmann, R. (1997). *The process-centered school: Sustaining a renaissance community*. Thousand Oaks, CA: Corwin Press. (ED 407 721)

Cox, P. (1983). *Inside-out and outside-in: Configurations of assistance and their impact on school improvement efforts*. Paper presented at the annual meeting of the American Educational Research Association, Montreal, Quebec, Canada. (ED 250 780)

Craig, R. (1996). *The ASTD training and development handbook: A guide to human resource development*. New York, NY: McGraw-Hill.

Cusick, P. (1973). *Inside high school*. Toronto, Ontario, Canada: Holt, Rinehart, & Winston.

D'Aprix, R. (1996). *Communicating for change: Connecting the workplace with the marketplace*. San Francisco, CA: Jossey-Bass.

Danzberger, J., Kirst, M., & Usdan, M. (1992). *Governing public schools: New times, new requirements*. Washington, DC: Institute for Educational Leadership. (ED 353 654)

Darling-Hammond, L. (1997). School reform at the crossroads: Confronting the central issues of teaching. *Educational Policy, 11*(2), 151-166. (EJ 547 270)

de Tarde, G. (1903). *The laws of imitation* (E. Parsons, Trans.). New York, NY: H. Holt & Company.

Directorate for Education and Human Resources. (1994). *Foundation for the future*. Washington, DC: National Science Foundation. (ED 370 808)

Ellsworth, J. (1997). Technology and change for the information age. *The Technology Source* [On-line journal]. Available: http://horizon.unc.edu/ts/vision/1997-10.asp

Ellsworth, J. (1998). Factors affecting participant reactions to new training devices. *Dissertation Abstracts International, 59*(08), 2938A. (University Microfilms No. AAI99-03405)

Elmore, R. (1980). *Complexity and control: What legislators and administrators can do about implementing public policy*. Washington, DC: National Institute of Education.

Ely, D. (1976). Creating the conditions for change. In S. Faibisoff and G. Bonn (Eds.), *Changing times: Changing libraries* (pp. 150-162). Champaign, IL: University of Illinois Graduate School of Library Science. (ED 183 139)

Ely, D. (1990a). Conditions that facilitate the implementation of educational technology innovations. *Journal of Research on Computing in Education, 23*(2), 298-305. (EJ 421 756)

Ely, D. (1990b). The diffusion and implementation of educational technology in developing nations: Cross-cultural comparisons of Indonesia, Chile, and Peru. *Instructional Developments, 1*(1), 9-12. (EJ 331 469)

Elzinga, D., Gulledge, T., & Lee, C. (1999). *Business process engineering: Advancing the state of the art.* Norwell, MA: Kluwer Academic Publishers.

Etzioni, A. (1993). *The spirit of community: Rights, responsibilities, and the communitarian agenda.* New York, NY: Crown Publishers.

Field, M. (1988). *Bringing about curriculum change.* Blagdon, United Kingdom: Further Education Staff College. (ED 324 549)

Flamholtz, E., & Randle, Y. (1998). *Changing the game: Organizational transformations of the first, second, and third kinds.* New York, NY: Oxford University Press.

Foley, J. (1997). *Success in restructuring: A step-by-step recipe.* Paper presented at the annual meeting of the Association for Supervision and Curriculum Development, Scottsdale, AZ. (ED 409 607)

Freidus, H., & Grose, C. (1998). *Implementing curriculum change: Lessons from the field.* Paper presented at the annual meeting of the American Educational Research Association, San Diego, CA. (ED 422 606)

Fuhrman, S., Clune, W., & Elmore, R. (1988). Research on education reform: Lessons on the implementation of policy. *Teachers College Record, 90*(2), 237-257.

Fullan, M. (1980). *The role of human agents internal to school districts in knowledge utilization.* San Francisco, CA: Far West Laboratory For Educational Research and Development. (ED 203 459)

Fullan, M. (1982). *The meaning of educational change.* New York, NY: Teachers College Press. (ED 218 247)

Fullan, M. (1988). *What's worth fighting for in the principalship: Strategies for taking charge in the elementary school principalship.* Toronto, Ontario, Canada: Ontario Public School Teachers' Federation. (ED 342 127)

Fullan, M. (1993). Why teachers must become change agents. *Educational Leadership, 50*(6), 12-17. (EJ 459 419)

Fullan, M. (1994). *School development and the management of change series: Vol. 10. Change forces: Probing the depths of educational reform.* Bristol, PA: Falmer Press. (ED 373 391)

Fullan, M., & Hargreaves, A. (1996). *What's worth fighting for in your school?* (Rev. ed.). New York, NY: Teachers College Press. (ED 401 622)

Fullan, M., & Newton, E. (1988). School principals and change processes in the secondary school. *Canadian Journal of Education, 13*(3), 404-422. (EJ 396 071)

Fullan, M., & Stiegelbauer, S. (1991). *The new meaning of educational change.* New York, NY: Teachers College Press. (ED 354 588)

Gardner, J. (1991). *Building community.* Washington, DC: American Institutes for Research.

Gardner, J. (1994). *The importance of community.* Palo Alto, CA: American Institutes for Research.

Garland, K. (1991). Diffusion and adoption of instructional technology. In G. Anglin (Ed.), *Instructional technology: Past, present, and future* (pp. 253-258). Englewood, CO: Libraries Unlimited, Incorporated.

Gayeski, D. (1999). Learned disabilities: How to re-invent your training system and revise its real lessons. *Performance Improvement, 38*(1), 6-9.

Gjerde, P. (1983). *An Interactional model for resistance to change in educational institutions.* Paper presented at the annual meeting of the American Psychological Association, Anaheim, CA. (ED 234 917)

Goddu, R. (1976). *Developing effective extension agents: Experience concerns.* Durham, NH: New England Program in Teacher Education. (ED 127 309)

Hahn, C. (1974). Relationships between potential adopters' perceptions of social studies innovations and their adoption of these innovations in Indiana, Ohio, Georgia, and Florida. *Dissertation Abstracts International, 35*(09), 5679A. (University Microfilms No. AAI75-05558)

Halal, W., & Smith, R. (1998). *The infinite resource: Creating and leading the knowledge enterprise.* San Francisco, CA: Jossey-Bass.

Hall, G. (1978). *Implications for planned dissemination, implementation, and evaluation revealed in the SRI/NDN evaluation and Levels of Use of the innovation studies.* Paper presented at the annual meeting of the American Educational Research Association, Toronto, Ontario, Canada. (ED 190 626)

Hall, G., George, A., & Rutherford, W. (1977). *Measuring Stages of Concern about the innovation: A manual for use of the SoC Questionnaire.* Austin, TX: The University of Texas at Austin, Research and Development Center for Teacher Education. (ED 147 342)

Hall, G., & Hord, S. (1987). *Change in schools: Facilitating the process.* Albany, NY: State University of New York Press. (ED 332 261)

Hall, G., Loucks, S., Rutherford, W., & Newlove, B. (1975). Levels of Use of the innovation: A framework for analyzing innovation adoption. *Journal of Teacher Education, 26*(1), 52-56. (EJ 115 168)

Hall, G., Newlove, B., George, A., Rutherford, W., & Hord, S. (1991). *Measuring change facilitator Stages of Concern: A manual for use of the CFSoC Questionnaire.* Greeley, CO: Center for Research on Teaching and Learning. (ED 353 307)

Hall, G., & Rutherford, W. (1983). *Client concerns: A guide to facilitating institutional change.* Austin, TX: The University of Texas at Austin, Research and Development Center for Teacher Education. (ED 251 728)

Hall, G., Wallace, R., & Dossett, W. (1973). *A developmental conception of the adoption process within educational institutions* (Report No. 3006). Austin, TX: The University of Texas at Austin, Research and Development Center for Teacher Education.

Halloran, M. (1984). *Class size and academic achievement.* (ED 260 845)

Hamilton, J., & Thompson, A. (1992). The adoption and diffusion of an electronic network for education. In M. Simonson and K. Jurasek (Eds.), *Proceedings of selected research paper presentations at the convention of the Association for Educational Communications and Technology, Washington, DC.* (ED 347 991)

Hammer, M. (1996). *Beyond reengineering: How the process-centered organization is changing our work and our lives.* New York, NY: Harper Business.

Hammer, M., & Champy, J. (1993). *Reengineering the corporation: A manifesto for business revolution.* New York, NY: Harper Business.

Harris, J. (1997). Who to hook and how: Advice for teacher trainers. *Learning and Leading with Technology, 24*(7), 54-57. (EJ 544 740)

Harvey, B. (1994). *The effect of class size on achievement and retention in the primary grades: Implications for policy makers.* Paper presented at the annual meeting of the North Carolina Association for Research in Education, Greensboro, NC. (ED 369 172)

Harvey, T., & Wehmeyer, L. (1990). *Checklist for change: A pragmatic approach to creating and controlling change.* Needham Heights, MA: Allyn & Bacon.

Haryono, A. (1990). Lecturer's perceptions of the conditions that facilitate the adoption and implementation of an instructional innovation introduced through a training program in higher education in Indonesia. *Dissertation Abstracts International, 52*(06), 2036A. (University Microfilms No. AAI91-26117)

Havelock, R. (1971). *Training for change agents: A guide to design of training programs in education and other fields.* Ann Arbor, MI: Ann Arbor Institute for Social Research. (ED 056 259)

Havelock, R. (1973). *The change agent's guide to innovation in education.* Englewood Cliffs, NJ: Educational Technology Publications. (ED 071 413)

Havelock, R., & Zlotolow, S. (1995). *The change agent's guide,* Second Edition. Englewood Cliffs, NJ: Educational Technology Publications. (ED 381 886)

Hawley, C. (1997). Systemic change in education: A road map. *Educational Technology, 37*(6), 57-64. (EJ 555 776)

Haynes, K., & Blomstedt, R. (1986). *The principal and educational change.* (ED 280 144)

Hebard, C. (1998). A story of real change. *Training & Development, 52*(7), 47-50 [On-line journal]. Available: http://www.astd.org/CMS/templates/index.html?template_id=1&articleid=12380 (ED 567 153)

Hillery, G. (1972). *Social structure and resistance to change.* Paper presented at the Third World Congress for Rural Sociology, Baton Rouge, LA. (ED 068 245)

Hinnant, E., & Oliva, L. (1997). Strategies for the integration of technology into teaching. In J. Morrison (Ed.), *Technology tools for today's campuses* [CD-ROM]. Redmond, WA: Microsoft Corporation.

Hirth, M. (1996). Systemic reform, equity, and school finance reform: Essential policy linkages. *Educational Policy, 10*(4), 468-479. (EJ 535 730)

Hirumi, A. (1995). Systems theory lesson [On-line]. Available: http://ide.ed.psu.edu/change/lessonoutline.html

Holloway, R. (1978). *Perceived characteristics of an innovation.* Paper presented at the annual meeting of the American Educational Research Association, Toronto, Ontario, Canada. (ED 150 716)

Holmes Group. (1995). *Tomorrow's schools of education: A report of the Holmes Group.* East Lansing, MI: Author. (ED 399 220)

Honig, B. (1994). How can Horace best be helped? *Phi Delta Kappan, 75*(10), 790-796. (EJ 486 337)

Hope, W. (1995). Microcomputer technology: Its impact on teachers in an elementary school. *Dissertation Abstracts International, 56*(03), 779A. (University Microfilms No. AAI95-26491) (ED 384 336)

Hord, S., Rutherford, W., Huling-Austin, L., & Hall, G. (1987). *Taking charge of change.* Alexandria, VA: Association for Supervision and Curriculum Development. (ED 282 876)

Horsley, D., Terry, W., Hergert, L., & Loucks-Horsley, S. (1991). *Managing change in rural schools: An action guide.* Andover, MA: Regional Laboratory for Educational Improvement of the Northeast & Islands. (ED 340 553)

Hull, C., & Rudduck, J. (1980). *Introducing innovation to pupils.* Norwich, United Kingdom: University of East Anglia, Centre for Applied Research in Education. (ED 188 953)

Humphreys, P. (1997). *Decision support in organizational transformation: IFIP TC8 WG8.3 International Conference on Organizational Transformation and Decision Support.* London, United Kingdom: Chapman & Hall.

Hutchins, C. (1994). State systems of education and systemic change. In C. Reigeluth & R. Garfinkle (Eds.), *Systemic change in education* (pp. 15-25). Englewood Cliffs, NJ: Educational Technology Publications. (ED 367 055)

Information Infrastructure Working Group. (1996). *Supporting Minnesota's information infrastructure* [On-line]. Available: http://www.state.mn.us/ebranch/admin/iiwgr.html

Jacobus, K. (1997). *A study of the change process utilized by Colorado high school principals: The concordance of practice and theory.* Paper presented at the annual meeting of the American Educational Research Association, Chicago, IL. (ED 407 742)

Jenks, C. (1994). Evaluating an educational system systemically. In C. Reigeluth & R. Garfinkle (Eds.), *Systemic change in education* (pp. 35-41). Englewood Cliffs, NJ: Educational Technology Publications. (ED 367 055)

Johnson, R. (1969). *Resistance: A precondition for change.* (ED 027 898)

Jorgensen, M. (1993). The promise of alternative assessment. *School Administrator, 50*(11), 17-23. (EJ 475 772)

Juechter, W., Fisher, C., & Alford, R. (1998). Five conditions for high-performance cultures. *Training & Development* [On-line journal]. Available: http://www.astd. org/CMS/templates/index.html?template_id=1&articleid=11674

Kalapothakos, A. (1996). *Pre-kindergarten to eighth grade teachers become change agents through active participation in school reform.* Unpublished doctoral practicum, Nova Southeastern University. (ED 401 014)

Kaufman, C., & Paulston, R. (1991). Hungarian education in transition. Paper presented at the annual conference of the American Educational Research Association, Chicago, IL. (ED 335 275)

Kaufman, R., Watkins, R., Triner, D., & Smith, M. (1998). The changing corporate mind: Organizations, visions, mission, purposes, and indicators on the move toward societal payoff. *Performance Improvement Quarterly, 11*(3), 32-44.

Kearns, K. (1992). Innovations in local governments: A socio-cognitive network approach. *Knowledge and Policy, 5*(2), 45-67.

Kell, D., Harvey, G., & Drexler, N. (1990). *Educational technology and the restructuring movement: Lessons from research on computers in classrooms.* Paper presented at the annual conference of the American Educational Research Association, Boston, MA. (ED 326 195)

Kember, D., & Mezger, R. (1990). The instructional designer as a staff developer: A course team approach consistent with a Concerns-Based Adoption Model. *Distance Education, 11*(1), 50-70. (EJ 415 316)

Kemp, J. (1995). *A school changes.* Washington, DC: Association for Educational Communications and Technology.

Kemp, J. (1996). School restructuring: Your school can do it! *TechTrends, 41*(1), 12-15. (EJ 518 403)

Kirkpatrick, D. (1994). *Evaluating training programs: The four levels.* San Francisco, CA: Berret-Koehler. (ED 382 790)

Klir, G. (1969). *An approach to general systems theory.* New York, NY: Van Nostrand Reinhold Company.

Kramlinger, T. (1998). How to deliver a change message. *Training & Development, 52*(4), 44-47. (EJ 562 252)

Krueger, R. (1994). *Focus groups: A practical guide for applied research.* Thousand Oaks, CA: Sage Publications.

LaGuardia, C., & Mitchell, B. (1998). *Finding common ground: Creating the library of the future without diminishing the library of the past.* New York, NY: Neal-Schuman Publishers. (ED 417 746)

Leibfried, K., & McNair, C. (1992). *Benchmarking: A tool for continuous improvement.* New York, NY: Harper Business.

Leithwood, K., & Montgomery, D. (1982). The role of the elementary school principal in program improvement: A review. *Review of Educational Research, 52*(3), 309-339. (EJ 273 688)

Lindquist, J. (1978). *Strategies for change.* Berkeley, CA: Pacific Soundings Press. (ED 200 113)

Lippitt, R., Watson, J., & Westley, B. (1958). *The dynamics of planned change: A comparative study of principles and techniques.* New York, NY: Harcourt, Brace.

Loucks, S. (1983). *The Concerns-Based Adoption Model (CBAM)* (Series Paper No. 2). Chapel Hill, NC: University of North Carolina–Chapel Hill, Technical Assistance Development System. (ED 233 524)

Louis, K., & Rosenblum, S. (1981). Linking R&D with schools: A program and its implications for dissemination and school improvement policy. Washington, DC: National Institute of Education. (ED 207 262)

Manning, G., Curtis, K., & McMillen, S. (1996). *Building community: The human side of work.* Cincinnati, OH: Thomson Executive Press.

Marlow, E., & Wilson, P. (1997). *The breakdown of hierarchy: Communicating in the evolving workplace.* Boston, MA: Butterworth-Heinemann.

Maromonte, K. (1996). *Building the invisible quality corporation: The executive guide to transcending TQM.* Westport, CT: Quorum Books.

Marovitz, M. (1994). The diffusion of educational television at the United States Military Academy. *Dissertation Abstracts International, 55*(08), 2354A. (University Microfilms No. AAI94-33994)

Marsh, D., Pelland, R., Melle, M., & Cooke, M. (1985). *Utilizing teacher concerns to mediate staff development efforts.* Paper presented at the annual meeting of the American Educational Research Association, Chicago, IL. (ED 263 070)

McIntyre, W., & Marion, S. (1989). *The relationship of class size to student achievement: What the research says* (Occasional Paper Series No. 3). Orono, ME: University of Maine, Orono College of Education. (ED 323 643)

McNamara, E., Grant, C., & Wasser, J. (1998). Putting it all together. *Hands On, 21*(1), 10-13. (EJ 566 728)

Means, B., Blando, J., Olson, K., Middleton, T., Morocco, C., Remz, A., & Zorfass, J. (1993). *Using technology to support education reform.* Washington, DC: Association for Educational Communications and Technology. (Reprinted from OERI Contract No. RR91172010, Washington, DC: U.S. Government Printing Office) (ED 364 220)

Millard, J. (1977). *Small classes? What research says about effective class sizes and possible alternatives to small classes.* Ankeny, IA: Heartland Education Agency. (ED 133 897)

Miller, N. (1994). Toward a common vision: The change process in practice. In C. Reigeluth & R. Garfinkle (Eds.), *Systemic change in education* (pp. 147-154). Englewood Cliffs, NJ: Educational Technology Publications. (ED 367 055)

Minogue, M., Polidano, C., & Hulme, D. (1998). *Beyond the new public management: Changing ideas and practices in governance.* Northampton, MA: E. Elgar.

Mitchell, R. (1994). Measuring up: Student assessment and systemic change. In C. Reigeluth & R. Garfinkle (Eds.), *Systemic change in education* (pp. 127-135). Englewood Cliffs, NJ: Educational Technology Publications. (ED 367 055)

Mitchell, R. (1995). *The promise of performance assessments: How to use backlash constructively.* Paper presented at the annual meeting of the American Educational Research Association, San Francisco, CA. (ED 382 677)

Mitchell, S. (1988). *Applications of the Concerns-Based Adoption Model in program evaluation.* Paper presented at the annual meeting of the American Education Research Association, New Orleans, LA. (ED 301 940)

Mone, E., & London, M. (1998). *HR to the rescue: Case studies of HR solutions to business challenges.* Houston, TX: Gulf.

Moore, G., & Benbasat, I. (1990). *An examination of the adoption of information technology by end-users: A diffusion of innovations perspective* (Working Paper 90-MIS-012). Vancouver, British Columbia, Canada: University of British Columbia, Department of Commerce and Business Administration.

Morgan, R. (1994). Educational reform: Top-down or bottom-up? In C. Reigeluth & R. Garfinkle (Eds.), *Systemic change in education* (pp. 43-50). Englewood Cliffs, NJ: Educational Technology Publications. (ED 367 055)

Newell, S. (1992, April). *Science teachers' perspectives on alternate assessment.* Paper presented at the annual meeting of the American Educational Research Association, San Francisco, CA. (ED 346 159)

Newton, D. (1992). *Whole Language: What is It?* (ED 354 494)

Nies, J., & LaBrecque, S. (1980). *Creating change.* Washington, DC: Home Economics Education Association. (ED 199 567)

Office of Educational Research and Improvement. (1994). *Intermediate benchmarks for systemic reform in mathematics and science education.* Washington, DC: U.S. Department of Education. (ED 405 177)

Olivier, M. (1971). *A review of literature: Training and the change process. (ED 083 142)*

Pipho, C. (1994). School finance in a transformed education system. In C. Reigeluth & R. Garfinkle (Eds.), *Systemic change in education* (pp. 103-108). Englewood Cliffs, NJ: Educational Technology Publications. (ED 367 055)

Poole, W. (1991). *Resistance to change in education: Themes in the literature.* Unpublished manuscript, Syracuse University. (ED 330 307)

Poole, W. (1995). Reconstructing the teacher-administrator relationship to achieve systemic change. *Journal of School Leadership, 5*(6), 595-596. (EJ 516 001)

Porter, A., & Read, W. (1998). *The information revolution: Current and future consequences.* Greenwich, CT: Ablex.

Powell, D., & Hyle, A. (1997). Principals and school reform: Barriers to inclusion in three secondary schools. *Journal of School Leadership, 7*(4), 301-326. (EJ 547 325)

Price Waterhouse Change Integration Group. (1995). *Better change: Best practices for transforming your organization.* Burr Ridge, IL: Irwin Professional.

Quality Resources/The Kraus Organization. (1994). *Beyond the basics of reengineering: Survival tactics for the '90s.* White Plains, NY: Industrial Engineering and Management Press, Institute of Industrial Engineers.

Read, C. (1994). Conditions that facilitate the use of shared decision-making in schools. *Dissertation Abstracts International, 55*(08), 2239A. (University Microfilms No. AAI94-34003)

Reigeluth, C. (1994). Introduction: The imperative for systemic change. In C. Reigeluth & R. Garfinkle (Eds.), *Systemic change in education* (pp. 3-11). Englewood Cliffs, NJ: Educational Technology Publications. (ED 367 055)

Reigeluth, C., & Garfinkle, R. (1994a). Envisioning a new system of education. In C. Reigeluth & R. Garfinkle (Eds.), *Systemic change in education* (pp. 59-70). Englewood Cliffs, NJ: Educational Technology Publications. (ED 367 055)

Reigeluth, C., & Garfinkle, R., Eds. (1994b). *Systemic change in education.* Englewood Cliffs, NJ: Educational Technology Publications. (ED 367 055)

Richie, M. (1994). *Quality management for educational technology services.* Washington, DC: Association for Educational Communications and Technology. (ED 382 158)

Riley, M. (1995). Conditions that facilitate implementation of a career development program to promote gender equity in middle and junior high schools. *Dissertation Abstracts International, 56*(09), 3440A. (University Microfilms No. AAI95-44945)

Rogers, E. (1962). *Diffusion of innovations.* New York, NY: The Free Press.

Rogers, E. (1973). *Communication strategies for family planning.* New York, NY: The Free Press.

Rogers, E. (1995). *Diffusion of innovations,* Fourth Edition. New York, NY: The Free Press.

Rose, S. (1982). Barriers to the use of educational technologies and recommendations to promote and increase their use. *Educational Technology, 22*(12), 12-15.

Ross, J., & Regan, E. (1990). Self-reported strategies of experienced and inexperienced curriculum consultants: Exploring differences. *The Alberta Journal of Educational Research, 36*(2), 157-180. Rubinstein, R., Hersh, H., & Ledgard, H. (1984). *The human factor: Designing computer systems for people.* Burlington, MA: Digital Press.

Rundell, C. (1994). To start a school: NASDC as a catalyst for systemic change. In C. Reigeluth & R. Garfinkle (Eds.), *Systemic change in education* (pp. 53-58). Englewood Cliffs, NJ: Educational Technology Publications. (ED 367 055)

Rutherford, W. (1986). *Teachers' contributions to school improvement: Reflections on fifteen years of research* (Report No. 3219). Austin, TX: University of Texas at Austin, Research and Development Center for Teacher Education.

Ryan, B., & Gross, N. (1943). The diffusion of hybrid seed corn in two Iowa communities. *Rural Sociology, 8,* 15-24.

Salisbury, D. (1996). *Five technologies for educational change.* Englewood Cliffs, NJ: Educational Technology Publications.

Sarason, S. (1982). *The culture of the school and the problem of change* (Rev. ed.). Needham Heights, MA: Allyn & Bacon.

Schieman, E. & Fiordo, R. (1990). *Barriers to adoption of instructional communications technology in higher education.* Paper presented at the Australian Communications Conference, Melbourne, Australia. (ED 329 244)

Schön, D. (1983). *The reflective practitioner: How professionals think in action.* New York, NY: Basic Books.

Seligman, M. (1991). *Learned optimism.* New York, NY: Pocket Books.

Senge, P. (1990). *The fifth discipline: The art and practice of the learning organization.* New York, NY: Doubleday.

Senge, P., Kleiner, A., Roberts, C., Ross, R., Roth, G., & Smith, B. (1999). *The dance of change: The challenges of sustaining momentum in learning organizations.* New York, NY: Currency/Doubleday.

Sevilla, J., & Marsh, D. (1992). *Inquiry-oriented science programs: New perspectives on the implementation process.* Paper presented at the annual meeting of the American Educational Research Association, San Francisco, CA. (ED 381 371)

Shih, M., & Zvacek, S. (1991). Distance education in Taiwan: A model validated. In M. Simonson & C. Hargrave (Eds.), *Proceedings of selected research paper presentations at the convention of the Association for Educational Communications and Technology, Orlando, FL.* (ED 335 013)

Shneiderman, B. (1987). *Designing the user interface: Strategies for effective human-computer interaction.* Reading, MA: Addison-Wesley.

Shotsberger, P., & Crawford, A. (1996). *An analysis of the validity and reliability of the Concerns Based Adoption Model for teacher concerns in education reform.* Paper presented at the annual meeting of the American Educational Research Association, New York, NY. (ED 400 278)

Sims, R. (1998). *Accountability and radical change in public organizations.* Westport, CT: Quorum Books.

Slotnik, W. (1993). Core concepts of reform. *Executive Educator, 15*(12), 32-34. (EJ 474 263)

Smith, M., O'Day, J., & Fuhrman, S. (1994). State policy and systemic school reform. In C. Reigeluth & R. Garfinkle (Eds.), *Systemic change in education* (pp. 109-118). Englewood Cliffs, NJ: Educational Technology Publications. (ED 367 055)

Smith, W., & Andrews, R. (1989). *Instructional leadership: How principals make a difference.* Alexandria, VA: Association for Supervision and Curriculum Development. (ED 314 826)

Southeastern Regional Vision for Education. (1992). *What teachers have to say about creating innovations in education: Proceedings from the Sharing Success Forum, Orlando, FL.* (ED 348 755)

Spence, W. (1994). *Innovation: The communication of change in ideas, practices and products.* London, United Kingdom: Chapman & Hall.

Stephens, E. (1994). The "new" federal and state education agenda. In G. Karim & N. Weate (Eds.), *Toward the 21st century: A rural education anthology, Vol. 1.* Oak Brook, IL: North Central Regional Education Lab. (ED 401 076)

Stiegelbauer, S. (1982). *Acculturation and the change process: An exploratory formulation from an applied model for research and facilitation.* Paper presented at the annual meeting of the American Educational Research Association, New York, NY. (ED 222 514)

Stolovitch, H., & Keeps, E. (1999). *Handbook of human performance technology: A comprehensive guide for analyzing and solving performance problems in organizations.* San Francisco, CA: Jossey-Bass/Pfeiffer.

Strebel, P. (1992). *Breakpoints: How managers exploit radical business change.* Boston, MA: Harvard Business School Press.

Theron, A., & van der Westhuizen, P. (1996). *The management of resistance to change and polarity in educational organizations.* Paper presented at the annual meeting of the American Educational Research Association, New York, NY. (ED 396 394)

Thompson, J. (1994). Systemic education reform. ERIC Digest Number 90 [On-line]. Available: http://www.ed.gov/databases/ERIC_Digests/ed370178.html (ED 370 178)

Thompson, S. (1998). Moving from publicity to engagement. *Educational Leadership, 55*(8), 54-57. (EJ 565 131)

Thornton, S., & Spiesberger, B. (1994). *Transforming schools: Finding success for students at risk through systemic change.* Sacramento, CA: Resources in Special Education. (ED 383 156)

Tichy, N., & Cohen, E. (1998). The teaching organization. *Training & Development, 52*(7), 26-37. (EJ 567 152)

Tilkin, S., & Hyle, A. (1997). *The change to inclusion: Five case studies in one district.* Paper presented at the annual meeting of the University Council of Educational Administration, Orlando, FL. (ED 415 635)

Toffler, A. (1980). *The third wave.* New York, NY: Morrow.

Toffler, A. & Toffler, H. (1993). *War and anti-war: Survival at the dawn of the twenty-first century.* Boston, MA: Little, Brown & Company.

Valente, T. (1995). *Network models of the diffusion of innovations.* Cresskill, NJ: Hampton Press.

van den Berg, R. (1993). The Concerns-Based Adoption Model in the Netherlands, Flanders and the United Kingdom: State of the art and perspective. *Studies in Educational Evaluation, 19*(1), 51-63. (EJ 461 978)

van Fleet, C., & Durrance, J. (1993). Public library leaders and research: Mechanisms, perceptions, and strategies. *Journal of Education for Library and Information Science, 34*(2), 137-152. (EJ 464 414)

von Bertalanffy, L. (1956). General system theory. *General Systems, 1,* 1-10.

Waldrop, P., & Adams, T. (1988). *Overcoming resistance to the use of instructional computing in higher education.* (ED 296 656)

Wasley, P., Hampel, R., & Clark, R. (1997). The puzzle of whole-school change. *Phi Delta Kappan, 78*(9), 690-697. (EJ 544 328)

Watkins, K., & Marsick, V. (1993). *Sculpting the learning organization: Lessons in the art and science of systemic change.* San Francisco, CA: Jossey-Bass. (ED 365 852)

Watkins, R., Leigh, D., Foshay, R., & Kaufman, R. (1998). Kirkpatrick plus: Evaluation and continuous improvement with a community focus. *Educational Technology Research and Development, 46*(4), 90-96. (EJ 582 179)

Webster's New Collegiate Dictionary. (1979). Springfield, MA: G. & C. Merriam Company.

Wesley, M., & Franks, M. (1996). *Advanced adoption of computer technology in the classroom and teachers' participation in voluntary innovation adoption activities.* Paper presented at the annual meeting of the Mid-South Educational Research Association, Tuscaloosa, AL. (ED 402 907)

Wiggam, L. (1994). Expanding the sphere: The importance of effective communications in change. In C. Reigeluth & R. Garfinkle (Eds.), *Systemic change in education* (pp. 155-161). Englewood Cliffs, NJ: Educational Technology Publications. (ED 367 055)

Williams, S. (1994). Do charter schools offer real promise or false hope? In C. Reigeluth & R. Garfinkle (Eds.), *Systemic change in education* (pp. 83-93). Englewood Cliffs, NJ: Educational Technology Publications. (ED 367 055)

Zakariya, S. (1996). Change agent. *Executive Educator, 18*(1), 10-15. (EJ 516 062)

Zaltman, G., & Duncan, R. (1977). *Strategies for planned change.* New York, NY: John Wiley and Sons.

Bibliography

ERIC Documents

Barr, R., & Parrett, W. (1997). *How to create alternative, magnet, and charter schools that work.* Bloomington, IN: National Educational Service. (ED 419 266)

In the early 1970s, pessimism about public education in the United States was on the rise. To counter this outlook, researchers held a conference to identify public schools that were humane, caring, and effective–and from this conference arose a heightened awareness of alternative schools and their place in education. Subsequent years of investigating these effective schools produced numerous insights, many of which are offered in this book. Chapter 1 offers an overview of the difficulties that plagued and continue to trouble public education. Chapter 2 examines these places and offers examples of what makes alternative schools so appealing. Chapter 3 focuses on why these schools are so effective, and Chapter 4 profiles models of established alternative schools. How to start an alternative school is the focus of Chapter 5, and this chapter is followed by an examination of magnet schools and charter schools. Six appendices contain answers to frequently asked questions, evaluation criteria, names of support organizations, sample alternative schools and programs, sample charter schools, and charter school support contacts.

Beck, C., & Schornack, G. (1998). *Understanding educational change: A systems model approach.* Paper presented at the Second North American Conference on the Learning Paradigm, San Diego, CA. (ED 420 906)

This paper explores the use of a series of heuristic models that identify the interrelated components of the broader educational process. This heuristic schema was designed so that educators can examine the purpose and limitations associated with models and subsequently enhance their ability to guide changes within their own institutional setting. The paper begins examining the purpose and limitations associated with models as a means of analysis. Building on a systems perspective, it then discusses the way in which the communication process expands a basic system. The paper suggests that the Learning Paradigm, as well as the Educational Process, follow the Rhetorical Process. Since the Educational Process essentially extends the Rhetorical Process, the categories for analysis in the Learning Paradigm parallel the elements of the Rhetorical Process. Developing these categories more completely yields the Educational Process, thus leading to the identification of the interrelated elements that comprise an educational system. An elaboration of these elements constitutes the bulk of the paper. Since educational change requires extensive communication, the Transactional Model of Communication is presented to identify the difficulties encountered in reaching consensus.

Benham, M. (1999). *Case studies for school administrators: Managing change in education.* Lancaster, PA: Technomic Publishing Company, Inc. (ED 429 332)

This book examines case-based learning in educational leadership courses, discusses case-based learning as an educational tool, exemplifies methods of writing a case study, and contains fourteen case studies by teachers and administrators. "Stakeholders in a House of Cards," by Audrey Burgher, discusses integrating technology with innovation. "Reforming Vocational Educational Programs: Change Among a Veteran Staff," by Sally Lib, looks at curriculum updating. "South Side Middle School: A Magnet Program in an Urban Setting," by Margaret Flowers, reviews implementation of an urban magnet school. "An Example of Curriculum Change through Manipulation," by Megan Russo, explores English curriculum revision. "Red-Green School District Bond Proposal," by Jan C. Amsterburg, chronicles a bond proposal and outcome. "Change from the Outside In," by Cary Trexler, focuses on infusion of outside resources. "Restructuring: An Exercise in Futility?" by Robert Van Camp, examines common planning time for teachers. "Block-Scheduling Failure at Montgomery High," by Maria Schleeter, examines attempts to reduce teachers' workload. "Murder at Seneca School," by Linda Amato, relates a shooting incident resulting from a teacher's layoff. "The New Principal: Innovation for Innovation's Sake," by Karen Huff, describes the firing of a new principal. "The Parking Lot Case: A Case of Principal Succession," by Stephen Marsden, looks at the effects of changing parking lot assignments. "It's for Children: Successful Inclusion Programs," by Norma Schutzki, examines mainstreaming emotionally impaired students. "A Case of Change: Strategic Planning," by Darleen Tanner, looks at developing grassroots empowerment. "To Be or Not To Be a Middle School," by Ann Tebo, discusses middle-school restructuring. Case studies also include commentaries by the case-author, a teacher-leader or administrator, and an educational scholar-researcher. Each study and set of commentaries is followed by a list of references.

Brandt, R. (1999). *No one best way–but many very good ways.* Paper presented at the annual conference and exhibit of the Association for Supervision and Curriculum Development, San Francisco, CA. (ED 430 732)

Noting that variety in education may be seen as a basic mechanism for change, this paper examines four important developments in public education: (1) site-based decision making; (2) charter schools; (3) whole school designs; and (4) parent choice. The paper maintains that site-based decision making should involve giving schools authority and responsibility for solving their own problems and then leading them to improve rather than just leaving schools alone to solve their problems. The paper further notes that although the growth of charter schools illustrates the potential for future entrepreneurs' efforts in education, there probably will not be any entirely new models of education invented. The paper advocates whole school programming, or comprehensive school reform, and describes examples of successful implementation of externally developed and designed school programs. Also noted is the importance of careful evaluation to determine if such programs produce results, and concern that the leadership and support needed to successfully implement educational models may be underestimated. Finally, the paper suggests that some degree of choice is an essential part of the emerging model of schooling and that parent choice is necessary with greater variety of educational models. The paper also maintains that education can be successful only when parents and teachers share a common philosophy, and advocates the development of a model moderating individual choice by limiting available choices to those approved by a responsible public agency. A recommendation for working toward deliberate educational variety concludes the paper.

Brown, D., McIntyre, W., & Perry, C. (1996). *Systemic change and the role of school boards.* Paper presented at the annual meeting of the American Educational Research Association, New York, NY. (ED 399 105)

Since 1992, Maine has received National Science Foundation Statewide Systemic Initiative (SSI) program monies. SSI is a model for improvement of mathematics and science education based on systemic reform. The SSI initiative in Maine has created seven "Beacon School" sites that vary in size and location including high poverty areas, urban areas, and rural areas. Each site is supported by a grant of $50,000 per year for five years plus two full-time on-site facilitators. In view of Maine's long history of local control of education, this study examined whether the SSI program influenced nine local school boards responsible for Beacon School sites to change policies, agendas, or behaviors. School board policy audits examined the adoption date of new or revised policies and analyzed current policies related to organizational structure, decision making, resources, professional development, and instruction. Secondly, a review of school board minutes from prior to project implementation through the first two project years examined what issues were addressed and what kind of decisions or actions took place. Data indicate that the SSI program impacted local policy makers as evidenced by a decrease in budget actions and an increase in personnel and academic/curriculum actions at board meetings; an increase in the number of policies adopted or revised related to communication, decision making, and instruction; and increased board interest and time spent discussing the Beacon project and systemic change. The findings suggest that school boards can be responsive to programs supportive of systemic change and that boards themselves, through their policy-setting mandates, can play a positive role in engendering systemic change. Includes data tables.

Brunner, I., & Davidson, B. (1998). *The dissemination of educational innovations: New insights into the coaching model.* Paper presented at the annual meeting of the American Educational Research Association, San Diego, CA. (ED 425 523)

Ways in which program innovators, policy developers, and educational researchers think about and engage in disseminating innovations to schools can prove a major barrier to reform. A process for effective dissemination using the coaching model in the accelerated schools program is described here. Accelerated schools draw on three principles: unity of purpose, empowerment coupled with responsibility, and building on strengths. To help spread this philosophy, educators from the schools and from the central office are trained as primary disseminators. The rapid growth of accelerated schools is mainly due to these trained coaches who either work at the district level or who are responsible for the implementation of the accelerated schools model at their own school. An examination of an evolving coaching model at the University of New Orleans Accelerated Schools Center, a comparison of the effectiveness of district coaches versus in-house coaches, and an overview of the coaching model at the National Center for Accelerated Schools shows that the coaching model must be adapted for certain conditions. The National Center requires a large pool of highly qualified applicants to work full-time at offsite schools, which would not be feasible in smaller school districts.

Cibulka, J., & Kritek, W. (1996). *Coordination among schools, families, and communities: Prospects for educational reform.* Albany, NY: State University of New York Press. (ED 395 718)

Establishing coordination among schools, families, and communities has emerged as a major policy issue in the debate over the quality of education and how the restructuring of education should be accomplished. This book explores coordination of services for children and youth between and among schools, families, and community groups and agencies, as one process for dealing with the broad set of educational and social problems. The articles in the book are divided into three parts: models of coordination, organizational and management issues, and evaluation and critiques of coordination as a reform. Following an introduction by William Kritek which examines the impetus for renewed interest in coordination and its role in school reform, the article titles are: (1) "The Kentucky Family Resource Centers: The Challenges of Remaking Family-School Interactions" (Claire Smrekar); (2) "Visible Differences and Unseen Commonalities" (H. Dickson Corbet and others); (3) "Conflict and Consensus" (Paul Heckman and others); (4) "The Best of Both

Worlds" (Shirley Brice Heath and Milbrey McLaughlin); (5) "Educating Homeless Children" (Rebecca Newman and Lynn Beck); (6) "Structure and Strategies: Toward an Understanding of Alternative Models for Coordinated Children's Services" (Robert Crowson and William Lowe Boyd); (7) "The Principal and Community-School Connections in Chicago's Radical Reform" (Mark Smylie and others); (8) "Schools as Intergovernmental Partners" (Carolyn Herrington); (9) "Institutional Effects of Strategic Efforts at Community Enrichment" (Hanne Mawhinney); (10) "School-Business-University Collaboratives" (Patrick Galvin); (11) "Reforming American Education Policy for the Twenty-First Century" (Deborah Verstegen); (12) "We're Not Housed in an Institution, We're Housed in the Community" (Colleen Capper); (13) "Schools and Community Connections" (Gail Chase Furman and Carol Merz); (14) "Connecting Schools and Communities through Interagency Collaboration for School-Linked Services" (Debra Shaver and others); (15) "Beyond Consensus: Mapping Divergent Views of Systems and Power in Collaboratives" (Maureen McClure and others). A concluding article, "Toward an Interpretation of School, Family, and Community Connections: Policy Challenges" (James Cibulka) is included. Each of the articles contains notes and/or references.

Clark, K. (1996). *Human systems engineering: A leadership model for collaboration and change.* Paper presented at the National Conference of the Association for Global Business, Dallas, TX. (ED 401 448)

Human systems engineering (HSE) was created to introduce a new way of viewing collaboration. HSE emphasizes the role of leaders who welcome risk, commit to achieving positive change, and help others achieve change. The principles of HSE and its successful application to the collaborative process were illustrated through a case study representing a collaboration of leaders from a private-sector firm (XXsys Technologies, Inc.), the University of California at San Diego, the California Department of Transportation, and the National Institute for Standards and Technology for the purpose of applying composites for seismic retrofitting of bridge columns. The case study demonstrated that the HSE model differs from the strategic alliance model by virtue of the fact that strategic alliances focus on accomplishing a common goal whereas HSE emphasizes the recognition and achievement of individual goals for collaborating partners. The case study further established that HSE focuses on the following: individual goals rather than the common goal; maximum rather than minimum risk; the process rather than its outcomes; positive change rather than change in any form; people who do the job rather than getting the job done; and relying on the strengths of all participants rather than balancing strengths and weaknesses.

Cooper, R., Slavin, R., & Madden, N. (1998). *Success for all: Improving the quality of implementation of whole-school change through the use of a national reform network*. Paper presented at the annual meeting of the American Educational Research Association, Chicago, IL. (ED 420 107)

The role and importance of national reform network participation in the implementation of one of the most successful U.S. whole-school reform efforts–Success for ALL (SFA)–is profiled here. The paper explores this educational network beyond professional development and examines the relationship between participation in SFA's national reform network activities and the quality of program implementation. Part 1 briefly describes the SFA model for school change and its major components. Then, after presenting a theoretical framework for understanding educational networks and how they can be used in supporting whole-school change, the analysis turns to how network activities are used to facilitate quality implementation of SFA. Two types of network activities are explored: (1) participation in a national conference; and (2) participation in local support network activities. The findings illuminate key connections between network participation and the quality implementation of whole-school change. It is suggested that national reform network activities play a key role in the development and expansion of whole-school change models. Appended is a list of the variables explored under the headings outcome measures, program structure, and reading curriculum or strategies.

Education Commission of the States. (1998). *Comprehensive school reform: Criteria and questions*. Denver, CO: Author. (ED 428 428)

This booklet is designed to offer state and district policymakers a thoughtful set of questions to ask about school reform models and the organizations that develop them. The questions follow the criteria for school-wide reform as spelled out in the federal legislation. Policymakers are encouraged to consider these questions as they work with developers of school reform programs to effectively implement CSRD, the Comprehensive School Reform Development Project. CSRD is a program that allocates funds to states through Title I and the Fund for the Improvement of Education resources.

Educational Research Service. (1998). *Comprehensive models for school improvement: Finding the right match and making it work*. Arlington, VA: Author. (ED 422 632)

Comprehensive school improvement is based on reorganizing and revitalizing the entire school rather than focusing on specific student populations or programs. An overview of seventeen school wide reform programs is provided in this book. The purpose of the text is to give education leaders basic information about some of the best-known externally developed programs available. Each overview is based largely on promotional materials provided by the sponsoring organizations. The guide opens with a synopsis of the trend toward comprehensive school improvement–including notes on federal funding–and details how to choose the right comprehensive program for a school. The profiles of the seventeen comprehensive school-improvement programs are offered next, with much of the information being provided in a question-and-answer format. Whether or not a school or district should design its own comprehensive school-improvement program is addressed and some essential elements of homegrown programs are discussed. The section includes information about the components researchers recommend, including those in any comprehensive model. The text concludes with strategies for successfully implementing comprehensive school-improvement programs. A list of additional resources to aid further research is given.

Fullan, M. (1997). *The challenge of school change: A collection of articles.* Arlington Heights, IL: IRI/Skylight Training and Publishing. (ED 409 640)

Educators must combine a deeper analysis and understanding of the key concepts of change with a commitment and set of ideas for action. The articles in this book provide critical analysis and empirical and theoretical observations about successful school change. The articles explore the theories, leadership, and implementation strategies in educational reform. They address the problems that have led to the school-change movement and offer solutions and proposals for reform. Section 1 establishes some of the new theories of change. Section 2 takes a critical approach to examining new forms of leadership for change among educators. Section 3 offers examples of implementation at the school and community levels, drawing on recent empirical work. The final section introduces two new concepts–emotion and hope–arguing that the future of reform must embody these deeper personal and human characteristics in the educational reform process. Following the introduction, articles include: (1) "Rethinking Educational Change" (Andy Hargreaves); (2) "The Complexity of the Change Process" (Michael Fullan); (3) "Cultures of Teaching and Educational Change" (Andy Hargreaves); (4) "Chaotic Reflexivity" (Helen Gunter); (5) "Leadership for Change" (Michael Fullan); (6) "Teacher's Professional Development in a Climate of Educational Reform" (Judith Warren Little); (7) "Getting School-Based Management Right" (Priscilla Wohlstetter); (8) "Learning From School Restructuring" (Penelope L. Peterson, Sarah J. McCarthy, and Richard F. Elmore); (9) "Finding the Way: Structure, Time, and Culture in School" (Tom Donahoe); (10) "School/Family/Community Partnerships" (Joyce L. Epstein); and (11) "Emotion and Hope: Constructive Concepts for Complex Times" (Michael Fullan). References accompany each chapter; an index is included.

Gaff, J. (1999). *General education: The changing agenda; The academy in transition.* Washington, DC: Association of American Colleges and Universities. (ED 430 438)

The intent of this discussion paper is to provide a survey of emerging trends in general education reform at institutions of higher education. Ten themes are identified: (1) rethinking the major; (2) concern with student learning beyond course content; (3) an increased emphasis on diversity; (4) the importance of technology; (5) efficiency and effectiveness; (6) the need for more emphasis on implementation strategies in improving general education; (7) new administrative models; (8) the necessity of program assessment; (9) combining of change initiatives; and (10) convergence of two movements: one to improve general education and the other concerned with accountability, fiscal responsibility, and prudent management.

Gelberg, D. (1997). *The "business" of reforming American schools.* Albany, NY: State University of New York Press. (ED 422 637)

This book's central thesis is that the relationship between school managers and teachers predicts the type of education offered children. That is, education can be seen as a handing down of information, or it can be viewed as a cooperative affair. The text is divided into two parts: 1895-1925 and 1961-1995. Chapter 1, which discusses America's most commonly held beliefs, values, and assumptions at the turn of the century, is followed by a detailed description of the earlier design and implementation of school reform, a type of reform championed by a coalition of businessmen, school leaders, and education professors. A competing vision of school reform is then discussed in Chapter 3, in which the emphasis is on education for individual development and democracy. The second part of the book presents discussions on reforming education. It discusses the 1960s and the challenges to schools, the influence of the management model on education reform, and an analysis of how the now popular pro-efficiency model of education had its origins in the early 20th century. A case study illustrates this pro-efficiency model.

Gross, S. (1998). *Staying centered: Curriculum leadership in a turbulent era.* Alexandria, VA: Association for Supervision and Curriculum Development. (ED 420 094)

This book covers ten exemplary curriculum development sites, ranging from those that follow detailed state guidelines to those with few external mandates. All the examples are public schools, have been involved in the process of curriculum leadership for several years, and are geographically diverse. The book is organized around four questions: (1) "How did these institutions start the process of curriculum leadership?"; (2) "What successful curriculum plans have these schools and districts used?"; (3) "How do these sites sustain development over time?"; and (4) "How have these schools and districts survived turbulence and become stronger?" The book opens with an overview of how to get started in curriculum leadership and how the featured schools and school districts were able to implement their plans. The common characteristics that lead to success, as well as some key traits of effective administrators, teachers, and community groups, are profiled. Specific strategies for how these educators dealt with the disruption that accompanies significant change are likewise offered.

Havelock, R., Guskin, A., Frohman, M., Havelock, M., Hill, M., & Huber, J. (1969). *A comparative study of the literature on the dissemination and utilization of scientific knowledge.* Ann Arbor, MI: Center for Research on Utilization of Scientific Knowledge. (ED 029 171)

This report provides a framework for understanding the processes of innovation, dissemination, and knowledge utilization (D&U) and it reviews the relevant literature in education and other fields of practice within this framework. D&U is viewed as a transfer of messages by various media between resource systems and users. Major sections analyze characteristics of individuals and organizations that inhibit or facilitate this transfer. The process is interpreted at four levels: the individual, the interpersonal, the organization, and the social system. Additional chapters analyze messages, media, phase models, and knowledge-linking roles. Models of D&U can be grouped into three perspectives: (1) "Research, Development and Diffusion", (2) "Social Interaction", and (3) "Problem Solving." A "linkage" model is proposed as a synthesis. Successful linkage is achieved when user and resource system interact collaboratively, stimulating each other's problem solving behaviors. Seven factors highly related to successful D&U are: (1) linkage to internal and external resources; (2) degree of structure in resource system, user, message and medium; (3) openness of user and resource systems; (4) capacity to marshal diverse resources; (5) reward; (6) proximity to resources and other users; and (7) synergy, i.e., the variety, persistence, and synchronization of messages and media. Implications are drawn for research, development, practice, and policy.

Huberman, A., & Miles, M. (1984). *People, policies, and practices: Examining the chain of school improvement: Vol. IV. Innovation up close: A field study in twelve school settings–a study of dissemination efforts supporting school improvement.* Andover, MA: Network of Innovative Schools, Inc. (ED 240 716)

The fourth volume of a ten-volume report, this document provides a synthesis and analysis of in-depth ethnographic case studies of twelve school districts engaged in school improvement efforts in a subsample of the study's one hundred forty-six districts. All districts were implementing new practices, seven using National Diffusion Network innovations and five developing and implementing practices of their own design funded through Title IV-C Development Grants. Each stage of the implementation process is portrayed, from preadoption to institutionalization, when it occurred. The motivations, behaviors, and aspirations of school personnel involved in the improvement effort are explored; aspects of the implementation process, including factors affecting its success, are examined; and outcomes, including impact on students, are discussed. Four patterns leading to the success or failure of implementation are identified: "enforced, stabilized use," "overreaching," "blunting/downsizing," and "indifference/discouragement."

Lawson, H., & Briar-Lawson, K. (1997). *Connecting the dots: Progress toward the integration of school reform, school-linked services, parent involvement and community schools.* Oxford, OH: Institute for Educational Renewal. (ED 409 696)

This report describes the outcomes of research that investigated school reform, school-linked services, parent involvement, and community school programs in schools in thirty-six states. Results found that services were often added on to school sites without any intent to integrate them with school reform; teachers were not directly involved in services; co-locating service providers did not guarantee better quality of services; and technical assistance, capacity-building, and time for teachers were in short-supply. A model comprised of ten strategies, "The Family-Supportive Community School," is presented to enhance learning experiences for all students, including students with disabilities. The strategies include: (1) parent empowerment and family support; (2) paraprofessional jobs and career ladders for parents; (3) school readiness, parent education, and family support; (4) caring classrooms that improve children's learning while enhancing teachers' and parents' efficacy; (5) improved classroom supports for teachers and children; (6) collaborative leadership; (7) educational communities; (8) neighborhood development and community organization; (9) simultaneous renewal of higher education; and (10) technology enhancement and use. Appendices include family support premises and principles of family-centered practice, and examples of knowledge needs and orientations of teachers, principals, service providers, and parents in three kinds of schools.

Lenaghan, D. (1999). *Brave new world: A good news scenario for educational reform.* (ED 430 151)

A good news scenario about the future of education in the United States includes many things that are already being done and other things that can be dreamed of. One example is the "Awesome All-Stars Academy," a dream of a group of dedicated politicians, administrators, teachers, parents, community members, and students who took seriously their commission to produce and be educated citizens. The "Awesome" program was based on research in four fields: the changing work force, brain operations and intelligences, diversity among learners, and technological tools for instruction. "Awesome Academy" offers a learning environment that understands and practices teaching for learning. It includes the latest technologies for learning, features teachers who are master motivators and guides, and has a curriculum based on future work force needs and new understandings of the way students learn.

Louis, K., & Miles, M. (1990). *Improving the urban high school: What works and why.* New York, NY: Teachers College Press. (ED 327 623)

This study examines the leadership and management skills needed to improve urban high schools. Information was drawn from a national survey of 178 urban high school principals whose schools had been conducting serious improvement efforts for up to 4 years and in-depth case studies of five large high schools in the following urban areas: (1) Boston; (2) New York; (3) New Jersey; (4) Cleveland; and (5) Los Angeles. The following summary findings are discussed in terms of their implications for districts and schools and the issues of will and skill involved in implementation: (1) schools and their districts must be actively engaged with each other, but with few rules and much autonomy for the school to choose goals and strategies; (2) planning should be evolutionary and works best through a cross-role group of people who may not normally work together; (3) a shared vision of what the school is to become is an important feature guiding improvement; (4) from $50,000 to $100,000 annually for several years is needed for serious change efforts; and (5) problems must be confronted actively, promptly, and in depth. Discussions of the research methodology, nine tables of statistical data, and a list of 155 references are appended.

MacTaggart, T. (1996). *Restructuring higher education: What works and what doesn't in reorganizing governing systems.* San Francisco, CA: Jossey-Bass. (ED 408 882)

This book presents nine papers about changing the way public higher education is governed. After providing an overview of the recent history of governance restructuring or renewal in public higher education in the United States, the book focuses on restructuring in five states: North Dakota, Massachusetts, Alaska, Maryland, and Minnesota. Part 1 presents general discussions of restructuring, Part 2 presents the five case studies, and Part 3 contains papers on the lessons of restructuring. The following papers are included: (1) "Restructuring and the Failure of Reform" (Terrence J. MacTaggart) and (2) "Methods, Objectives, and Consequences of Restructuring"

(Richard J. Novak); (3) "Restructuring that Works: North Dakota" (Douglas M. Treadway); (4) "Where All Politics is Local: Massachusetts" (Patricia H. Crosson); (5) "Restructuring As a Way of Life: Alaska" (Patrick J. O'Rourke); (6) "The Human Side of Restructuring" Minnesota" (Terrence J. MacTaggart); and (7) "Restructuring and Its Aftermath: Maryland" (Robert Berdahl and Frank A. Schmidtlein); (8) "A Model for Successful Restructuring" (Aims C. McGuinness, Jr.); and (9) "Lessons for Leaders" (Terrence J. MacTaggart).

Marsh, D. (1999). *Preparing our schools for the 21st century: 1999 ASCD yearbook.* Alexandria, VA: Association for Supervision and Curriculum Development. (ED 427 414)

This yearbook offers a view of the key elements of schooling in the 21st century, outlining the nature of the change process that will be needed to create such schools. These key elements are drawn from the experience of educational reform in several countries and reflect a growing consensus about which elements will help all schools achieve both excellence and equity in student performance. Following an introduction by David D. Marsh, the yearbook is divided into three sections. Section 1, "New Directions for our Schools–Trends and Issues," contains the following essays: "Getting to the Heart of the Matter: Education in the 21st Century" (D. Eastin); "Education and the Demands of Democracy in the Next Millennium" (M. Tucker and J. Codding); "Education for the Public Good: Strategic Intentions for the 21st Century" (B. Caldwell); "Rethinking Civic Education for the 21st Century" (T. Clark); and "Diversity and Education for the 21st Century" (B. Williams). Section 2, "Creating a New Era–Educational Reform for the 21st Century," contains the following essays: "The Role of Standards in Educational Reform for the 21st Century" (P. Hill and C. Crevola); "Making Better Use of Resources for Educational Reform" (A. Odden); "Leadership in the 21st Century: Using Feedback To Maintain Focus and Direction" (S. King); and "Life Inside a School: Implications for Reform in the 21st Century" (M. Marsh). Section 3 contains one essay: "Using the Year 2000 in Schools: Celebrating, Synthesizing, and Reflecting".

Moore, N. (1996). *Using the Malcolm Baldrige Criteria to improve quality in higher education.* Paper presented at the Forum of the Association of Institutional Research, Albuquerque, NM. (ED 399 919)

This report discusses the Malcolm Baldrige (MB) Education Criteria, the award process, and the experiences of one institution–San Juan College (New Mexico)–that received an award at the state level. The Baldrige Criteria are based on 11 core values: (1) learning-centered education; (2) leadership; (3) continuous improvement and organizational learning; (4) faculty and staff participation and development; (5) partnership development; (6) design quality and prevention; (7) management by fact; (8) long-range view of the future; (9) public responsibility and citizenship; (10) fast response; and (11) results orientation. An institution under consideration for an award under the Baldrige Criteria must submit to the awarding agency a self-assessment report written around seven MB Criteria providing the framework for the core values, including leadership; information and analysis; strategic and operational planning; human resource development and management; education and business process management; school performance results; and student focus and satisfaction. In 1994 and 1995, San Juan College participated in the Quality New Mexico Award process. This process uses teams of evaluators who read, score, and write feedback comments on reports of organizations under consideration for an award. This document concludes that the Baldrige Criteria have provided a conceptual framework that focused the action planning process of San Juan College.

Myers, C., & Simpson, D. (1997). *Re-creating schools: Places where everyone learns and likes it.* Thousand Oaks, CA: Corwin Press, Inc. (ED 418 498)

Americans are increasingly disenchanted with what they perceive to be lackluster efforts to improve schools. Some new approaches are needed. Schools must be re-created by local school leaders and by teachers who will focus on their vision or visions of what their school culture, learning, and teaching would be like if all conditions were as they would like them to be. The ideas are contained in five chapters, which discuss the importance of envisioning the ideal school and address old myths about schools as factories. Schools are morally based communities–cultural constructs–and teaching is an experience-based intellectual construction. Teaching is a professional practice of problem identification and problem solving and teachers are ever-learning professionals. How-to steps on improving schools are presented, such as assessing current local school conditions sincerely and honestly. The book also describes the important dimension of evaluation and demonstrates ways to assess schools, teachers, and students that are consistent with the view of an ideal school.

National Association of College and University Business Officers. (1996). *Organizational paradigm shifts.* Washington, DC: Author. (ED 402 888)

This collection of essays explores a new paradigm of higher education. The first essay, "Beyond Re-engineering: Changing the Organizational Paradigm" (L. Edwin Coate), suggests a model of quality process management and a structure for managing organizational change. "Thinking About Consortia" (Mary Jo Maydew) discusses cooperative effort and organizational issues for consortia. In "Rethinking the Academy's Administrative Structure" (Jillinda J. Kidwell and David O'Brien), administrative inefficiencies and the business case for change are studied; included also is a case study of a budget experience at the Stanford University School of Medicine. "Meeting the Challenges of Change at Kent State" (Myron S. Henry) discusses fiscally driven changes to rethink curricula, administrative roles, and operations of major functional units. "New Paradigms in Student Affairs" (Paula M. Rooney and P. Gerard Shaw) briefly reviews the history of student affairs, describes changes currently underway at many institutions, and peeks at the future. "Organizational Restructuring at Carnegie Mellon University" (Patrick J. Keating, et al.) explores the university's creation and implementation of a strategy for process restructuring and suggests it as a model for other institutions facing similar problems. The final essay, "Academic Renewal at Michigan" (James Duderstadt) sees the modern research university as a complex, international conglomerate of highly diverse businesses.

New American Schools Development Corp. (1997). *Working towards excellence: Results from schools implementing New American Schools designs.* Arlington, VA: Educational Research Service. (ED 420 896)

This report presents eight different approaches adapted by schools to dramatically raise student achievement. The schools combine comprehensive, whole-school change with systems-level restructuring, to help a large proportion of schools around the country achieve excellence. The eight programs include (1) ATLAS (Authentic Teaching, Learning, and Assessment for all Students) Communities, which use pathways that serve as feeder patterns of schools serving students from pre-kindergarten to grade 12; (2) Purpose-Centered Education, which focuses all student learning on a complex and meaningful "purpose"; (3) Co-NECT schools, which provide a comprehensive, technology-supported framework for school restructuring; (4) Expeditionary Learning Outward Bound, which focuses on "learning expeditions" developed by teachers in each school; (5) the Los Angeles Learning Centers, a comprehensive kindergarten-through-12 model organized around curriculum, learning supports, and management; (6) Modern Red Schoolhouse, which encourages teachers to identify and nurture each child's potential; (7) the National Alliance for Restructuring Education, a partnership of states, school districts, and national organizations; and (8) Roots and Wings, a comprehensive restructuring program for elementary schools.

New American Schools Development Corp. (1998). *Blueprints for school success: A guide to New American Schools designs.* Arlington, VA: Educational Research Service. (ED 420 913)

New American Schools (NAS) is a nonprofit, nonpartisan organization that was founded by business leaders who wanted to improve the quality of public education. To explain how this organization works, an overview of its strategies for helping schools is provided here. The guide is intended for education leaders, policy makers, parents, and community members, and it offers background material on NAS, information about how its design teams assist schools, and suggestions on the selection and implementation of comprehensive school designs. The first section provides an overview of NAS, describing the basic principles guiding the NAS design teams, and suggests the benefits of working with a design team. Subsequent sections offer guidelines to help individual schools select and implement a comprehensive school-improvement design; guidelines for school districts, including a general overview of how school districts can support individual schools; and guidelines for states, which describe how states can help schools and districts tap federal funding for the implementation of research-tested, comprehensive school-improvement plans. The guide also offers descriptions of various NAS designs and describes how schools using designs teach the educational basics. An appendix offers some examples of "tools" that have proven useful in implementing designs.

Nicholls, G. (1997). *Collaborative change in education.* Sterling, VA: Stylus Publishing, Inc. (ED 408 932)

This book reviews key aspects–social, psychological, cultural, and contextual–of the development of collaborative partnerships between elementary/secondary schools and institutions of higher education, and examines especially the nature of collaboration as part of the framework of professional development. After an introductory chapter, the first chapter focuses on the professional teaching and research communities, suggesting the need for collaboration to improve each other's practice. Chapter 2 examines the nature of working in "partnership" and the role of initial teacher education in formalizing partnership agreements. Chapter 3 addresses issues in the collaboration of schools and higher education institutions. In Chapter 4 two case studies, a school-based curriculum development project in England and a school-based professional development project at a California high school, illustrate successes and failures of collaborative ventures. Chapter 5 offers some theoretical perspectives on collaborative partnerships in the context of educational change, both internally and externally imposed. Finally, Chapter 6 looks at the future of collaboration in suggesting that, despite trends toward greater prescription by external agencies and government legislation, there will also be increased opportunities for collaboration between institutions of higher education and schools.

Pourdavood, R., Cowen, L., & Svec, L. (1999). *Complexity of school reform: Order and chaos.* Paper presented at the annual meeting of the American Educational Research Association, Montreal, Quebec, Canada. (ED 430 286)

This paper reports on a case study that explored the process K-4 educators encountered as they attempted to implement recommendations from the National Council of Teachers of Mathematics (NCTM) Standards. The primary research questions of the study asked what triggers major school change, what complexities surround school change, and what sustains the reform process and allows/encourages it to evolve. Data sources for the study included transcripts of audiotapes from long interviews and follow-up interviews of key informants, field notes of university researchers, and related documents. Results show that initial changes in implementing the standards were mechanical–the lessons and materials did little to change teachers' existing beliefs and practices about mathematics. However, the reform took a different direction when some K-4 teachers "reinvented" mathematics instruction around key ideas and processes within a relevant context for children. Tensions emerged as some teachers' instructional practices began to look different from those of other classrooms, and teachers began to write lessons to supplement the district curriculum. Chaotic situations challenged conventional leadership strategies, interrupted stability of the school climate, and suggested an uncertain future. The reform seemed to depend on educators who believed in the need to restructure and reculture schools.

Rosenfeld, S., & Gravois, T. (1996). *Instructional consultation teams: Collaborating for change.* New York, NY: Guilford Publications. (ED 394 260)

This book presents a design for initiating, implementing, and institutionalizing a consultation-based service delivery system in school settings, based on the Instructional Consultation Teams (IC-Teams) model. It brings together the literature on school consultation and school change, for practitioners in general and special education and in school psychology seeking holistic and multilevel approaches to school reform. The first chapter describes the context for developing interdisciplinary consultation support services in relation to school and special education reform. Chapters 2 and 3 outline the essential dimensions of IC-Teams, which are a combined delivery system and consultation process implemented in over sixty schools in four states. In Chapter 4 the role of the change facilitator is considered, elaborating on the skills required in facilitating transition to a new service delivery system. The staged-based design for that transition is the focus of Chapters 5 through 8, which provide more specific guidance for initiating, training, implementing, and institutionalizing IC-Teams. Each of these chapters examines issues and concerns involved in facilitating the transition and outlines evaluation procedures. Chapter 9 summarizes the major issues and themes of the book. Appendices contain a variety of forms and materials useful to facilitators.

Schmuck, R., & Miles, M. (1972). *Handbook of organizational development in schools.* Palo Alto, CA: The National Press. (ED 071 167)

This text has been written primarily as a handbook for organizational specialists in school districts, for those learning to become organizational specialists, and for teachers of organizational specialists. For the most part, each chapter and each major section has been organized to be understood and used independently from the rest of the book. The first two chapters describe the theory of organizations and the specific activities used for planning interventions in school organizations. Chapters three through eight present a rationale and the methods for improving the school organization functions of clarifying communication, establishing goals, uncovering and working with conflict, improving group meetings, solving problems, and making decisions. Each of these chapters contains ideas for planning as well as action guides for actual practice in the field. Two final chapters discuss two of the most important skills of the organizational specialist the design and the evaluation of a training program. One chapter presents ideas on how to go about putting together sequences of training activities into coherent designs; it also serves as a summary of the core chapters. The last chapter provides information for evaluating interventions and the particular aspects of any training design.

Stanford, B. (1998). *Charting school change: Improving the odds for successful school reform*. Thousand Oaks, CA: Corwin Press, Inc. (ED 418 497)

Although models of successful school innovations exist, some reformers are giving up on the public schools. To address this problem, some suggestions for educators who want usable concepts to reform education are presented. The book is intended for the busy professionals devoted to education–teachers, administrators, curriculum specialists, and college faculty–and explains complex theories using diagrams and examples. It draws on the author's experiences in teaching humanities and builds a unified theory by selecting different combinations of disciplines. Part 1 addresses the need for a new conceptual framework and introduces the basic concepts of self-organizing systems, showing how these concepts can help interpret common phenomena in school reform. Some of the specific issues it addresses include reasons behind dysfunctional systems and the mechanism by which systems transform themselves. Part 2 is a practical handbook for applying systems concepts to specific dimensions of school change. Each chapter looks at a specific part of the change process from a self-organizing-system perspective. Selected issues covered include creating a vision for change, building partnerships, and the important role of conflict in systems change.

Talley, S., & Martinez, D. (1998). *Tools for schools: School reform models supported by the National Institute on the Education of At-Risk Students*. Washington, DC: National Institute on the Education of At-Risk Students. (ED 418 174)

The school reform models presented in this publication have been supported, at some time in their development and dissemination, by the National Institute on the Education of At-Risk Students in the Office of Educational Research and Improvement, U.S. Department Education. As part of its mission, the Institute supports the development of research-based knowledge and strategies promoting excellence and equity in the education of children and youth placed at risk of educational failure. The Institute supports a coordinated and comprehensive program of educational research primarily through national research and development centers, multi-year contracts, and a field-initiated studies program. This publication represents the compilation of information about twenty-seven school reform models that have received support for development, expansion, adaptation, or evaluation through the Institute's research program. The primary purpose of this publication is to provide information to practitioners and policymakers who have decision-making authority for improving the performance of schools with significant at-risk student populations. The information provided on each of the models is intended to give readers a fairly in-depth view of what is required for a school to implement the model. Each model description was prepared by the model's developer through a format developed by the Institute and identifies contact persons and other sources that may be accessed for additional information. The document is divided into three sections: (1) "Comprehensive School Reform Models"; (2) "Classroom and Curriculum Redesign Models"; and (3) "Professional Development Reform Models." The first appendix groups the models by center/program affiliation, grade levels, and educational priorities. The second appendix presents information on the National Institute on the Education of At-Risk Students and its mission, program, and staff.

Tutt, B., & Carter, S. (1999). *Understanding and using change forces.* Paper presented at the annual meeting of the American Association of Colleges for Teacher Education, Washington, DC. (ED 428 049)

As local, state, and national educational reform continues to impact professional educators and others who support student learning, all professionals are faced with responding to change in a positive way. The study of educational change over the last thirty years has brought educators to a paradigm breakthrough in terms of how they think and act in relation to change. Fullan's vision of change, which includes eight lessons, embraces the chaotic nature of the forces of change at all levels of society. Since 1995, Missouri's William Woods University has sponsored the Connections Project, which helps regional and area schools ensure that all students succeed in school. Connections is a professional development resource for educators, counselors, administrators, human service providers, and others who work with children and families. In 1998, the Connections staff conducted training sessions for education professionals that highlighted Michael Fullan's research and ideas and encouraged participants to develop group models of the change process. Participants completed surveys on their understanding of Fullan's lessons and their applicability to the school site. Responses indicated that respondents understood Fullan's lessons of change and believed they could affect change using them, but many had not used the lessons in their classroom/school/community since participating in the professional development. Some of the school sites had left the Connections project.

Wallace, B., & Braunger, J. (1998). *Teacher stories of curriculum change.* Portland, OR: Northwest Regional Educational Lab. (ED 424 205)

This report presents stories, written by teachers in the northwestern United States, about their experiences with curriculum over the years. The stories come from several groups, including four teachers who wrote as individuals, one pair of close colleagues, and one interview with a team of educators. The teachers responded to questions about how their curriculum experiences affected their convictions about student learning; how their convictions affected their teaching; how curriculum helped them grow as teachers; what happened to change their understandings and philosophies during their teaching; and how the changes influenced their students. Several common themes grew out of the stories. One of the universal themes was the growing awareness of the impact of students themselves on curriculum. The support and encouragement of other teachers and administrators was essential to several teachers' change processes. Teachers identified time as a major factor in their explorations of curriculum and their process of change. Self-awareness was another universal theme. Several stories showed the effects of modeling on teachers and students. Teachers noted working on cooperative teams as a major challenge that they faced. Teachers' thinking was stretched by the influence of students whose experiences and cultural backgrounds differed from their own. After an introduction by Barbara Wallace, the stories include: "If they can say Stegosaurus..." (Teri Houghton); The Power of Reflection (Gail Gilchrist); Choosing the Road Less Traveled (Susan Seaman); Navigating Sameness (Karen Mitchell); On Change as a Constant: An Interview with a Curriculum Development Team (Jane Braunger); and Caution: Women at Work (Margaret Marsh and Linda Kidd).

Williams, B. (1997). *Initiating curricular change in the professions: A case study in nursing.* Paper presented at the annual meeting of the American Educational Research Association, Chicago, IL. (ED 411 718)

This paper describes the initiation of curricular change in the undergraduate nursing program at the University of Alberta in Edmonton, in light of significant changes in the health care delivery system. In 1995, the program's Administrative Council adopted a Facilitated Deliberative Inquiry consensus model to manage a review of the curriculum and guide change, organizing a Deliberative Group of faculty, student, alumnae, employer, and consumer representatives. The group recommended that the curriculum evolve to a problem-based learning (PBL) model that would integrate essential concepts from support course disciplines. To counter a lack of strong faculty support for the change, open forums, individual meetings, and workshops on PBL were held. The curricular change eventually garnered 80 percent approval among faculty. It is concluded that effective curricular change requires the support of deans and senior administrators, careful choice of a consultant, the segregation of function and authority among faculty, the selective dissemination of specific recommendations when they are still in draft form, a high level of faculty involvement, and early positive experiences with the proposed changes.

ERIC Journal Articles

Birrell, J., Ostlund, M., Eagan, M., Young, J., Cook, P., DeWitt, P., & Tibbitts, C. (1998). Collaboration, communities, and covey: A model for personal and professional change. *Clearing House, 71*(6), 359-362. (EJ 568 515)

Reports on one school-university partnership that used S. Covey's "The 7 Habits of Highly Effective People" as a framework for initiating and sustaining teacher-education reform in an elementary school. Discusses how the collaboration overcame a difficult start involving distrust of the university. Shows how the project illuminates three important considerations regarding collaborative reform and organizational learning.

Bohen, S., & Stiles, J. (1998). Experimenting with models of faculty collaboration: Factors that promote their success. *New Directions for Institutional Research, 25*(4), 39-55. (EJ 577 732)

Although interdisciplinary approaches to complex problems are not new to Harvard University (Massachusetts), there is new interest in structured faculty collaboration. Some of the barriers to faculty teamwork are explored, models that enable interaction outside traditional departmental confines are examined, and some ways that other colleges and universities can encourage similar work are discussed.

Bol, L., Nunnery, J., Lowther, D., Dietrich, A., Pace, J., Anderson, R., Bassoppo-Moyo, T., & Phillipsen, L. (1998). Inside-in and outside-in support for restructuring: The effects of internal and external support on change in the New American Schools. *Education and Urban Society, 30*(3), 358-384. (EJ 572 907)

Teachers' perceptions of support provided for implementation of the New American Schools models in the Memphis City (Tennessee) school district are examined in relation to the effectiveness of these models. Via questionnaires and focus group interviews, teachers indicated professional development, teacher collaboration, and resources to be important support sources for positive reform outcomes.

Boss, S. (1998). The wisdom of working together. *Northwest Education, 4*(2), 2-9. (EJ 578 201)

Community revitalization efforts based on partnerships between educators, civic leaders, local employers, entrepreneurs, and parents are gaining momentum. Local schools play a leading role in many of these. Discusses three models of school/community interaction, how relationships build social capital, mapping community assets, getting started, and developing good communication between partners. Contains three online resources.

Cookson, P. (1998). Stewards of the future. *American School Board Journal, 185*(9), 34-36. (EJ 571 762)

Schools must stick to core issues—those concerned with teaching and learning and provision of material resources to maximize intellectual and personal growth. They must develop a fluid change model and a vision promoting abolition of violence, humanitarian standards, and global justice. Schools should also adopt a developmental learning cycle.

Cummings, K., Dragna, F., & Hanson, R. (1996). The Aggie and the ecstasy: A descriptive analysis of the process of general education reform at a land grant university. *Journal of General Education, 45*(4), 319-334. (EJ 543 273)

Presents a case study illustrating processes used to implement curriculum reform at North Dakota State University. Describes methods used to develop the general education curriculum and to collect and relay information within the university. Provides a model of the involvement of academic departments in the process.

Donlevy, J., & Donlevy, T. (1997). Teachers, technology, and training: Perspectives on education and school reform—a focus on the sociological perspective. *International Journal of Instructional Media, 24*(1), 1-14. (EJ 569 032)

Reviews four perspectives that education and school-reform writings fall under—technological, psychological, ideological, and sociological—and looks at the implications of each for the role of the teacher. Focuses on the descriptive, prescriptive, and communitarian aspects of the sociological perspective and suggests ways that teacher-preparation programs can be improved.

Edwards, T. (1996). Implications of a model for conceptualizing change in mathematics teachers' instructional practices. *Action in Teacher Education, 18*(2), 19-30. (EJ 536 843)

A model for conceptualizing teacher change was developed during a two-year study of mathematics teachers' implementation of an innovative curriculum. Based on constructivist views of teaching and learning, the model suggested that one way to promote change in teaching practice is to structure interactions among teachers to promote reflective thinking.

Hall, G. (1992). The local educational change process and policy implementation. *Journal of Research in Science Teaching, 29*(8), 877-904. (EJ 453 551)

In this article, implications for policy, development, and implementation of educational change are offered, along with suggested directions for research. The author contends that all involved need to work together; they need to develop a holistic view of the system and work with an approach that engages interactive partners in the educational change process.

Khan, B. (1997). The designing matrix: A systemic tool for understanding the visions and images of new educational systems. *Performance Improvement, 36*(2), 32-36. (EJ 539 719)

Discusses the redesign of educational systems and presents a designing matrix to help select boundaries of a new system. A conceptual framework for exploring educational system boundaries is described, systems models are discussed, and the three cells of the matrix are explained.

Olson, L. (1998). Models for reform. *American Educator, 22*(3), 18-19. (EJ 578 727)

A growing number of researchers are questioning the usefulness of reform strategies that do not provide teachers with specific information about how to implement changes. The replication of successful programs depends on giving teachers the tools they need to carry out reforms by explaining them in detail.

Plank, D., Scotch, R., & Gamble, J. (1996). Rethinking progressive school reform: Organizational dynamics and educational change. *American Journal of Education, 104*(2), 79-102. (EJ 522 453)

Develops a model of progressive school reform based on recent work in institutionalist theory. The authors present findings from preliminary empirical tests of the model, which provide strong support for an institutionalist account and considerably weaker support for political explanations of reform.

Sakofs, M. (1998). Painting and Christopher Columbus: A story about metaphors for school change. *Journal of Experiential Education, 21*(2), 108-111. (EJ 580 360)

Uses metaphors of the preparation necessary for painting and for Columbus's journey into the unknown to suggest a model for planning and promoting school reform. Steps include definition of preexisting conditions, assessment of the situation, immersion (communication and trust building among stakeholders), and coordinated strategic and tactical planning.

Speck, M. (1996). Best practice in professional development for sustained educational change. *ERS Spectrum, 14*(2), 33-41. (EJ 527 481)

This is based on recent research in professional development, adult learning theory, shared leadership, effective schools, and the change process. The model views increased student learning as the goal; schools as the unit of change; professional development as a diverse, ongoing process; and educator involvement as essential.

Squires, D., & Kranyik, R. (1996). The Comer program: Changing school culture. *Educational Leadership, 53*(4), 29-32. (EJ 517 889)

Site-management designs generally fail to establish structures and processes that help school communities work through cultural change. The Comer School Development Program succeeds because it supports a change in school culture and focuses on children's development, not just their speech, language, and intellectual capabilities. Lessons from Dallas schools are discussed.

Valente, T., & Rogers, E. (1995). The origins and development of the diffusion of innovations paradigm as an example of scientific growth. *Science Communication, 16*(3), 242-273. (EJ 499 788)

Describes some of the history of rural sociological research on the diffusion of agricultural innovations, and shows how research followed (and deviated from) the Kuhnian concept of paradigm development. Examines the Iowa Hybrid Seed Corn Study, which contributed to the rise of sociological diffusion research.

van de Ven, A., & Rogers, E. (1988). Innovations and organizations: Critical perspectives. *Communicaion Research, 15*(5), 632-651. (EJ 379 897)

Presents an overview of research on innovations and organizations. Criticizes past research and calls for a focus on process research in future investigations, moving from a stage-by-stage conception of the innovation process to a dynamic, continuous conception in which the variables involved are sequenced and analyzed through time.

Wertheimer, R., & Zinga, M. (1998). Applying chaos theory to school reform. *Internet Research, 8*(2), 101-114. (EJ 566 619)

Presents a case study of the ideology, strategies and process of the "Common Knowledge: Pittsburgh" project in its attempt at school reform in an urban school district. Reflects on the project's activities, and uses its experience to develop a conceptual framework based on chaos theory, as developed in mathematics and science, for discussing educational reform efforts.

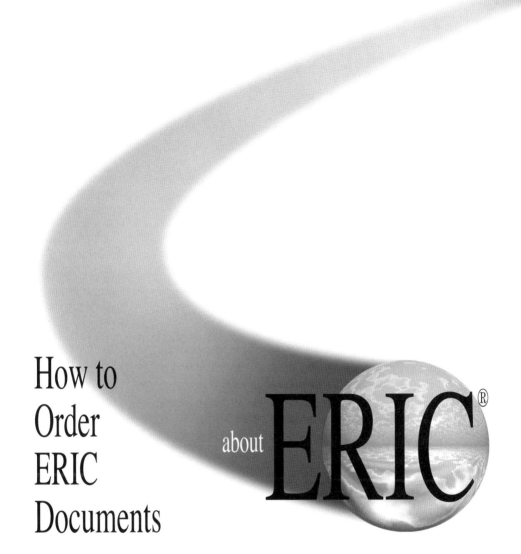

How to Order ERIC Documents

about ERIC®

Individual copies of ERIC documents are available in either microfiche or paper copy from the ERIC Document Reproduction Service (EDRS), 7420 Fullerton Road, Suite 110, Springfield, VA 22153-2852; some are available only in microfiche. Information needed for ordering includes the ED number, the number of pages, the number of copies wanted, the unit price, and the total unit cost. Sales tax should be included on orders from Maryland, Virginia, and Washington, DC.

Please order by ED number, indicate the format desired (microfiche or paper copy), and include payment for the price listed plus shipping. Call EDRS at 1-800-443-ERIC (or 703-440-1400) or e-mail EDRS customer service department: service@edrs.com, for information on pricing, shipping costs and/or other services offered by the contractor.

Inquiries about ERIC may be addressed to the ERIC Clearinghouse on Information & Technology, 621 Skytop Road, Suite 160, Syracuse University, Syracuse, NY 13244-5290 (800-464-9107), e-mail: eric@ericir.syr.edu; or ACCESS ERIC, 2277 Research Boulevard, 7A, Rockville, MD 20850 (800-LET-ERIC), e-mail: acceric@inet.ed.gov

Journal Articles

Copies of journal articles can be found in library periodical collections; through interlibrary loan; from the journal publisher; or from article reprint services such as the UMI/InfoStore (1-800-248-0360), UnCover Company (1-800-787-7979), or Institute for Scientific Information (ISI) (1-800-336-4474). Information needed for ordering includes the author, title of article, name of journal, volume, issue number, page numbers, date, and EJ number for each article. Fax services are available.

What is ERIC?

ERIC, the Educational Resources Information Center, is a national education information system sponsored by the Office of Educational Research and Improvement in the U.S. Department of Education. The main product of ERIC is a bibliographic database containing citations and abstracts for more than 1 million documents and journal articles published since 1966. Most of the document literature cited in ERIC can be read in full text at any of the 900+ libraries or institutions worldwide holding the ERIC microfiche collection. In addition, users can purchase copies of ERIC documents from the ERIC Document Reproduction Service. Journal articles cited in ERIC can be obtained at a subscribing library, through interlibrary loan, or from an article reprint service.

How Do I Find Information in ERIC?

The ERIC Database can be searched manually through its two print indexes, Resources in Education (RIE) and Current Index to Journals in Education (CIJE). Over 3,000 libraries and information centers subscribe to one or both of these monthly indexes. The database can also be searched online: (a) through a computer based information retrieval service; (b) by CD-ROM; (c) on a locally mounted system, which may be accessible through the Internet; or (d) Internet: http://ericir.syr.edu/Eric/.

What is ERIC/IT?

The ERIC Clearinghouse on Information & Technology, or ERIC/IT, is one of 16 clearinghouses in the ERIC system. It specializes in library and information science and educational technology. ERIC/IT acquires, selects, catalogs, indexes, and abstracts documents and journal articles in these subject areas for input into the ERIC database.

Among the topics covered in library and information science are:
- Management, operation, and use of libraries and information centers
- Library technology and automation
- Library education
- Information policy
- Information literacy
- Information storage, processing and retrieval
- Networking

Topics covered in educational technology include:
- Design, development, and evaluation of instruction
- Computer-assisted instruction
- Hypermedia, interactive video, and interactive multimedia
- Telecommunications
- Film, radio, television, and other audio-visual media
- Distance education
- Simulation and gaming

What is Available From ERIC/IT?

Each year, ERIC/IT publishes Monographs, Minibibliographies, and Digests in the fields of educational technology and library and information science. Our semiannual newsletter, ERIC/IT Update, announces new clearinghouse products and developments, and ERIC/IT Networkers provide helpful information for using ERIC-related resources on the Internet.

Publications
- Digests, providing brief overviews of topics of current interest and references for further reading
- Monographs, featuring trends and issues analyses, synthesis papers and annotated bibliographies
- ERIC/IT Update, a semi-annual newsletter

User Services
- Response to inquiries about ERIC and matters within the ERIC/IT scope area
- Workshops and presentations about ERIC and database searching
- Assistance in searching the ERIC database

AskERIC
- Internet-based question answering service for educators
- AskERIC Virtual Library, an Internet site of education-related information resources including lesson plans, InfoGuides, listservs and much more
    E-mail: *askeric@askeric.org*
    Internet: *http://www.askeric.org*

Would You Like to Submit Your Work to ERIC?

Have you written materials related to educational technology or library and information science that you would like to share with others? ERIC/IT would be interested in reviewing your work for possible inclusion in the ERIC database. We actively solicit documents from researchers, practitioners, associations, and agencies at national, state, and local levels. ERIC documents include the following and more:

- Research Reports
- Program Descriptions
- Instructional Materials
- Conference Papers
- Teaching Guides
- Opinion Papers

How Do I Find Out More?

For additional information about ERIC or about submitting documents, or for a current publications list, contact:

ERIC Clearinghouse on Information & Technology
621 Skytop Road, Suite 160
Syracuse University
Syracuse, New York 13244-5290
R. David Lankes, Director
Telephone: (315) 443-3640   Fax: (315) 443-5448   (800) 464-9107
E-mail: *eric@ericir.syr.edu*   WWW URL: *http://ericir.syr.edu/ithome*

Questions about the ERIC system can also be directed to:
ACCESS ERIC
2277 Research Boulevard, 6L
Rockville, Maryland 20850
Telephone: (800) LET-ERIC
E-mail: *acceric@accesseric@accesseric.org*
        http://www.accesseric.org

ERIC Clearinghouses
- Adult, Career, and Vocational Education
- Assessment and Evaluation
- Community Colleges
- Counseling and Student Services
- Disabilities and Gifted Education
- Educational Management
- Elementary and Early Childhood Education
- Higher Education
- Information & Technology
- Languages and Linguistics
- Reading, English, and Communication
- Rural Education and Small Schools
- Science, Mathematics, and Environmental Education
- Social Studies/Social Science Education
- Teaching and Teacher Education
- Urban Education

Support Components
- ERIC Document Reproduction Service
  Telephone: (800) 443-ERIC (3742)
- ERIC Processing and Reference Facility
  Telephone: (800) 799-ERIC (3742)

Index

A

C

D

E

J

Z

315 SURVIVING CHANGE: A Survey of Educational Change Models